WHO WAS RESPONSIBLE FOR
THE DEATH OF BJORN FAULKNER
ON THE NIGHT OF JANUARY 16TH?

If this play's sense of life were to be verbalized, it would say, in effect: "Your life, your achievement, your happiness, *your person* are of paramount importance. Live up to your highest vision of yourself no matter what the circumstances you might encounter. An exalted view of self-esteem is a man's most admirable quality."

—Ayn Rand, from her Introduction
to *Night of January 16th*

AYN RAND

Three Plays

Night of January 16th

Ideal

Think Twice

A SIGNET BOOK

SIGNET
Published by New American Library, a division of
Penguin Group (USA) Inc., 375 Hudson Street,
New York, New York 10014, USA
Penguin Group (Canada), 10 Alcorn Avenue, Toronto,
Ontario M4V 3B2, Canada (a division of Pearson Penguin Canada Inc.)
Penguin Books Ltd., 80 Strand, London WC2R 0RL, England
Penguin Ireland, 25 St. Stephen's Green, Dublin 2,
Ireland (a division of Penguin Books Ltd.)
Penguin Group (Australia), 250 Camberwell Road, Camberwell, Victoria 3124,
Australia (a division of Pearson Australia Group Pty. Ltd.)
Penguin Books India Pvt. Ltd., 11 Community Centre, Panchsheel Park,
New Delhi - 110 017, India
Penguin Group (NZ), cnr Airborne and Rosedale Roads, Albany,
Auckland 1310, New Zealand (a division of Pearson New Zealand Ltd.)
Penguin Books (South Africa) (Pty.) Ltd., 24 Sturdee Avenue,
Rosebank, Johannesburg 2196, South Africa

Penguin Books Ltd., Registered Offices:
80 Strand, London WC2R 0RL, England

First published by Signet, an imprint of New American Library,
a division of Penguin Group (USA) Inc.

First Printing, April 2005
10 9 8 7 6 5 4 3 2 1

Contents

Editor's Note

This volume collects all three of Ayn Rand's original stage plays in one volume. *Night of January 16th* includes her own introduction from a previous edition. *Ideal* and *Think Twice* are reprinted from *The Early Ayn Rand* and include the prefaces written by Leonard Peikoff for that volume.

Although she is famous for her bestselling novels, many of her readers are not aware that Ayn Rand's first stage play, *Night of January 16th,* was produced in Hollywood in 1934 and had a lengthy and successful run on Broadway in 1935, before her first novel was published. The purpose of this collection is to bring Ayn Rand's achievements as a writer of dramatic art to the attention of a wider audience of readers—and thereby enrich their enjoyment of her creative power.

Inquiries about professional production rights for these plays should be directed to: Curtis Brown Ltd., Ten Astor Place, New York, NY 10003.

—Richard E. Ralston
August 2004

Night of January 16th

INTRODUCTION

If I were to classify *Night of January 16th* in conventional literary terms, I would say that it represents, not Romantic Realism, but Romantic Symbolism. For those acquainted with Objectivist aesthetics, I can name a more precise classification: *Night of January 16th* is not a philosophical, but a sense-of-life play.

A sense of life is a preconceptual equivalent of metaphysics, an emotional, subconsciously integrated appraisal of *man's relationship to existence*. I emphasize this last because it is a man's attitude toward life that constitutes the core and motor of his subconscious philosophy. Every work of fiction (and wider: every work of art) is the product and expression of its author's sense of life. But it may express that sense of life translated into conceptual, i.e., philosophical, terms, or it may express only an abstract emotional sum. *Night of January 16th* is a pure, untranslated abstraction.

This means that its events are not to be taken *literally*; they dramatize certain fundamental psychological characteristics, deliberately isolated and emphasized in order to convey a single abstraction: the characters' attitude toward life. The events serve to feature the *motives* of the characters' actions, regardless of the particular forms of action—i.e., the motives, not their specific concretization. The events feature the confrontation of two extremes, two opposite ways of facing existence: passionate self-assertiveness, self-confidence, ambition, audacity,

3

independence—versus conventionality, servility, envy, hatred, power-lust.

I do not think, nor did I think it when I wrote this play, that a swindler is a heroic character or that a respectable banker is a villain. But for the purpose of dramatizing the conflict of independence versus conformity, a criminal—a social outcast—can be an eloquent symbol. This, incidentally, is the reason of the profound appeal of the "noble crook" in fiction: He is the symbol of the rebel as such, regardless of the kind of society he rebels against, the symbol—for most people—of their vague, undefined, unrealized groping toward a concept, or a shadowy image, of man's self-esteem.

That a career of crime is not, in fact, the way to implement one's self-esteem is irrelevant in sense-of-life terms. A sense of life is concerned primarily with consciousness, not with existence—or rather: with the way a man's consciousness faces existence. It is concerned with a basic frame of mind, not with rules of conduct.

If this play's sense of life were to be verbalized, it would say, in effect: "Your life, your achievement, your happiness, *your person* are of paramount importance. Live up to your highest vision of yourself no matter what the circumstances you might encounter. An exalted view of self-esteem is a man's most admirable quality." How one is to live up to this vision—how this frame of mind is to be implemented in action and in reality—is a question that a sense of life cannot answer: *that* is the task of philosophy.*

Night of January 16th is not a philosophical treatise on morality: that basic frame of mind (and its opposite) is all that I wanted to convey.

This play was written in 1933. It started in my mind with the idea of writing a courtroom drama, a murder trial, in which the jury would be drawn from the audience and would vote on the verdict. Obviously, the factual evidence

---

*For a fuller discussion of the nature and functions of a sense of life, I refer you to my articles "Philosophy and Sense of Life" and "Art and Sense of Life," in my book *The Romantic Manifesto*.

of the defendant's guilt or innocence had to be evenly balanced in order to make either verdict possible. But a jury's disagreement about inconclusive facts could not be of any possible interest or significance. The issue at stake, therefore, had to be psychological.

The springboard for the story was the collapse of Ivar Kreuger—or, more precisely, the public reaction to that collapse.

On March 12, 1932, Ivar Kreuger, the Swedish "Match King," committed suicide. His death was followed by the crash of the vast financial empire he had created, and by the revelation that that empire was a gigantic fraud. He had been a mysterious figure, a "lone wolf," celebrated as a man of genius, of unswerving determination and spectacular audacity. His fall was like an explosion that threw up a storm of dust and muck—a storm of peculiarly virulent denunciations.

It was not his shady methods, his ruthlessness, his dishonesty that were being denounced, but his *ambition.* His ability, his self-confidence, the glamorous aura of his life and name were featured, exaggerated, overstressed, to serve as fodder for the hordes of envious mediocrities rejoicing at his downfall. It was a spree of gloating malice. Its leitmotif was not: "How did he fall?" but: "How did he dare to rise?" Had there been a world press at the time of Icarus and Phaëthon, *this* was the kind of obituary they would have received.

In fact, Ivar Kreuger was a man of unusual ability who had, at first, made a fortune by legitimate means; it was his venture into politics—mixed-economy politics—that destroyed him. Seeking a world monopoly for his match industry, he began to give large loans to various European governments in exchange for a monopoly status in their countries—loans which were not repaid, which he could not collect and which led him to a fantastic juggling of his assets and bookkeeping in order to conceal his losses. In the final analysis, it was not Kreuger who profiteered on the ruin of the investors he had swindled; the profiteers were sundry European governments. (But when governments pursue such policies, it is not called a swindle: it is called "deficit financing.")

At the time of Kreuger's death, it was not the political aspects of his story that interested me, but the nature of those public denunciations. It was not a crook that they were denouncing, but greatness as such; it was greatness as such that I wanted to defend.

This, then, was my assignment in *Night of January 16ᵗʰ*: to dramatize the sense of life that was vaguely symbolized by Ivar Kreuger, and set it against the sense of life blatantly revealed by his attackers.

Bjorn Faulkner, the hero who never appears in the play, is not Ivar Kreuger; he is what Ivar Kreuger might have been or, perhaps, ought to have been. The two sides in the play are represented, on the one hand, by Bjorn Faulkner and Karen Andre, his secretary-mistress who is on trial for his murder—and, on the other, by John Graham Whitfield and his daughter. The factual evidence for and against the accused is (approximately) balanced. The issue rests on the credibility of the witnesses. The jury has to choose which side to believe, and this depends on every juror's own sense of life.

Or, at least, so I hoped. I was aware, even then, that most people would not see the issue in such terms, that most people are not that consistent, neither in their conscious convictions, nor in their choice of values, nor even in their sense of life. I was aware that they would probably miss the basic antithesis and would judge on the spur or color or drama of the moment, attaching no further significance to their verdict.

I knew also that a sense-of-life issue was not the best way to implement the idea of a trial by an audience-jury, and that some explicit controversial issue would be better, such as birth control or mercy-killing or "trial marriages." But here I truly had no choice. For the life of me, I could not have invented a story dealing with some narrow issue. My own sense of life demanded a theme involving great figures and crucial fundamentals; I could not arouse myself to any interest in anything less—then or now.

The motive of my writing has always been the presentation of an ideal man. I did not regard Bjorn Faulkner as an ideal. But I was not ready to attempt the portrait of an ideal man; his first appearance in my writing is Howard Roark in *The Fountainhead,* followed by the heroes of *Atlas Shrugged.* What I *was* ready to write about was a woman's feeling for her ideal man, and this I did in the person of Karen Andre.

Those interested in tracing my personal development will observe the sense-of-life consistency of this play with my subsequent novels. But my novels deal with more than a sense of life: they involve a conscious philosophy, i.e., a conceptually defined view of man and of existence. And, to illustrate the translation of a sense of life into conceptual terms: if Bjorn Faulkner were to make the same mistakes in terms applicable to actual life, he would become Gail Wynand, the most tragic character in *The Fountainhead;* or, if Bjorn Faulkner were to be an ideal businessman, he would become Francisco d'Anconia of *Atlas Shrugged.*

I am still asked, once in a while—and it always astonishes me—whether I intended Karen Andre to be found guilty or not guilty. I did not think that there could be any doubt about *my* verdict: of course, *she is not guilty.* (But this need not deter any prospective viewer or reader from pronouncing his own judgment: in this matter, to each his own sense of life.)

The original title of this play was *Penthouse Legend.*

This is still its best title; it gives some indication of the play's nonrealistic, symbolic nature. But it was changed twice, first to *Woman on Trial,* then to *Night of January 16th.* In both cases, the producers assured me that my original title would be a serious handicap to the play; one of them claimed that the public was antagonized by the word "Legend" and he cited the failure of some movies which had used that word in their titles. I thought that this was nonsense, but I did not want the producers to work

under the pressure of doubt or fear in regard to an issue
about which they felt very strongly, but which I considered unimportant.

Today, I regret it. *Night of January 16ᵗʰ* is an empty,
meaningless title. It was, however, the least offensive one
of those suggested to me at the time. I could not change it
later: the play had become too famous.

In a way, that title is appropriate to the practical history
of the play: for me, it was empty, meaningless—and very
painful.

The play's history began with a series of rejections by
New York's theatrical producers. I was living in Hollywood at the time, but I had an agent who kept sending the
play to one producer after another. What I regarded as the
most original feature of the play was the idea of drawing
the jury from the audience. It was precisely because of this
idea that the producers rejected the play: the jury gimmick
would not work, they said, the public would not go for it, it
would "destroy the theatrical illusion."

Then, simultaneously, I received two offers for the
play: one from A. H. Woods, a well-known New York producer; the other from E. E. Clive, a British actor who ran a
modest stock company at the Hollywood Playhouse. But
Woods wanted the right to make changes in my play at his
sole discretion. So I rejected his offer and signed a contract with Clive.

The play was produced at the Hollywood Playhouse in
the fall of 1934, under the title *Woman on Trial*. The role
of Karen Andre was played by Barbara Bedford, a star of
the silent movies. E. E. Clive directed it and played a small
part; he was a brilliant character actor, who loved my play
and seemed to understand it, at least to the extent of knowing that there was something unusual about it. To this day,
I deeply appreciate his attitude. But, as a producer, he was
badly handicapped by lack of funds. The production was
competent, but somewhat unexciting: unstylized and too
naturalistic. The play received good reviews and had a
modestly successful run.

At its conclusion, A. H. Woods renewed his offer for a

Broadway production. The contract clause regarding script changes was reworded, but in a highly ambiguous manner; my agent assured me that the new clause meant that all changes were to be made by mutual consent. I did not think so; I was fairly certain that it still gave Woods the control he wanted, but I decided to take the chance, relying on nothing but my power of persuasion.

The rest of the play's history was hell.

The entire period before and after the play's opening was a sickening struggle between Woods and me. I managed to prevent the worst of the changes he wanted to introduce, and I managed to preserve the best of the passages he wanted to eliminate, but that was all I could do. So the play became an incongruous mongrel slapdashed out of contradictory elements.

Woods was famous as a producer of melodramas, some of which had been good, some dreadful. Melodrama was the only element of my play that he understood, but he thought that there wasn't enough of it. So, "to liven it up," he introduced, in small touches, a junk heap of worn, irrelevant melodramatic devices that clashed with the style, did not advance the action and served only to confuse the audience—such as a gun, a heat test to determine its erased serial number, a flashy gun moll, etc. (The gun moll was introduced, in the last act, to throw doubt on the testimony of Guts Regan, which, of course, she did not accomplish. I did not write that bit, it was written by the play's director.) Woods actually believed that only guns, fingerprints and police matters could hold an audience's attention, but "speeches" could not. To his credit as a showman, I can say only that he thought the jury gimmick was a great idea, which is what made him buy the play.

This was my first (but not last) encounter with the literary manifestation of the mind-body dichotomy that dominates today's culture: the split between the "serious" and the "entertaining"—the belief that if a literary work is "serious," it must bore people to death; and if it is "entertaining," it must not communicate anything of importance. (Which means that "the good" has to be painful, and that pleasure has to be mindlessly low-grade.) A. H. Woods was a faithful adherent of that school of thought, so that it was useless to mention the word "thought" to him, or "idea" or "philosophy" or "sense of life" in connection with any theatrical matter. It would be inexact to say that he was antagonistic to such concepts: he was completely tone-deaf to them. I was naive enough to be shocked by it. Since then, I have observed the same tone-deafness in regard to this dichotomy (though, usually, on its other side) in men who had less excuse for it than A. H. Woods: in college professors. At the time, I fought against that dogma to the limit of my brain and endurance. I am still fighting that battle today, with the same intensity, but without the painful, incredulous astonishment of youth.

In regard to casting, Woods' judgment was better than his literary views. He gave the part of Karen Andre to a talented unknown, a young actress he had discovered—Doris Nolan. She was very attractive in the right way, she was an unusually good type for the part and gave an excellent performance. The male lead, the part of Guts Regan, was played by Walter Pidgeon. This was my one contribution to the casting. At that time, which was the period of transition from the silent movies to the talkies, Pidgeon was regarded as through in Hollywood and was playing in a summer stock theater in the East. He had been one of my favorites in the silent movies (where he had played strong, glamorous, aristocratic villains) and I had seen him on the stage in Hollywood, so I suggested that Woods go to see him in summer stock. Woods' first reaction was: "Aw, he's through," but he went. To give him credit, Woods was so impressed with Pidgeon's performance that he signed him for *Night of January 16ᵗʰ* at once (and told me: "Aw, that guy's great"). Shortly after our opening, Pidgeon signed a long-term movie contract with M-G-M, which was his new start in pictures, the beginning of his rise to stardom. He told me later that he owed that contract to his performance as Guts Regan. (I regret that M-G-M confined him to the homey, "*Mister* Miniver" type of role; he deserved better than that.)

This was one of the few pleasant incidents connected with *Night of January 16th*. By the time the play opened on Broadway (in September of 1935), it was dead, as far as I was concerned. I could feel nothing for it or about it except revulsion and indignation. It was not merely a mangled body, but worse: it was a mangled body with some of its torn limbs still showing a former beauty and underscoring the bloody mess. On opening night, I sat in the back row, yawning—not out of tension, but out of genuine boredom, since it was an event that had no value-meaning for me any longer.

The play received mixed reviews; it did not become a hit, but what was regarded as a "success." It ran for six months. What made it successful and talked about was, of course, the jury gimmick. On opening night, Woods had arranged in advance for a jury of celebrities (of whom the only one I remember was Jack Dempsey, the former heavyweight champion). For the first couple of weeks thereafter, he kept a jury of stooges on hand backstage, just in case the members of the audience did not volunteer. But he soon found the precaution unnecessary: his office was besieged by requests from celebrities and others who wanted to sit on that jury; there were more volunteers than he could accommodate.

One interesting incident of the play's run was a benefit performance given for the blind. (I did not attend it: I could not bear to see the play again, but I was told about it.) All the members of the jury and most of the audience were blind; the foreman of the jury was Helen Keller. Graham McNamee, a famous newscaster, acted as a narrator to describe visual information, when needed. The verdict that night was "Guilty."

As to the general record of verdicts during the play's run in New York, they were 3 to 2 in favor of acquittal—according to the stage manager, who kept a tally.

That winter, Woods launched two road companies (starting out of Chicago and Los Angeles) and a third company in London; all of them did very well.

The Chicago production remains in my mind for the

unexpected reason that a drama critic, Ashton Stevens, gave me the only review that pleased me in my entire career. I have received reviews that might be called better and some that I deeply appreciated, but none of them said the things I would have wanted to be said. I learned to expect nothing from reviewers because of the so-called favorable reviews, not because of the illiterate smears. What I liked about Ashton Stevens' piece was that he understood the *technique* of drama, knew what it takes and praised me for the best aspects of the play's structure; he praised me for an attribute which only a viewer in full focus can appreciate: ingenuity. He treated the play as a melodrama, since that is all it had become; I am inclined to believe that his sense of life was probably the opposite of mine, since he wrote: "It is not as close and upclimbing a piece as [*The Trial of*] *Mary Dugan*. Nor as heart-tearing. None of the characters is lovable."

But here is what I love *him* for: "But it is the fastest courtroom melo I ever saw. It shoots its stuff from a dozen angles, and every shot is a surprise.

"The biggest and best surprise is when the prisoner— the tense, Roman-medal-faced Karen Andre—crashes and crumbles as Gunman ('Guts') Regan rushes up the aisle and into court and informs her that the man she is accused of murdering IS dead. That, ladies and gentlemen of the audience, is a S E C O N D - A C T   C U R T A I N. [Typography his.] . . .

"You see, the play flattered the cunning of the audience. It permitted us to anticipate with some success. But it never left us right for more than a jiffy. . . . There is a kind of genius in the play." (If there was, in the version he saw, I marvel at his ability to see it.)

The play was unusually successful in summer stock: in its first summer (1936), it was presented by eighteen theaters, and was a leading favorite for many summers thereafter. One bright spot of the summer of 1936 was a week at a theater in Stony Creek, Connecticut, where the part of Guts Regan was played by my husband, Frank O'Connor.

In subsequent years, the play was presented, in various

translations, in most European countries. In World War II, it was presented by the U.S.O. for the American troops occupying Berlin. It is still being given occasionally in various parts of the world, with or without my knowledge; at least, I receive unexpected royalties from it, once in a while. And, once in a while, it is still played here, in summer stock. It has been presented on the radio and twice (by two different companies) on television.

The amateur market of this play belongs on the horror side of its history. The amateur rights were sold to a publishing house that issued an adapted, "cleaned up" version. The amateur market, they claimed at the time, consisted of church, school and college groups that worked under a strict kind of censorship (I do not know who imposed it): these groups were not allowed to mention a love affair or a mistress, or to smoke onstage, or to swear, etc. For instance, they were not allowed to use the word "Guts," so that my character's name was changed to "Larry" Regan. That version of my play was adapted by the publishing house; it was not to be sold in bookstores or to the public, but was to be sold *only* to amateur groups for amateur performances. Once in a while, I hear—with somewhat helpless indignation—that some fan of mine has somehow obtained a copy of that version. So I want to state formally, for the record and as a public notice, that the amateur version of *Night of January 16th* is not written by me and is not part of my works.

The movie version of this play is another horror story. I had nothing to do with its screen adaptation. There is nothing of mine in that movie, except the names of some of the characters and the title (which was not mine). The *only* line of dialogue from my play which appears in the movie is: "The court will now adjourn till ten o'clock tomorrow morning." The cheap, trashy vulgarity of that movie is such that no lengthier discussion is possible to me.

Through all those years, while the play was becoming famous, I felt a painfully growing embarrassment: I did not want to be associated with it or to be known as its author. I thought, at the time, that I had merely been unlucky in my producer and in the kind of people I had to deal with. Today, I know better: I know that it could not have been different, granting the nature of my work and of today's cultural trends. But don't let anyone ever approach me about making changes in my work: I learned my lesson the hard way.

For twenty-five years, I never looked at a script of this play, and winced whenever it was mentioned. Then, in 1960, Nathaniel Branden asked me to let him give a reading of the play at Nathaniel Branden Institute, in response to requests from students. I could not let him read the A. H. Woods version, so I had to prepare a definitive version of the play. I compared the original script of *Penthouse Legend,* the script of *Woman on Trial* (which was the same, but with some cuts made by me) and the script of *Night of January 16th.* I was somewhat astonished by the result: in this final, definitive version, I had to cut out *everything* that had been contributed by the Woods production (except one line change and the title). I cut out, of course, the gun moll, the gun and all the cruder elements of that sort; but I did not expect to find that even small lines and minor touches were jarringly wrong and had to be discarded.

I felt an odd kind of sadness: my mind went back to a certain argument I had with Woods during the rehearsals. We were sitting in the front row of an empty theater and he was saying indignantly: "How can you be so stubborn? How can you argue with me? This is your first play and I've been in the theater for forty years!" I explained to him that it was not a matter of personalities, age or experience, not a matter of *who* said it, but of *what* was said, and that I would give in to his office boy, if the boy happened to be *right.* Woods did not answer; I knew even then that he did not hear me.

The final, definitive version of *Night of January 16th* is closest, in content, to the script of *Woman on Trial.* I made no changes in story or substance; the additional changes I made were mainly grammatical. That final version is the one now published here, in this book.

I am glad to see it published. Up to now, I had felt as if it were an illegitimate child roaming the world. Now, with this publication, it becomes legitimately mine.

And, although it has played all over the world, I feel as if it were a play that has never been produced.

—Ayn Rand
New York, June 1968

NOTE TO PRODUCER

This play is a murder trial without a prearranged verdict. The jurors are to be selected from the audience. They are to witness the play as real jurors and bring in a verdict at the end of the last act. Two short endings are written for the play—to be used according to the verdict.

The play is built in such a way that the evidence of the defendant's guilt or innocence is evenly balanced and the decision will have to be based upon the jurors' own values and characters. The two parties opposed in the trial are as radically antagonistic as will be members of any audience, where some will sympathize with the wife, others with the mistress. Either decision will bring the protest of the opposite side; the case is bound to arouse arguments and discussions, for its underlying conflict is the basic conflict of two different types of humanity. It is really the audience who is thus put on trial. In the words of the defense attorney: "Who is on trial in this case? Karen Andre? No! It's you, ladies and gentlemen of the jury, who are here on trial. It is your own souls that will be brought to light when your decision is rendered!"

The jurors' seats are to be on the stage, as in a real courtroom. Thus we give the public all the excitement of a murder trial. We heighten the public's interest by leaving the decision in its own hands and add to the suspense by the fact that no audience, at any performance of the play, can be sure of its outcome.

A NOTE FROM AYN RAND'S EXECUTOR

In 1973, for a production of *Night of January 16th* under the title of *Penthouse Legend,* Ayn Rand made several dozen relatively small editorial changes in the text of the play, mostly with a view to updating the language. Judging from correspondence of hers that has recently been discovered, Miss Rand regarded these changes as definitive. They are, therefore, being incorporated in all future printings, beginning with this one.

—Leonard Peikoff
May 1985

CHARACTERS

JUDGE HEATH
DISTRICT ATTORNEY FLINT
DEFENSE ATTORNEY STEVENS
KAREN ANDRE
DR. KIRKLAND
JOHN HUTCHINS
HOMER VAN FLEET
ELMER SWEENEY
MAGDA SVENSON
NANCY LEE FAULKNER
JOHN GRAHAM WHITFIELD
JAMES CHANDLER
SIEGURD JUNGQUIST
"GUTS" REGAN
COURT ATTENDANTS

Place   New York Courtroom

Time   Present

18

Night of January 16th

ACT I

The stage represents a New York courtroom. It faces the audience, so that the public is in the position of spectators in a real courtroom. In the center of the back is the Judge's desk on a high platform; behind it is the door to the Judge's chambers; by the side of the desk, at left, is the witness stand, facing the audience; behind it is the door to the jury room. In front of the Judge's desk is the desk of the Court Reporter; at right—the desk of the Court Clerk. Behind it is the door through which witnesses enter the courtroom. Farther downstage, at right, is a table for the defendant and attorneys; at left—another table for the prosecution. At the wall, left, are the twelve seats for the jurors. Farther downstage is a door through which spectators enter the courtroom. At the opposite wall, at right, are a few chairs for spectators. Steps lead down from the stage in the right and left aisles. When the curtain rises the court session is ready to open, but the JUDGE *has not yet made his appearance. The prosecution and defense are ready at their respective tables.*

DISTRICT ATTORNEY FLINT *is a heavy, middle-aged man with the kindly appearance of a respectable father of a family and the shrewd, piercing manner of a pawn-broker.* DEFENSE ATTORNEY STEVENS *is tall, gray-haired, displaying the grooming and sophisticated grace of a man of the world. He is watching his client, who does not pay any attention to him and, sitting at the defense table, calmly, almost insolently studies the*

19

audience. The client, the defendant KAREN ANDRE, *is twenty-eight. One's first impression of her is that to handle her would require the services of an animal trainer, not an attorney. Yet there is nothing emotional or rebellious in her countenance; it is one of profound, inexorable calm; but one feels the tense vitality, the primitive fire, the untamed strength in the defiant im- mobility of her slender body, the proud line of her head held high, the sweep of her tousled hair. Her clothes are conspicuous by their severe, tailored simplicity; a very costly simplicity, one can notice, but not the elegance of a woman who gives much thought to her clothes, rather that of one who knows she can make any rag attractive and does it unconsciously.*

When the curtain rises the lights in the audience do not go out.

BAILIFF: Court attention!

[EVERYONE *rises as* JUDGE HEATH *enters.* BAILIFF *raps*]

Superior Court Number Eleven of the State of New York. The Honorable Judge William Heath presiding.

[*The* JUDGE *takes his seat.* BAILIFF *raps and* EVERYONE *sits down*]

JUDGE HEATH: The people of the State of New York versus Karen Andre.
FLINT: Ready, your Honor.
STEVENS: Ready, your Honor.
JUDGE HEATH: Mr. Clerk, draw a jury.

[*The* CLERK *steps to the proscenium with a list in his hand, and addresses the audience*]

CLERK: Ladies and gentlemen, you are to be the jurors in this case. Twelve of you will be drawn to perform this duty. You will kindly step up here, take your seats, and receive your instructions from Judge Heath.

[*He reads twelve names. The* JURORS *take their places. If some are unwilling and do not appear, the* CLERK *calls a few more names. When the jurors are seated, the lights in the audience go out.* JUDGE HEATH *addresses the jury*]

JUDGE HEATH: Ladies and gentlemen, you are the jurors who will try this case. At its close, you will retire to the jury room and vote upon your verdict. At the end of each day's session, you will remain seated until the Bailiff escorts you to the jury room. I instruct you to listen to the testimony carefully and pronounce your judgment to the best of your ability and integrity. You are to determine whether the defendant is Guilty or Not Guilty and her fate rests in your hands . . . The District Attorney may now proceed.

[DISTRICT ATTORNEY FLINT *rises and addresses the jury*]

FLINT: Your Honor! Ladies and gentlemen of the jury! On the sixteenth of January, near midnight, when the lights of Broadway blazed an electric dawn over the festive crowds below, the body of a man came hurtling through space and crashed—a disfigured mess—at the foot of the Faulkner Building. That body had been Sweden's great financier—Bjorn Faulkner. He fell fifty stories from his luxurious penthouse. *A suicide,* we were told. A great man unwilling to bend before his imminent ruin. A man who found a fall from the roof of a skyscraper shorter and easier than a descent from his tottering throne of the world's financial dictator. Only a few months ago, behind every big transaction of gold in the world, stood that well-known figure: young, tall, with an arrogant smile, with kingdoms and nations in the palm of one hand—and a whip in the other. If gold is the world's life blood, then Bjorn Faulkner, holding all its dark, hidden arteries, regulating its ebb and flow, its every pulsation, was the heart of the world. Well, ladies and gentlemen, the world has just had a heart attack. And like all heart attacks, it was rather sudden. No one

suspected the gigantic swindle that lay at the foundation
of the Faulkner enterprises. A few days after his death,
the earth shook from the crash of his business; thousands of investors were stricken with the paralysis
which follows an attack, when that monstrous heart
stopped beating. Bjorn Faulkner had had a hard struggle
facing the world. But he had a much harder struggle to
face in his heart, a struggle which this trial will have to
uncover. Two women ruled his life—and death. Here is
one of them, ladies and gentlemen.

[*Points at* KAREN]

Karen Andre, Faulkner's efficient secretary and notorious mistress. But six months ago Faulkner came to
America to get a loan and save his fortune. Fate sent
him a means to save his own heart—in the person of the
lovely girl who is now his widow, Nancy Lee Faulkner,
only daughter of John Graham Whitfield, our great philanthropist. Faulkner thought he had found salvation and
a new life in the virtuous innocence of his young bride.
And the best proof of it is that two weeks after his wedding he dismissed his secretary—Karen Andre. He was
through with her. But, ladies and gentlemen, one is not
easily through with a woman like Karen Andre. We can
only guess what hatred and revenge smouldered in her
heart; but they leaped into flame on the *night of January
sixteenth*. Bjorn Faulkner *did not* kill himself. He was
murdered. Murdered by the very delicate and capable
hands which you see here before you.

[*He points at* KAREN]

The hands that helped to raise Bjorn Faulkner high over
the world; the hands that threw him down, from as great
a height, to crash into a pavement cold as this woman's
heart. That, ladies and gentlemen, is what we are going
to prove.

[FLINT *pauses; then calls*]

Our first witness will be Doctor Kirkland.

CLERK: Dr. Kirkland!

[DR. KIRKLAND, *elderly, kindly, and indifferent, makes his way toward the witness stand*]

You solemnly swear to tell the truth, the whole truth and nothing but the truth so help you God?

KIRKLAND: I do.

FLINT: Kindly state your name.

KIRKLAND: Thomas Kirkland.

FLINT: What is your occupation?

KIRKLAND: Medical examiner of this county.

FLINT: In the course of your duty, what were you called upon to do on the night of January sixteenth?

KIRKLAND: I was called to examine the body of Bjorn Faulkner.

FLINT: What did you find?

KIRKLAND: A body mangled to an extreme degree.

FLINT: What did you establish as the cause of death?

KIRKLAND: A fall from a great height.

FLINT: How long had Faulkner been dead when you examined his body?

KIRKLAND: I reached it about half an hour after the fall.

FLINT: Judging by the condition of the body, could you say exactly how long it had been dead?

KIRKLAND: No, I could not. Owing to the cold weather, the blood had coagulated immediately, which makes a difference of several hours impossible to detect.

FLINT: Therefore, it is possible that Faulkner had been dead longer than half an hour?

KIRKLAND: It is possible.

FLINT: Could his death have been caused by anything other than this fall?

KIRKLAND: I found no evidence of it.

FLINT: For instance, had his skull been broken before the fall, would you be able to tell it by examining the body?

KIRKLAND: No. Owing to the condition of the body, it would be impossible to determine.

FLINT: That's all, Doctor.

STEVENS: Did you find any trace of any such earlier wound in your examination of the body, Doctor Kirkland?

KIRKLAND: No, I did not.

STEVENS: Did you find any indication that death might have been caused by anything other than the fall?

KIRKLAND: No, I did not.

STEVENS: That's all.

[DR. KIRKLAND *leaves the stand and exits*]

FLINT: John Hutchins!

CLERK: John Hutchins!

[HUTCHINS *is a timid, elderly man, neat, but almost shabby; he walks to the stand shyly, cringing, nervously fingering his hat in both hands*]

You solemnly swear to tell the truth, the whole truth and nothing but the truth so help you God?

HUTCHINS: Yes, sir, I do.

FLINT: What is your name?

HUTCHINS: [*Timidly*] John Joseph Hutchins.

FLINT: And your occupation?

HUTCHINS: I'm the night watchman in the Faulkner Building, sir.

FLINT: Did Mr. Faulkner have business offices in that building?

HUTCHINS: Yes, sir.

FLINT: Do you know who owned the penthouse on the roof of the building?

HUTCHINS: Certainly, sir. Mr. Faulkner did.

FLINT: And who lived there?

HUTCHINS: Mr. Faulkner and Miss Andre, sir. That is, before Mr. Faulkner's marriage.

FLINT: And after the marriage?

HUTCHINS: After the marriage, Miss Andre lived there— alone.

FLINT: Have you ever seen Mr. Faulkner calling on Miss Andre after his marriage?

HUTCHINS: Only once, sir.

FLINT: And that was?

HUTCHINS: On the night of January sixteenth.

FLINT: Tell us about it, Mr. Hutchins.

HUTCHINS: Well, sir, it was about ten thirty and—

FLINT: How did you know the time?

HUTCHINS: I come on duty at ten, sir, and it was no more than a half hour after. The entrance door bell rang. I went down to the lobby and opened the door. It was Miss Andre, and Mr. Faulkner was with her. I was surprised, because Miss Andre has her own key and, usually, she opens the door herself.

FLINT: Was she alone with Mr. Faulkner?

HUTCHINS: No, sir. There were two other gentlemen with them.

FLINT: Who were they?

HUTCHINS: I don't know, sir.

FLINT: Had you ever seen them before?

HUTCHINS: No, sir, never.

FLINT: What did they look like?

HUTCHINS: They were tall and sort of slender, both of them. One had sharp cheekbones, as I remember. The other one—I couldn't see his face at all, sir, on account of his hat being all crooked over his eyes. He must have had a bit too much, sir, meaning no disrespect.

FLINT: Just what do you mean?

HUTCHINS: Well, he was a bit tight, sir, if I'm permitted to say so. He wasn't very steady on his feet, so that Mr. Faulkner and the other gentleman had to help him. They almost dragged him into the elevator.

FLINT: Did Mr. Faulkner look worried?

HUTCHINS: No, sir. On the contrary, he seemed very happy.

FLINT: Did he look like a man contemplating suicide?

STEVENS: We object, your Honor!

JUDGE HEATH: Objection sustained.

FLINT: Did the others in the party seem happy, too?

HUTCHINS: Yes, sir. Miss Andre was smiling. And Mr. Faulkner laughed when they went up in the elevator.

FLINT: Did you see any of them leave, that night?

HUTCHINS: Yes, sir. The first one left about fifteen minutes later.

FLINT: Who was that?

HUTCHINS: The drunken one, sir. He came down in the elevator, all by himself. He didn't seem quite so drunk no more. He could walk, but he staggered a little.

FLINT: Did you see where he went?

HUTCHINS: Well, I wanted to help him to the door, seeing the condition he was in, but he noticed me coming and he hurried out. He got into a car parked right at the entrance and did he step on it! But I'm sure he didn't go far. The cops must've got him.

FLINT: What makes you think that?

HUTCHINS: Well, I noticed a car that started right after him.

[KAREN *comes to life, suddenly, out of her frozen calm. She jumps up and throws her question at* HUTCHINS]

KAREN: What car?

JUDGE HEATH: The defendant will please keep quiet.

[STEVENS *whispers to* KAREN, *making her sit down*]

FLINT: If Miss Andre will let me do the questioning, I may satisfy her curiosity. I was just going to ask what car, Mr. Hutchins?

HUTCHINS: It was a big black sedan, sir. It was parked two cars away from him.

FLINT: Who was in it?

HUTCHINS: I saw only one man.

FLINT: What makes you think he was after the first car?

HUTCHINS: Well, I couldn't be sure he was, sir. It just looked funny they started together like that.

FLINT: Did you see that other guest of Miss Andre's leaving, too?

HUTCHINS: Yes, sir. It wasn't more than ten minutes later when he came out of the elevator.

FLINT: What did he do?

HUTCHINS: Nothing unusual, sir. He seemed to be in a hurry. He went right out.

FLINT: And then what happened?

HUTCHINS: I started on my round of the building; and then, it must have been an hour later, I heard screams outside, in the street. I rushed down and as I came into the lobby, I saw Miss Andre running out of the elevator, her gown all torn, sobbing wild-like. I ran after her. We pushed through the crowd outside and *there* was Mr. Faulkner all over the pavement.

FLINT: What did Miss Andre do?

HUTCHINS: She screamed and fell on her knees. It was horrible, sir. I've never seen a body smashed like that.

FLINT: That is all, Mr. Hutchins.

STEVENS: You said that you had never seen Mr. Faulkner calling on Miss Andre after his marriage, with the exception of that night. Now, tell me, do you always see every visitor who comes into the building at night?

HUTCHINS: No, sir. I'm not in the lobby all of the time, I have my rounds to make. If the guest has a key, he can come in and I wouldn't see him at all.

STEVENS: In other words, Miss Andre might have had any number of visitors, Mr. Faulkner included, whom you never saw come in?

HUTCHINS: Yes, sir, quite right.

STEVENS: That is all.

[HUTCHINS *leaves the stand and exits*]

FLINT: Homer Van Fleet!

CLERK: Homer Van Fleet!

[HOMER VAN FLEET *makes his appearance. He is tall, not very young, and can be best described by the word "correct." His clothes are correct—smart, but not flashy; his manner is correct—cool, exact, strictly business-like. He is diffident and dignified at the same time*]

You solemnly swear to tell the truth, the whole truth and nothing but the truth so help you God?

VAN FLEET: I do.

FLINT: Your name?

VAN FLEET: Homer Herbert Van Fleet.

FLINT: Occupation?

VAN FLEET: Private investigator.

FLINT: What was your last assignment?

VAN FLEET: Shadowing Mr. Bjorn Faulkner.

FLINT: By whom were you hired to do it?

VAN FLEET: By Mrs. Bjorn Faulkner.

[*A slight reaction in the courtroom*]

FLINT: Were you shadowing Mr. Faulkner on the night of January sixteenth?

VAN FLEET: I was.

FLINT: Kindly tell us about it.

VAN FLEET: I'll start with six thirteen p.m.

FLINT: How do you know the time, Mr. Van Fleet?

VAN FLEET: Part of my duties. Had to record it and report to Mrs. Faulkner.

FLINT: I see.

VAN FLEET: [*He speaks briskly, precisely, as if reporting to an employer*] Six thirteen p.m. Mr. Faulkner leaves home on Long Island. Wears formal dress suit. Drives car himself, alone. Special notation: Unusual speed all the way to New York.

FLINT: Where does Mr. Faulkner go?

VAN FLEET: He drives up to the Faulkner Building and goes in. It is now seven fifty-seven p.m., all offices closed. I wait outside, in my car. Nine thirty-five p.m. Mr. Faulkner comes out with Miss Andre. Miss Andre is dressed formally. Special notation: Miss Andre is wearing a corsage of orchids of unusual proportions. They drive away.

FLINT: Where do they go?

VAN FLEET: No one is perfect in this world.

FLINT: What do you mean?

VAN FLEET: I mean I lost track of them. Due to Mr. Faulkner's speed and to an accident.

FLINT: What accident?

VAN FLEET: My left fender crashing into a truck; damages for which fender charged to Mrs. Faulkner.

FLINT: What did you do when you lost track of them?

VAN FLEET: Returned to the Faulkner Building and waited.

FLINT: When did they return?

VAN FLEET: Ten thirty p.m. exactly. A gray car follows them. Mr. Faulkner gets out and helps Miss Andre. While she rings the bell, he opens the door of the gray car; a tall gentleman in formal clothes steps out, and together they help out a third gentleman, the latter wearing a dark gray sport coat. Special notation: The aforementioned gentleman shows signs of inebriation. They all go into the Faulkner Building.

FLINT: Then what did you do?

VAN FLEET: Left my car and went into Gary's Grill, across the street from the Faulkner Building. I must explain that I allow myself time to take nourishment every four hours while on duty and four hours had elapsed since we left Long Island. I sat at a window and watched the Faulkner entrance door.

FLINT: What did you observe?

VAN FLEET: Nothing—for fifteen minutes. Then the man in the gray coat comes out and starts the car—the gray car. Obviously in a hurry. Drives south.

FLINT: Did you see the other stranger leave?

VAN FLEET: Yes, ten minutes later. He gets into a car which stands at the curb. I don't know how it got there, but there it is and he seems to have the keys, for he gets in and drives away. South.

FLINT: Have you ever seen Mr. Faulkner with these two men before?

VAN FLEET: No. First time I ever saw them.

FLINT: What did you do when they left?

VAN FLEET: I wait. Mr. Faulkner is now alone up in the penthouse with Miss Andre. I'm curious—professionally. Decide to do some closer investigating. Have a special observation post; had used it before.

FLINT: And where is that?

VAN FLEET: At the Sky Top. Night club, roof of Brooks Building, three doors from Faulkner's. There's an open gallery there, off the dance floor. You go out and you can see the Faulkner penthouse clear as the palm of your hand. I go out, I look and I yell.

FLINT: What do you see?

VAN FLEET: No lights. Karen Andre's white gown shimmering in the moonlight. She is hoisting a man's body up on the parapet. A man in evening clothes. Faulkner. He's unconscious. No resistance. She pushes him with all her strength. He goes over the parapet. Down. Into space.

FLINT: Then what do you do?

VAN FLEET: I rush back into the dining room. Yell about what I'd seen. A crowd follows me down to the Faulkner Building. We find the bloody mess on the pavement and Miss Andre sobbing over it, fit to move a first-night audience.

FLINT: Did you speak to her?

VAN FLEET: No. The police arrive and I report what I'd seen, as I've told you here.

FLINT: Your witness.

[STEVENS *gets up and walks slowly toward* VAN FLEET, *eyeing him steadily*]

STEVENS: Can you kindly tell us, Mr. Van Fleet, when did you start in the employ of Mrs. Faulkner?

VAN FLEET: October thirteenth last.

STEVENS: Can you tell us the date of Mr. and Mrs. Faulkner's wedding?

VAN FLEET: October twelfth. The day before.

STEVENS: Exactly. *Just the day before.* In other words, Mrs. Faulkner hired you to spy on her husband the day after their wedding?

VAN FLEET: So it seems.

STEVENS: What were Mrs. Faulkner's instructions when you were hired?

VAN FLEET: To watch every action of Mr. Faulkner and report in detail.

STEVENS: Any special attention to Miss Andre?

VAN FLEET: Not specified.

STEVENS: Had Mr. Faulkner been calling on Miss Andre after his marriage?

VAN FLEET: Yes. Frequently.

STEVENS: In the daytime?

VAN FLEET: Seldom.

STEVENS: Did you report that to Mrs. Faulkner?

VAN FLEET: I did.

STEVENS: What was Mrs. Faulkner's reaction to these reports?

VAN FLEET: Mrs. Faulkner is a lady and, as such, she has no reactions.

STEVENS: Did she seem worried?

VAN FLEET: I don't believe so. [*He declaims in a slightly unnatural manner*] Mr. Faulkner was the most devoted of husbands and he loved his wife dearly.

STEVENS: Just how do you know that?

VAN FLEET: Those are Mrs. Faulkner's own words.

STEVENS: Now, Mr. Van Fleet, can you tell us exactly what time you started for the Sky Top Night Club on the evening of January sixteenth?

VAN FLEET: At eleven thirty-two exactly.

STEVENS: How long a walk is it from the Faulkner Building to the Sky Top?

VAN FLEET: Three minutes.

STEVENS: What time was it when you came out to the balcony at the Sky Top?

VAN FLEET: Eleven fifty-seven.

STEVENS: So it took you exactly twenty-five minutes to get to the balcony. What were you doing the rest of the time?

VAN FLEET: Of course, they have a dance floor at the Sky Top . . . and other things.

STEVENS: Did you take advantage of the . . . "other things"?

VAN FLEET: Well, I just had a couple of drinks, if I understand the drift of your curiosity. But it doesn't mean that you can say I was intoxicated.

STEVENS: I have said nothing of the kind—as yet. Now, then, you saw Miss Andre pushing Mr. Faulkner off the roof, and it was a little distance away, in the darkness, and you were . . . well, shall we say you just had a couple of drinks?

VAN FLEET: The drinks had nothing to do with it.

STEVENS: Are you quite certain that she was *pushing* him? Isn't it possible that she was *struggling* with him?

VAN FLEET: Well, it's a funny way of struggling. If I were struggling with a man, I wouldn't be hoisting him up by his . . . I wouldn't be hoisting him up, I mean.

STEVENS: Mr. Van Fleet, what were Mrs. Faulkner's instructions to you before you came here to testify?

VAN FLEET: [*With indignation*] I received no instructions of any kind. I may inform you that Mrs. Faulkner is not here to instruct me, were she inclined to do so. She has been taken to California by her father—to rest her shattered nerves.

STEVENS: Mr. Van Fleet, do you think that Mr. Faulkner's suicide is very flattering to Mrs. Faulkner?

FLINT: We object!

JUDGE HEATH: Objection sustained.

STEVENS: Mr. Van Fleet, can you tell us how much a witness to Mr. Faulkner's *murder* would be worth to Mrs. Faulkner?

FLINT: [*Jumping up*] We object, your Honor!

JUDGE HEATH: Objection sustained.

VAN FLEET: I should like to remind Mr. Stevens that he may be sued for making insinuations such as these.

STEVENS: I made no insinuation, Mr. Van Fleet. I merely asked a question in a general way.

VAN FLEET: Well, I would like to inform you—in a general way—that perjury is not part of a private investigator's duties.

STEVENS: No special notations to the rule?

VAN FLEET: None!

STEVENS: That is all, Mr. Van Fleet.

KAREN: Not quite. I want you to ask him two more questions, Stevens.

STEVENS: Certainly, Miss Andre. What are the questions?

[KAREN *whispers to* STEVENS; *he is astonished*]

STEVENS: What kind of a car do you drive, Mr. Van Fleet?

VAN FLEET: [*Astonished, too*] A brown Buick two-door sedan. Last year's model. Old but serviceable.

[KAREN *whispers to* STEVENS]

STEVENS: Did you see any car following the gentleman in the gray coat when he drove away, Mr. Van Fleet?

VAN FLEET: I cannot recall that I did. The traffic was quite heavy at that time.

STEVENS: That's all, Mr. Van Fleet.

[VAN FLEET *exits*]

FLINT: Inspector Sweeney!

CLERK: Inspector Sweeney!

[POLICE INSPECTOR SWEENEY, *round-faced, somewhat naive, walks to the stand*]

You solemnly swear to tell the truth, the whole truth and nothing but the truth so help you God?

SWEENEY: I do.

FLINT: Your name?

SWEENEY: Elmer Sweeney.

FLINT: Your occupation?

SWEENEY: Inspector of Police.

FLINT: On the night of January sixteenth were you called upon to investigate Bjorn Faulkner's death?

SWEENEY: Yes, sir. I was one of the first officers to reach the spot.

FLINT: Did you question Miss Andre?

SWEENEY: Not right away. Before I could do anything, that fellow Van Fleet rushed up to me and yelled that he had seen Karen Andre throw Faulkner off the roof.

FLINT: How did Miss Andre react to this?

SWEENEY: She was stunned. She stood there, her eyes wide fit to burst. And then, cross my heart, sir, she started laughing. I thought she'd went crazy.

FLINT: What did you do?

SWEENEY: I ordered her held for questioning and we took her up with us in the elevator—to examine the penthouse. What a joint!

FLINT: Did you find anything unusual?

SWEENEY: Unusual—yes, sir. The bedroom.

FLINT: Ah, and what did you find in the bedroom?

SWEENEY: Nightgowns, sir. Lace nightgowns, just about made of thin air. A crystal bathtub in the bathroom. And we turned the shower on—and the water was perfumed.

FLINT: [*Smiling*] You misunderstood my question, Inspector. I wasn't referring to the esthetic values of the penthouse. I asked if you found anything unusual that could be connected with Bjorn Faulkner's death?

SWEENEY: Yes, sir. In the living room.

FLINT: And what was that?

SWEENEY: A letter. It was lying in plain sight on a table. It was sealed and the address said: "To whomsoever finds it first."

[FLINT *takes a letter from the* CLERK *and hands it to* SWEENEY]

FLINT: Is this the letter?

SWEENEY: Yes, sir.

FLINT: Will you kindly read it to the jury?

SWEENEY: [*Reading*] "If any future historian wants to record my last advice to humanity, I'll say that I found only two enjoyable things on this earth whose every door was open to me: My whip over the world and Karen Andre. To those who can use it, the advice is worth what it has cost mankind. Bjorn Faulkner."

FLINT: [*Handing letter to* CLERK] Submitted as evidence.

JUDGE HEATH: Accepted as Exhibit A.

FLINT: Did you question Miss Andre about this letter?

SWEENEY: I did. She said that Faulkner wrote the letter and left it there, on the table, and ordered her not to touch it, then went out to the roof garden. She struggled with him, when she saw what he was going to do, but she couldn't stop him.

FLINT: Did you ask her who had been with them that night?

SWEENEY: I did. She said two gentlemen had: they were friends of Mr. Faulkner and *she had never seen them before*. He picked them up in a night club, that evening, and brought them along. She said their names were "Jerry White" and "Dick Saunders."

FLINT: Did you try to find any gentlemen by these names among Mr. Faulkner's acquaintances?

SWEENEY: We did. We found that no one had ever heard of them.

FLINT: And Miss Andre told you, as she did at the inquest, that she had never seen these two men before?

SWEENEY: Yes, sir.

FLINT: Was she very emphatic about that?

SWEENEY: Yes, sir. *Very.*

FLINT: That is all, Inspector.

STEVENS: Miss Andre told you that she had struggled with Faulkner to prevent his suicide. Did you notice any evidence of a struggle in her clothes?

SWEENEY: Yes, sir. Her dress was torn. It had diamond shoulder straps, and one of them was broken, so that she had to hold the dress up with one hand.

STEVENS: What did you think of that?

SWEENEY: [*Embarrassed*] Do I have to answer?

STEVENS: You certainly do.

SWEENEY: Well . . . I wished he had broken the other strap, too.

STEVENS: I meant, did you think that the dress looked as though it had been torn in a struggle?

SWEENEY: It looked like it, yes, sir.

STEVENS: Now, can you tell us why on earth you turned the shower on in the bathroom?

SWEENEY: [*Embarrassed*] Well, you see, we heard Faulkner had wine instead of water in it.

STEVENS: [*Laughing*] You mustn't believe all the legends you hear about Bjorn Faulkner . . . That's all, Inspector.

[SWEENEY *leaves the stand and exits*]

FLINT: Magda Svenson!
CLERK: Magda Svenson!

[MAGDA SVENSON *enters and waddles toward the witness stand. She is fat, middle-aged, with tight, drawn lips, suspicious eyes, an air of offended righteousness. Her clothes are plain, old-fashioned, meticulously neat*]

You solemnly swear to tell the truth, the whole truth and nothing but the truth so help you God?

MAGDA: [*Speaks with a pronounced Swedish accent*] I swear. [*She takes the Bible, raises it slowly to her lips, kisses it solemnly, and hands it back, taking the whole ceremony with a profound religious seriousness*]

FLINT: What is your name?

MAGDA: You know it. You just call me.

FLINT: Kindly answer my questions without argument. State your name.

MAGDA: Magda Svenson.

FLINT: What is your occupation?

MAGDA: I am housekeeper.

FLINT: By whom were you employed last?

MAGDA: By Herr Bjorn Faulkner and before that his father.

FLINT: How long have you been employed by them?

MAGDA: I been in the family thirty-eight years. I remember Herr Bjorn since he was little child.

FLINT: When did you come to America?

MAGDA: I been here five years.

FLINT: What were the duties Mr. Faulkner assigned to you?

MAGDA: I keep penthouse for him. He visit here every year or so. I stay even after he go, when he get married. But I never employed by this one.

[*She points at* KAREN *with undisguised hatred*]

FLINT: Now, Mrs. Svenson, what—

MAGDA: [*Offended*] *Miss* Svenson.

FLINT: I beg your pardon, Miss Svenson. What do you know about Miss Andre's relations with Mr. Faulkner?

MAGDA: [*With forceful indignation*] Decent woman like me shouldn't know about such things. But sin is shameless in this world.

FLINT: Tell us about it, Miss Svenson.

MAGDA: From very first day this woman appeared, she was sleeping with Herr Faulkner. It isn't good thing when a man forgets line between his bed and his desk. And she put her claws tight on both. Sometimes, they talked loans and dividends in bed; other times, the door to his office was locked and, under the window shades that was pulled down, I seen her lace pants on the window sill.

STEVENS: [*Jumping up*] Your Honor! We object!

FLINT: I think Miss Andre should have objected many years ago!

STEVENS: Such line of testimony is outrageous!

FLINT: These are facts pertaining to the vital question of their relationship and—

JUDGE HEATH: [*Rapping his gavel*] Silence, gentlemen! I shall ask the witness to word her testimony more carefully.

MAGDA: Sin is sin any name you call it, Judge.

FLINT: Miss Svenson, do you know of any instance when Miss Andre's conduct was detrimental to Mr. Faulkner in other ways than moral?

MAGDA: I do so. You try count up all money he waste on that woman.

FLINT: Can you tell us an instance of Mr. Faulkner's extravagance?

MAGDA: I tell you. He had a platinum gown made for her. Yes, I said platinum. Fine mesh, fine and soft as silk. She wore it on her naked body. He would make a fire in the fireplace and he would heat the dress and then put it on her. It cooled and you could see her body in silver sheen, and it been more decent if she had been naked. And she ask to put it on as hot as she can stand, and if it burned her shameless skin, she laughed like the pagan she is, and he kissed the burn, wild like tiger!

STEVENS: Your Honor! We object! This testimony is irrelevant and only tends to prejudice the jury against Miss Andre!

KAREN: [*Very calmly*] Let her talk, Stevens.

[*She looks at the jury and for a swift moment we see a smile, mischievous, tempting, radiant, a surprise in this cold business woman, revealing an entirely different type of femininity*]

Perhaps it may prejudice the jury in my favor.

[*Commotion in the courtroom.* STEVENS *stares at* KAREN. JUDGE HEATH *strikes his gavel*]

FLINT: Mr. Stevens has my sympathy. His client is not an easy one to handle.

JUDGE HEATH: Silence! Objection overruled.

FLINT: Did you observe Mr. Faulkner's attitude toward his marriage?

MAGDA: He was happy for first time in his life. He was happy like decent man what found right road.

FLINT: Did you know of anything that made him worry in those days, that could bring him to suicide eventually?

MAGDA: No. Nothing.

FLINT: Now, tell us, Miss Svenson, did you observe Miss Andre's attitude toward Mr. Faulkner's marriage?

MAGDA: She silent, like stone statue. She—

[*There is a commotion in the courtroom.* NANCY LEE FAULKNER *appears at the spectators' door at left.* NANCY LEE FAULKNER *is twenty-two, blond, slender, delicate, perfect as a costly porcelain statuette. Her exquisite white skin is a contrast to the somber, unrelieved black of her clothes; they are clothes of mourning, severe and in perfect taste.* EVERYONE *in the courtroom stares at her.* KAREN *turns toward her slowly. But* NANCY LEE *does not look at* KAREN. FLINT *cannot restrain an exclamation of astonishment*]

FLINT: Mrs. Faulkner!

NANCY LEE: [*She speaks in a soft, slow voice*] I understand you wanted to call me as a witness, Mr. Flint?

FLINT: I did, Mrs. Faulkner, but I thought you were in California.

NANCY LEE: I was. I escaped.

FLINT: You escaped?

NANCY LEE: Father was concerned over my health. He wouldn't allow me to come back. But I want to do my duty toward the memory of . . . [*Her voice trembles a little*] my husband. I'm at your disposal, Mr. Flint.

FLINT: I can only express my deepest appreciation, Mrs. Faulkner. If you will kindly take a seat, we will be ready for you in just a little while.

NANCY LEE: Thank you.

[*She takes one of the spectators' chairs at the wall, at right*]

FLINT: [*To* MAGDA] You were telling us about Miss Andre's attitude toward Mr. Faulkner's marriage, Miss Svenson.

MAGDA: I said she keep silent. But I hear her crying one night, after marriage. Crying, sobbing—and that the first and only time in her life.

FLINT: Did she seem to . . . suffer much?

MAGDA: Suffer? No. Not her. One man more or less make no much difference to her. I seen her unfaithful to Herr Faulkner on the night of his wedding.

[*Reaction in the courtroom. Even* KAREN *takes notice, a little startled*]

FLINT: Unfaithful? With whom?

MAGDA: I don't know the man. I seen him first time the night of Herr Faulkner's wedding.

FLINT: Tell us about it.

MAGDA: I gone to wedding. Ah, it was beautiful. My poor Herr Bjorn so handsome and the young bride all white and lovely as lily. [*Sniffles audibly*] I cried like looking at my own children. [*Her voice changes; she points at* KAREN *ferociously*] But *she* not go to wedding!

FLINT: Did Miss Andre stay at home?

MAGDA: She stay home. I come back early. I come in servants' door. She not hear me come. She was home. But she was not alone.

FLINT: Who was with her?

MAGDA: *He* was. The man. Out on the roof, in the garden. It was dark, but I could see. He holding her in his arms and I think he want to crush her bones. He bent her back so far I think she fall into her reflection in the pool. And then he kiss her and I think he never get his lips off hers.

FLINT: And then?

MAGDA: She step aside and say something. I cannot hear, she speak very soft. He not say word. He just take her hand and kiss it and hold it on his lips so long I get tired waiting and go back to my room.

FLINT: Did you learn the name of that man?

MAGDA: No.

FLINT: Did you see him again?

MAGDA: Yes. Once.

FLINT: And when was that?

MAGDA: The night of January sixteenth.

[*A movement in the courtroom*]

FLINT: Tell us about it, Miss Svenson.

MAGDA: Well, *she* very strange that day. She call me and said I have the rest of day off. And I been suspicious.

FLINT: Why did that make you suspicious?

MAGDA: My day off is Thursday and I not asked for second day. So I said I not need day off, and she said she not need me. So I go.

FLINT: What time did you go?

MAGDA: About four o'clock. But I want to know secret. I come back.

FLINT: When did you come back?

MAGDA: About ten at night. The house dark, she not home. So I wait. Half hour after, I hear them come. I seen Herr

Faulkner with her. So I afraid to stay. But before I go I seen two gentlemen with them. One gentleman, he drunk. I not know him.

FLINT: Did you know the other one?

MAGDA: The other one—he was tall and lanky and had sharp cheekbones. He was the man I seen kissing Miss Andre.

FLINT: [*Almost triumphant*] That's all, Miss Svenson.

[MAGDA *is about to leave the stand.* STEVENS *stops her*]

STEVENS: Just a minute, Miss Svenson. You still have to have a little talk with me.

MAGDA: [*Resentfully*] For what? I say all I know.

STEVENS: You may know the answers to a few more questions. Now, you said that you had seen that stranger kissing Miss Andre?

MAGDA: Yes, I did.

STEVENS: You said it was dark, that night when you saw him for the first time?

MAGDA: Yes, it was dark.

STEVENS: And, on the night of January sixteenth, when you were so ingeniously spying on your mistress, you said that you saw her come in with Mr. Faulkner, and you hurried to depart in order not to be caught. Am I correct?

MAGDA: You have a good memory.

STEVENS: You just had a swift glance at the two gentlemen with them?

MAGDA: Yes.

STEVENS: Can you tell us what the drunken gentleman looked like?

MAGDA: How can I? No time to notice face and too dark at door.

STEVENS: So! It was too dark? And you were in a hurry? And yet you were able to identify a man you had seen but once before?

MAGDA: [*With all the strength of her righteous indignation*] Let me tell you, mister! I'm under oath as you say,

and I'm religious woman and respect oath. But I said it
was the same man and I say it again!

STEVENS: That is all. Thank you, Miss Svenson.

[MAGDA *leaves the stand, carefully avoiding looking at*
KAREN. *There is a little hush of expectancy as all eyes
turn to* NANCY LEE FAULKNER. FLINT *calls solemnly,
distinctly*]

FLINT: Mrs. Faulkner!

[NANCY LEE *rises and walks to the stand slowly, as if
each step taxed her strength. She is calm, but gives the
impression that the ordeal is painful to her and that she
is making a brave effort to do her duty*]

CLERK: You solemnly swear to tell the truth, the whole
truth and nothing but the truth so help you God?

NANCY LEE: I do.

FLINT: What is your name?

NANCY LEE: Nancy Lee Faulkner.

FLINT: What relation were you to the late Bjorn Faulkner?

NANCY LEE: I was . . . his wife.

FLINT: I realize how painful this is to you, Mrs. Faulkner,
and I appreciate your courage, but I will have to ask you
many questions that will awaken sad memories.

NANCY LEE: I am ready, Mr. Flint.

FLINT: When did you first meet Bjorn Faulkner?

NANCY LEE: In August of last year.

FLINT: Where did you meet him?

NANCY LEE: At a ball given by my friend Sandra van
Renssler, in Newport.

FLINT: Will you kindly tell us about it, Mrs. Faulkner?

NANCY LEE: Sandra introduced us. I remember she said:
"Here's a tough one for you, Nancy. I wonder whether
you'll add *this* scalp to the well-known collection."
Sandra had always insisted on exaggerating my popu-
larity . . . I danced with him, that night. We danced in
the garden, under the trees, and stopped on the edge of a

pool. We were alone in the darkness, with the faint sound of the Blue Danube Waltz filling the silence. Mr. Faulkner reached up to pick a rose for me. As he tore it off, his hand brushed my bare shoulder. I don't know why, but I blushed. He noticed it and apologized, graciously, smiling. Then he took me back to the guests . . . I think we both felt a silent understanding, that night, for we did not dance again with each other.

FLINT: When did you see Mr. Faulkner again?

NANCY LEE: Three days later. I invited him to dine at my home on Long Island. It was a real Swedish meal—and I cooked it myself.

FLINT: Did you see him often after that?

NANCY LEE: Yes, quite often. His visits became more and more frequent until the day . . .

[*Her voice breaks*]

FLINT: Until the day?

NANCY LEE: [*Her voice barely above a whisper*] The day he proposed to me.

FLINT: Please tell us about it, Mrs. Faulkner.

NANCY LEE: We went driving, Mr. Faulkner and I, alone. It was a beautiful day, with a bright, cold sunshine. I was driving my car—and I felt so young, so happy that I grew reckless. I . . .

[*Her voice trembles; she is silent for a few seconds, as if fighting the pain of these memories, then resumes with a faint smile of apology*]

I'm sorry. It's a little . . . hard for me to think of . . . those days . . . I was reckless . . . reckless enough to lose my way. We stopped on a strange country road. I laughed and said: "We're lost. I've kidnapped you and I won't release you." He answered: "The ransom you want is not in circulation." Then, suddenly, he seized my hand and looking straight at me, said: "What's the use of pretending? I love you, Nancy . . ."

[*Her voice breaks into a sob. She buries her face in a lace handkerchief*]

FLINT: I'm so sorry, Mrs. Faulkner. If you wish to be dismissed now and continue tomorrow—

NANCY LEE: [*Raising her head*] Thank you, I'm all right. I can go on . . . It was then that I first learned about the desperate state of Mr. Faulkner's fortune. He said that he had to tell me the truth, that he could not ask me to marry him when he had nothing to offer me. But I . . . I loved him. So I told him that money had never meant anything to me.

FLINT: Did Mr. Faulkner feel hopeless about the future, when your engagement was announced?

NANCY LEE: No, not at all. He said that my faith in him and my courage helped him so much. I told him that it was our duty to save his enterprises, our duty to the world he had wronged, not to ourselves. I made him realize his past mistakes and he was ready to atone for them. We were entering a new life together, a life of unselfish devotion to the service and welfare of others.

FLINT: Did you remain in New York after your wedding?

NANCY LEE: Yes. We made our home in my Long Island residence. Mr. Faulkner gave up his New York penthouse.

FLINT: Did Mr. Faulkner tell you of his relations with Miss Andre?

NANCY LEE: No, not then. But he did, two weeks after our wedding. He came to me and said: "Dearest, there is a woman—there *was* a woman—and I feel I must tell you about her." I said: "I know it. You don't have to say a word if you'd rather not, dear."

FLINT: And what did Mr. Faulkner tell you?

NANCY LEE: He said: "Karen Andre is the cause and the symbol of my darkest years. I am going to dismiss her."

FLINT: What did you answer?

NANCY LEE: I said that I understood him and that he was right. "But," I said, "we must not be cruel. Perhaps you can find another position for Miss Andre." He said that he'd provide for her financially, but that he never wanted to see her again.

FLINT: He, therefore, dismissed Miss Andre voluntarily, of his own choice?

NANCY LEE: [*Proudly*] Mr. Flint, there are two kinds of women in this world. And *my* kind is never jealous of . . . the other.

FLINT: What was Mr. Faulkner's business situation after your marriage?

NANCY LEE: I'm afraid I don't understand much about business. But I know that Father made a loan—a very large loan—to my husband.

FLINT: Mrs. Faulkner, will you tell us whether you think it possible that your husband had any reason to commit suicide?

NANCY LEE: I think it totally impossible.

FLINT: Did he ever speak of his plans for the future?

NANCY LEE: We used to dream of the future, together. Even . . . even on the evening before his . . . his death. We were sitting by the fire, in his study, talking about the years ahead. We knew that we would not be wealthy for a long time, if ever. But we didn't care about that. We had renounced material concerns, with all their consequences: pride, selfishness, ambition, the desire to rise above our fellow-men. We wanted to devote our life to spiritual values. We were planning to leave the city, to be part of some modest community, to be like everyone else.

FLINT: And this was on the night of January fifteenth, the day before his death?

NANCY LEE: [*Feebly*] Yes.

FLINT: What did Mr. Faulkner do on the day of January sixteenth?

NANCY LEE: He spent it in town, on business, as usual. He came home late in the afternoon. He said that he had to attend a business banquet in New York that night, so he did not have dinner at home. He left at about six o'clock.

FLINT: What banquet was Mr. Faulkner supposed to attend?

NANCY LEE: He did not tell me and I didn't ask. I made it a
point never to interfere with his business.

FLINT: Did you notice anything peculiar when he said
goodbye to you, that night?

NANCY LEE: No, not a thing. He kissed me and said that
he'd try to come home early. I stood at the door and
watched him drive away. He waved to me as his car disappeared in the dusk. I stood there for a few minutes,
thinking of how happy we were, of what a perfect
dream our love had been, like a delicate idyll, like . . .
[*Her voice trembles*] I didn't know that our beautiful romance would . . . indirectly . . . through jealousy . . .
bring about his . . . his death.

[*She drops her head, hiding her face in her hands, sobbing audibly, as* STEVENS'S *voice booms out*]

STEVENS: Your Honor! We object! Move that that be
stricken out!

JUDGE HEATH: The witness's last sentence may go out.

FLINT: Thank you, Mrs. Faulkner. That is all.

STEVENS: [*Coldly*] Will you be able to answer a few questions now, Mrs. Faulkner?

NANCY LEE: [*Raising her tearstained face, proudly*] As
many as you wish, Mr. Stevens.

STEVENS: [*Softly*] You said that your romance was like a
perfect dream, didn't you?

NANCY LEE: Yes.

STEVENS: A sacred troth that regenerated a soul?

NANCY LEE: Yes.

STEVENS: A beautiful, uplifting relationship based on *mutual trust*?

NANCY LEE: [*Becoming a little astonished*] Yes.

STEVENS: [*Changing his voice, fiercely*] Then why did you
hire a detective to spy on your husband?

NANCY LEE: [*A little flustered*] I . . . that is . . . I didn't hire
a detective to spy on my husband. I hired him to protect
Mr. Faulkner.

STEVENS: Will you kindly explain that?

NANCY LEE: Well . . . you see . . . you see, some time ago, Mr. Faulkner had been threatened by a gangster—"Guts" Regan. I believe they call him that. Mr. Faulkner did not pay any attention to it—no one could intimidate him—and he refused to hire a bodyguard. But I was worried . . . so as soon as we were married, I hired Mr. Van Fleet to watch him. I did it secretly, because I knew that Mr. Faulkner would object.

STEVENS: How could a sleuth following at a distance protect Mr. Faulkner?

NANCY LEE: Well, I heard that the underworld has a way of finding out those things and I thought they would not attack a man who was constantly watched.

STEVENS: So all Mr. Van Fleet had to do was to watch Mr. Faulkner?

NANCY LEE: Yes.

STEVENS: Mr. Faulkner alone?

NANCY LEE: Yes.

STEVENS: Not Mr. Faulkner *and* Miss Andre?

NANCY LEE: Mr. Stevens, that supposition is insulting to me.

STEVENS: I haven't noticed *you* sparing insults, Mrs. Faulkner.

NANCY LEE: I'm sorry, Mr. Stevens. I assure you that was not my intention.

STEVENS: You said that Mr. Faulkner told you he never wanted to see Miss Andre again?

NANCY LEE: Yes, he did.

STEVENS: And yet, he called on her after his marriage, he called on her often and *at night.* Your detective told you that, didn't he?

NANCY LEE: Yes. I knew it.

STEVENS: How do you explain it?

NANCY LEE: I cannot explain it. How can I know what blackmail she was holding over his head?

STEVENS: How do you explain the fact that Mr. Faulkner lied to you about the business banquet on the night of January sixteenth and went directly to Miss Andre's house?

NANCY LEE: If I could explain that, Mr. Stevens, I might be able to save you the bother of this trial. We would have an explanation of my husband's mysterious death. All I know is that she made him come to her house for some reason which he could not tell me—and that he was found dead, that night.

STEVENS: Mrs. Faulkner, I want you to answer one more question.

NANCY LEE: Yes?

STEVENS: I want you to state here, under oath, that Bjorn Faulkner loved you.

NANCY LEE: Bjorn Faulkner was mine.

STEVENS: That is all, Mrs. Faulkner.

KAREN: [*Calmly, distinctly*] No. That's not all.

[*All eyes turn to her*]

Ask her one more question, Stevens.

STEVENS: What is it, Miss Andre?

KAREN: Ask her whether she loved him.

NANCY LEE: [*Sitting straight up, with the icy poise of a perfect lady*] I did, Miss Andre.

KAREN: [*Jumping to her feet*] Then how can you speak of *him* as you did? How can you sit here and lie, lie about him, when he can't come back to defend himself?

[JUDGE HEATH *strikes his gavel violently*. NANCY LEE *gasps and jumps to her feet*]

NANCY LEE: I won't stand for it! Why should I be questioned by . . . by the murderess of my husband!

[*She falls back on the chair, sobbing*. FLINT *rushes to her*]

KAREN: [*Calmly*] That's all.

FLINT: I'm so sorry, Mrs. Faulkner!

JUDGE HEATH: The court will now adjourn till ten o'clock tomorrow morning.

[EVERYONE *rises.* JUDGE HEATH *leaves the courtroom, while* FLINT *helps* NANCY LEE *down from the witness stand. As she passes by* KAREN, NANCY LEE *throws a defiant look at her.* KAREN *stands straight and says aloud, so that all heads turn to her*]

KAREN: One of us is lying. And we both know which one!

CURTAIN

ACT II

Same scene as at the opening of Act I. KAREN *is sitting at the defense table, as proudly calm as ever. When the curtain rises, the* BAILIFF *raps.*

BAILIFF: Court attention!

[JUDGE HEATH *enters.* EVERYONE *rises*]

Superior Court Number Eleven of the State of New York. The Honorable Judge William Heath presiding.

[JUDGE HEATH *sits down,* BAILIFF *raps, and* EVERYONE *resumes his seat*]

JUDGE HEATH: The people of the State of New York versus Karen Andre.
FLINT: Ready, your Honor.
STEVENS: Ready, your Honor.
JUDGE HEATH: The District Attorney may proceed.
FLINT: If your Honor please, the prosecution has one more witness to introduce. Mr. John Graham Whitfield!
CLERK: John Graham Whitfield!

[MR. WHITFIELD *comes in, followed by* NANCY LEE. MR. WHITFIELD *is tall, gray-haired, perfectly groomed, a thorough gentleman with the imperious manner of a wartime generalissimo.* NANCY LEE *walks in slowly, head downcast.* WHITFIELD *pats her hand affection-*

50

*ately as if to encourage her, as they part; he walks to the
witness stand, and she takes a chair at right*]

You solemnly swear to tell the truth, the whole truth and
nothing but the truth so help you God?

WHITFIELD: I do.

FLINT: What is your name?

WHITFIELD: John Graham Whitfield.

FLINT: What is your occupation?

WHITFIELD: I am president of the Whitfield National
Bank.

FLINT: Were you related to the late Bjorn Faulkner?

WHITFIELD: I was his father-in-law.

FLINT: It is obvious, Mr. Whitfield, that you are well quali-
fied to pass judgment on financial matters. Can you tell
us about the state of Mr. Faulkner's business at the time
preceding his death?

WHITFIELD: I shall say it was desperate, but not hopeless.
My bank made a loan of twenty-five million dollars to
Mr. Faulkner in an effort to save his enterprises. Need-
less to say, that money is lost.

FLINT: What prompted you to make that loan, Mr. Whitfield?

WHITFIELD: He was the husband of my only daughter; her
happiness has always been paramount to me. But my
motives were not entirely personal: realizing the count-
less tragedies of small investors that the crash would
bring, I considered it my duty to make every possible
effort to prevent it.

FLINT: Is it possible that you would have risked such a
considerable sum in Mr. Faulkner's enterprises if you
believed them hopelessly destined to crash?

WHITFIELD: Certainly not. It was a difficult undertaking,
but I had full confidence that my business acumen
would have prevented the crash—had Faulkner lived.

FLINT: He, therefore, had no reason to commit suicide as
far as his business affairs were concerned?

WHITFIELD: He had every reason for remaining alive.

FLINT: Now, Mr. Whitfield, can you tell us whether Mr.
Faulkner was happy in his family life, in his relations
with your daughter?

WHITFIELD: Mr. Flint, I would like to state that I have always regarded the home and the family as the most important institutions in our lives. You, therefore, will believe me when I tell you how important my daughter's family happiness was to me—and she had found perfect happiness with Mr. Faulkner.

FLINT: Mr. Whitfield, what was your opinion of Mr. Faulkner?

WHITFIELD: It is only fair to admit that he had many qualities of which I did not approve. We were as different as two human beings could be: I believe in one's duty above all; Bjorn Faulkner believed in nothing but his own pleasure.

FLINT: From your knowledge of him, Mr. Whitfield, would you say you consider it possible that Mr. Faulkner committed suicide?

WHITFIELD: I consider it absolutely impossible.

FLINT: Thank you, Mr. Whitfield. That is all.

STEVENS: Mr. Whitfield, were you very fond of your son-in-law?

WHITFIELD: Yes.

STEVENS: And you never disagreed with him, never lost your temper in a quarrel?

WHITFIELD: [*With a tolerant, superior smile*] Mr. Stevens, I never lose my temper.

STEVENS: If my memory serves me right, there was some kind of trouble at the time you made that stupendous loan to Mr. Faulkner. Wasn't there something said to the effect that you denied making the loan?

WHITFIELD: Purely a misunderstanding, I assure you. I must admit that Mr. Faulkner made a . . . somewhat unethical attempt to hasten that loan, which was quite unnecessary, since I granted it gladly—for my daughter's sake.

STEVENS: You said that your fortune has been badly damaged by the Faulkner crash?

WHITFIELD: Yes.

STEVENS: And your financial situation is rather strained at present?

WHITFIELD: Yes.

STEVENS: Then how could you afford to offer a one hundred thousand dollar reward for the arrest and conviction of "Guts" Regan?

FLINT: Objection! What has that got to do with the case?

WHITFIELD: Your Honor, I would like to have the privilege of explaining this.

JUDGE HEATH: Very well.

WHITFIELD: I did offer such a reward. I was prompted by a feeling of civic duty. The gentleman commonly known as "Guts" Regan is a notorious criminal. I offered that reward for evidence that would make his arrest and conviction possible. However, I agree with Mr. Flint that this has nothing to do with the present case.

STEVENS: Mr. Whitfield, can you tell us why you left for California in such a hurry before the beginning of this trial?

WHITFIELD: I think the answer is obvious. My daughter was crushed by the sudden tragedy. I hastened to take her away, to save her health, perhaps her life.

STEVENS: You love your daughter profoundly?

WHITFIELD: Yes.

STEVENS: You have always made it a point that her every wish should be granted?

WHITFIELD: I can proudly say yes.

STEVENS: When she—or you—desire anything, you don't stop at the price, do you?

WHITFIELD: We don't have to.

STEVENS: Then would you refuse to buy her the man she wanted?

FLINT: Your Honor! We—

WHITFIELD: Mr. Stevens!

STEVENS: You wouldn't stop if it took your entire fortune to break the first unbreakable man you'd ever met?

FLINT: Your Honor! We object!

JUDGE HEATH: Sustained.

STEVENS: Now, Mr. Whitfield, are you going to tell us that your money had nothing to do with Mr. Faulkner dismissing Miss Andre? That no ultimatum was delivered to him?

WHITFIELD: [*His tone is slightly less kindly and composed*

than before] You are quite mistaken in your insinuations. My daughter was no more jealous of Miss Andre than she would be of Mr. Faulkner's soiled underwear. All men have some at one time or another!

STEVENS: I'd be careful of statements such as these, Mr. Whitfield. Remember that your daughter paid for what Karen Andre got free!

FLINT: Your Honor! We—

[WHITFIELD *jumps to his feet; his face is distorted; he is shaking with fury.* JUDGE HEATH *raps his gavel, but to no avail.* NANCY LEE *jumps up, crying hysterically through* WHITFIELD'S *speech*]

NANCY LEE: Father! Father!

WHITFIELD: Why you . . . you God-damn, impudent . . . Do you know who I am? Do you know that I can crush you like a cockroach, as I've crushed many a better—

STEVENS: [*With insulting calm*] That is just what I wanted to prove. That is all. Thank you, Mr. Whitfield.

FLINT: Your Honor! We move that the defense counsel's outrageous remark which led to this incident be stricken out!

JUDGE HEATH: The remark may go out.

[WHITFIELD *leaves the stand and sits down next to* NANCY LEE; *she takes his hand and holds it affectionately, showing great concern*]

FLINT: [*Loudly, solemnly*] The people rest.

STEVENS: Move that the case be dismissed for lack of evidence.

JUDGE HEATH: Denied.

STEVENS: Exception . . . Ladies and gentlemen of the jury! We cannot pass judgment on Karen Andre without passing it on Bjorn Faulkner. He had put himself beyond all present standards; whether it was below or above them, is a question for each of us to decide personally. But I'll ask you to remember that he was the man who said he needed no justifications for his actions: *he* was the justification; the man who said that laws were made for the fun of breaking them. If you'll remember that, you will understand that the life into which he was thrown in his last few months was as impossible to him as that of a tiger in a vegetarian cafeteria. And to escape it, he would be driven to *the most desperate means*— including suicide!

[STEVENS *pauses, then calls*]

Our first witness will be James Chandler.
CLERK: James Chandler!

[CHANDLER, *middle-aged, precise, dignified, enters and takes the stand*]

You solemnly swear to tell the truth, the whole truth and nothing but the truth so help you God?
CHANDLER: I do.
STEVENS: Your name?
CHANDLER: James Chandler.
STEVENS: Your occupation?
CHANDLER: Handwriting expert of the New York Police Department.

[STEVENS *takes the letter read by* INSPECTOR SWEENEY *and hands it to* CHANDLER]

STEVENS: Do you recognize this letter?
CHANDLER: Yes. It is the letter found in Mr. Faulkner's penthouse on the night of his death. I have been called upon to examine it.
STEVENS: What were you asked to determine?
CHANDLER: I was asked to determine whether it was written by Mr. Faulkner.
STEVENS: What is your verdict?
CHANDLER: This letter was written by Bjorn Faulkner.
STEVENS: Your witness.
FLINT: Mr. Chandler, it has been called to your attention during the inquest that Miss Andre was in the habit of signing Faulkner's name to unimportant documents, at

the time she was employed as his secretary. Have you compared those signatures with Faulkner's real ones?

CHANDLER: I have.

FLINT: What is your opinion of them?

CHANDLER: I can compliment Miss Andre on her art. The difference is very slight.

FLINT: With Miss Andre's knowledge of Mr. Faulkner, is it possible that she could have forged this letter so perfectly as to escape detection?

CHANDLER: It is not probable; but it is possible.

FLINT: That is all.

[CHANDLER *exits*]

STEVENS: Siegurd Jungquist!

CLERK: Siegurd Jungquist!

[JUNGQUIST *enters and takes the stand. He is a man in his late thirties, a little timid in a quiet, reserved way, with a naive face and questioning, as if constantly wondering, eyes. He is Swedish and speaks with an accent*]

Do you solemnly swear to tell the truth, the whole truth and nothing but the truth so help you God?

JUNGQUIST: I do.

STEVENS: What is your name?

JUNGQUIST: Siegurd Jungquist.

STEVENS: What is your occupation?

JUNGQUIST: My last job was secretary to Herr Bjorn Faulkner.

STEVENS: How long have you held that job?

JUNGQUIST: Since beginning of November. Since Miss Andre left.

STEVENS: What was your position before that?

JUNGQUIST: Bookkeeper for Herr Faulkner.

STEVENS: How long did you hold that job?

JUNGQUIST: Eight years.

STEVENS: Did Mr. Faulkner give you Miss Andre's position when she was dismissed?

JUNGQUIST: Yes.

STEVENS: Did Miss Andre instruct you in your new duties?

JUNGQUIST: Yes, she did.

STEVENS: What was her behavior at that time? Did she seem to be angry, sorry or resentful?

JUNGQUIST: No. She was very calm, like always, and explained everything clearly.

STEVENS: Did you notice any trouble between Miss Andre and Mr. Faulkner at that time?

JUNGQUIST: [*Amused, with a kindly, but superior, tolerance*] Herr Lawyer, there can be no more trouble between Herr Faulkner and Miss Andre as between you and your face in the mirror!

STEVENS: Have you ever witnessed any business conferences between Mr. Faulkner and Mr. Whitfield?

JUNGQUIST: I never been present at conferences, but I seen Herr Whitfield come to our office many times. Herr Whitfield he not like Herr Faulkner.

STEVENS: What makes you think that?

JUNGQUIST: I heard what he said one day. Herr Faulkner was desperate for money and Herr Whitfield asked him, sarcastic-like, what he was going to do if his business crash. Herr Faulkner shrugged and said lightly: "Oh, commit suicide." Herr Whitfield looked at him, very strangely and coldly, and said, very slowly: "If you do, be sure you make a good job of it."

[*An* ATTENDANT *enters and hands a note to* STEVENS. STEVENS *reads it, shrugs, astonished; then turns to* JUDGE HEATH]

STEVENS: If your Honor please, I would like to report this incident which I consider as a hoax and whose purpose I would like to determine. A man has just called on the telephone and insisted on talking to me immediately. When informed that it was impossible, he gave the following message just brought to me. [*Reads note*] "Do not put Karen Andre on the stand until I get there." No signature.

[*The crash of her chair pushed back so violently that it falls makes all eyes turn to* KAREN. *She stands straight, eyes blazing, her calm poise shattered*]

KAREN: I want to go on the stand right away!

[*Reaction in the courtroom*]

FLINT: May I ask why, Miss Andre?
KAREN: [*Ignoring him*] Question me now, Stevens!
STEVENS: [*Very astonished*] I'm afraid it's impossible, Miss Andre. We have to finish the examination of Mr. Jungquist.
KAREN: Then hurry. Hurry.

[*She sits down, showing signs of nervousness for the first time*]

JUDGE HEATH: [*Rapping his gavel*] I shall ask the defendant to refrain from further interruptions.
STEVENS: Now, Mr. Jungquist, where were you on the night of January sixteenth?
JUNGQUIST: I was in our office in the Faulkner Building. I was working. I been working late for many nights.
STEVENS: What did you do when you heard of Mr. Faulkner's death?
JUNGQUIST: I want to call Herr Whitfield. I telephone his home in Long Island, but butler say he not home. I call his office in town, but no answer, no one there. I call many places, but not find Herr Whitfield. Then, I call his home again and I have to tell Mrs. Faulkner that Herr Faulkner committed suicide.
STEVENS: And when you told her that, what were Mrs. Faulkner's first words?
JUNGQUIST: She said: "For God's sake, don't give it to the newspapers!"
STEVENS: That is all.

[KAREN *jumps up, ready to go on the stand*]

FLINT: Just one moment please, Miss Andre. Why such hurry? Whom are you expecting?

[KAREN *sits down reluctantly, without answering*]

Mr. Jungquist, you have been employed by Bjorn Faulkner for over eight years, haven't you?

JUNGQUIST: Yes.

FLINT: Did you know all that time how crooked and criminal your boss's operations were?

JUNGQUIST: No, I did not.

FLINT: Do you know now that he was a criminal and a swindler?

JUNGQUIST: [*With the quiet dignity of a strong conviction*] No, I do not know *that*.

FLINT: You don't, eh? And you didn't know what all those brilliant financial operations of his were?

JUNGQUIST: I knew that Herr Faulkner did what other people not allowed to do. But I never wonder and I never doubt. I know it was not wrong.

FLINT: How did you know that?

JUNGQUIST: Because he was Herr Bjorn Faulkner.

FLINT: And he could do no wrong?

JUNGQUIST: Herr Lawyer, when little people like you and me meet a man like Bjorn Faulkner, we take our hats off and we bow, and sometimes we take orders; but we don't ask questions.

FLINT: Splendid, my dear Mr. Jungquist. Your devotion to your master is worthy of admiration. You would do anything for him, wouldn't you?

JUNGQUIST: Yes.

FLINT: Are you very devoted to Miss Andre, too?

JUNGQUIST: [*Significantly*] Miss Andre was dear to Herr Faulkner.

FLINT: Then such a little matter as a few lies for your master's sake would mean nothing to you?

STEVENS: We object, your Honor!

JUDGE HEATH: Objection sustained.

JUNGQUIST: [*With quiet indignation*] I not lied, Herr Lawyer. Herr Faulkner is dead and cannot tell me to lie.

But if I had choice, I lie for Bjorn Faulkner rather than tell truth for you!

FLINT: For which statement I am more grateful than you can guess, Herr Jungquist. That is all.

[JUNGQUIST *exits*]

STEVENS: [*Solemnly*] Karen Andre!

[KAREN *rises. She is calm. She steps up to the stand with the poise of a queen mounting a scaffold. The* CLERK *stops her*]

CLERK: You solemnly swear to tell the truth, the whole truth and nothing but the truth so help you God?

KAREN: [*Calmly*] That's useless. I'm an atheist.

JUDGE HEATH: The witness has to affirm regardless.

KAREN: [*Indifferently*] I affirm.

STEVENS: What is your name?

KAREN: Karen Andre.

STEVENS: What was your last position?

KAREN: Secretary to Bjorn Faulkner.

STEVENS: How long have you held that position?

KAREN: Ten years.

STEVENS: Tell us about your first meeting with Bjorn Faulkner.

KAREN: I answered his advertisement for a stenographer. I saw him for the first time in his office, on an obscure side street of Stockholm. He was alone. It was my first job. It was his first office.

STEVENS: How did Faulkner greet you?

KAREN: He got up and didn't say a word. Just stood and looked at me. His mouth was insulting even when silent; you couldn't stand his gaze very long; I didn't know whether I wanted to kneel or slap his face. I didn't do either. I told him what I had come for.

STEVENS: Did he hire you then?

KAREN: He said I was too young and he didn't like me. But he threw a stenographer's pad at me and told me to get down to work, for he was in a hurry. So I did.

STEVENS: And you worked all day?

KAREN: All day. He dictated as fast—almost faster than he could talk. He didn't give me time to say a word. He didn't smile once and he never took his eyes off me.

STEVENS: When did he first

[*He hesitates*]

KAREN: When did he first take me? That first day I met him.

STEVENS: How did that happen?

KAREN: He seemed to take a delight in giving me orders. He acted as if he were cracking a whip over an animal he wanted to break. And I was afraid.

STEVENS: Because you didn't like that.

KAREN: Because I liked it . . . So when I finished my eight hours, I told him I was quitting. He looked at me and didn't answer. Then he asked me suddenly if I had ever slept with a man. I said, No, I hadn't. He said he'd give me a thousand kroner if I would go into the inner office and take my skirt off. I said I wouldn't. He said if I didn't, he'd take me. I said, try it. He did. . . . After a while, I picked up my clothes; but I didn't go. I stayed. I kept the job.

STEVENS: And you worked, and lived, and rose to success together ever since?

KAREN: For ten years. When we made our first million kroner, he took me to Vienna. We sat in a restaurant where the orchestra played "Sing, Gypsy." When we made ten million, he took me to Delhi. We stood on the shore of the Ganges, on the steps of an old temple where men had been sacrificed to gods . . . When we made twenty-five million, he took me to New York. We hired a pilot to fly a plane above the city—and the wind waved Bjorn's hair as a banner over the world at his feet.

STEVENS: Can you tell us the extent of Mr. Faulkner's personal fortune at the height of his success?

KAREN: No, and he couldn't tell you himself: he had no personal fortune. He took what he wanted. When he owed money to one of his companies—it was crossed off the books and debited to the accounts of several other concerns. It was very simple. We prepared all the balance sheets ourselves.

STEVENS: Why did a man of Mr. Faulkner's genius resort to such methods?

KAREN: He wanted to build a gigantic net and to build it fast; a net over the world, held in his own hand. He had to draw unlimited sums of money; he had to establish his credit. So he paid dividends out of his capital, dividends much higher than we actually earned.

STEVENS: When did Mr. Faulkner's business difficulties start?

KAREN: Over a year ago.

STEVENS: What brought Mr. Faulkner to America, this time?

KAREN: A short term loan of ten million dollars from the Whitfield National Bank was due and we could not meet it. We had to have an extension. Whitfield refused it. Until his daughter came into the question.

STEVENS: How did that happen?

KAREN: Bjorn met her at a party. She made it obvious that she was greatly interested in him . . . Then, one day, he came to me and said: "Karen, we have only one piece of collateral left and you're holding it. You'll have to let me borrow it for a while." I said: "Certainly. What is it?" He said it was himself. I asked: "Nancy Whitfield?" and he nodded. I didn't answer at once—it wasn't very easy to say—then, I said: "All right, Bjorn." He asked: "Will that change things between us?" I said: "No."

STEVENS: Had Mr. Faulkner proposed to Miss Whitfield?

KAREN: No. She had proposed to him.

STEVENS: How did that happen?

KAREN: He told me about it. She took him for a drive and stopped on a lonely road. She said that they were lost, that she had kidnapped him and wouldn't release him. He answered that the ransom she wanted was not in circulation. Then she turned to him pointblank and said: "What's the use of pretending? I want you and you know it. You don't want me and I know that. But I pay for what I want, and I have the price." He asked: "And what is the price?" She said: "The extension of a certain ten million dollar loan which you'll need to save your business. If you stay out of jail as a swindler, it can be only in the custody of *Mrs. Bjorn Faulkner!*"

[NANCY LEE *jumps up, trembling with indignation*]

NANCY LEE: It's a lie! It's a shameless lie! How can you—
JUDGE HEATH: [*Striking his gavel*] Quiet, please! Anyone disturbing the proceedings will be asked to leave the courtroom!

[WHITFIELD *whispers to* NANCY LEE *and forces her to sit down, patting her hand*]

STEVENS: What was Mr. Faulkner's answer to that, Miss Andre?
KAREN: He said: "It will cost you an awful lot of money." She answered: "Money has never meant anything to me." Then he said: "Will you always remember that it's a business deal? You're not buying any feeling; you're not to expect any." And she answered: "I don't need any. You'll have your money and I'll have you." Such was the bargain.
STEVENS: Was Mr. Whitfield eager to accept that bargain?
KAREN: Bjorn said he thought Mr. Whitfield would have a stroke when his daughter's decision was announced to him. But Miss Whitfield insisted. She always had her way. It was agreed that the loan would be extended and that Whitfield would give Bjorn unlimited credit.
STEVENS: In other words, Faulkner sold himself as his last security?
KAREN: Yes. And like the others, it meant nothing to him.
STEVENS: Did you resent that marriage?
KAREN: No. I didn't. We had always faced our business as a war. We both looked at this as our hardest campaign.
STEVENS: Why did Mr. Faulkner dismiss you two weeks after his wedding?

KAREN: He was forced to do that. Whitfield refused to advance the money he had promised.

STEVENS: What reason did he offer for that refusal?

KAREN: The reason that Bjorn was keeping a mistress. It was Miss Whitfield's ultimatum: I had to be dismissed.

STEVENS: And did Mr. Whitfield grant the loan after you were dismissed?

KAREN: No. He refused it again. He attached what he called "a slight condition" to it.

STEVENS: What was that condition?

KAREN: He wanted the controlling interest in Bjorn's enterprises.

STEVENS: Did Faulkner agree to that?

KAREN: Bjorn said that he'd rather gather all his stock certificates into one pile—and strike a match.

STEVENS: And did Mr. Whitfield grant the loan?

KAREN: No, he didn't grant it. Bjorn took it.

STEVENS: How did he do that?

KAREN: By forging Mr. Whitfield's signature on twenty-five million dollars' worth of securities.

STEVENS: How do you know that?

KAREN: [*Calmly*] I helped him to do it.

[*Reaction in the courtroom.* STEVENS *is taken aback;* FLINT *chuckles*]

STEVENS: Did this help Mr. Faulkner?

KAREN: Only temporarily. Certain dividend payments were coming due. We couldn't meet them. Bjorn had stretched his credit to the utmost—and there was no more to be had.

STEVENS: How did Mr. Faulkner take this situation?

KAREN: He knew it was the end.

STEVENS: What were his plans?

KAREN: You don't find men like Bjorn Faulkner cringing before a bankruptcy commission. And you don't find them locked in jail.

STEVENS: And the alternative?

KAREN: He was not afraid of the world. He had defied its

every law. He was going to leave it when and how he pleased. He was—

[*The spectators' door at left flies open. A tall, slender, light-eyed young man in traveling clothes rushes in*]

REGAN: I told you to wait for me!

[KAREN *leaps to her feet with a startled cry.* FLINT, WHITFIELD, *and several* OTHERS *jump up.* FLINT *exclaims*]

FLINT: "Guts" Regan!
KAREN: [*Desperately*] Larry! Keep quiet! Please! Oh, please, keep quiet! You promised to stay away!

[JUDGE HEATH *raps his gavel—to no avail*]

REGAN: Karen, you don't understand, you don't—
KAREN: [*Whirling toward* JUDGE HEATH] Your Honor! I demand that this man not be allowed to testify!
FLINT: Why not, Miss Andre?
STEVENS: [*Rushing to* KAREN] Wait! Don't say a word!
KAREN: [*Ignoring him, shouting desperately over the noise*] Your Honor . . . !
REGAN: Karen!

[*To* STEVENS]

Stop her! For God's sake, stop her!
JUDGE HEATH: Silence!
KAREN: Your Honor! This man loves me! He'll do *anything* to save me! *He'll lie!* Don't believe a word he says!

[*She breaks off abruptly, looks at* REGAN *defiantly*]

REGAN: [*Slowly*] Karen, your sacrifice is useless: Bjorn Faulkner is dead.
KAREN: [*It is a wild, incredulous cry*] He's . . . dead?

REGAN: Yes.
KAREN: Bjorn . . . dead?
FLINT: Didn't you know it, Miss Andre?

[KAREN *does not answer. She sways and falls, uncon-scious, on the steps of the witness stand. Pandemonium in the courtroom*]

CURTAIN

ACT III

Same scene as at the opening of Acts I and II. Court session ready to open. NANCY LEE, WHITFIELD, *and* JUNGQUIST *occupy the spectators' seats.* KAREN *sits at the defense table, her head bowed, her arms hanging limply. Her clothes are black. She is calm—a dead, indifferent calm. When she moves and speaks, her manner is still composed; but it is a broken person that faces us now. The* BAILIFF *raps.*

BAILIFF: Court attention!

[JUDGE HEATH *enters.* EVERYONE *rises*]

Superior Court Number Eleven of the State of New York. The Honorable Judge William Heath presiding.

[JUDGE HEATH *sits down.* BAILIFF *raps and* EVERYONE *resumes his seat*]

JUDGE HEATH: The people of the State of New York versus Karen Andre.
STEVENS: Ready, your Honor.
FLINT: If your Honor please, I want to report that I have issued a warrant for Regan's arrest, as he is obviously an accomplice in this murder. But he has disappeared. He was last seen with the defense counsel and I would like to—
REGAN: [*Entering*] Keep your shirt on! [*He walks toward*

FLINT *calmly*] Who's disappeared? What do you suppose I appeared for, just to give you guys a thrill? You don't have to issue any warrants. I'll stay here. If she's guilty, I'm guilty. [*He sits down at the defense table*]

JUDGE HEATH: The defense may proceed.

STEVENS: Karen Andre.

[KAREN *walks to the witness stand. Her grace and poise are gone; she moves with effort*]

Miss Andre, when you took the stand yesterday, did you know the whole truth about this case?

KAREN: [*Faintly*] No.

STEVENS: Do you wish to retract any of your testimony?

KAREN: No.

STEVENS: When you first took the stand, did you intend to shield anyone?

KAREN: Yes.

STEVENS: Whom?

KAREN: Bjorn Faulkner.

STEVENS: Do you still find it necessary to shield him?

KAREN: [*Speaking with great effort*] No . . . it's not necessary . . . anymore.

STEVENS: Do you still claim that Bjorn Faulkner committed suicide?

KAREN: No. [*Forcefully*] Bjorn Faulkner did not commit suicide. He was murdered. I did not kill him. Please, believe me. Not for my sake—I don't care what you do to me now—but because you cannot let *his* murder remain unpunished! I'll tell you the whole truth. I've lied at the inquest. I've lied to my own attorney. I was going to lie here—but everything I told you so far has been true. I'll tell you the rest.

STEVENS: You had started telling us about Mr. Faulkner's way out of his difficulties, Miss Andre.

KAREN: I told you that he was going to leave the world. But he was not to kill himself. I did throw a man's body off the penthouse. But that body was dead before I threw it. It was not Bjorn Faulkner.

STEVENS: Please explain this to us, Miss Andre.

KAREN: Bjorn wanted to be officially dead. No searches or investigations were to bother him. He was to disappear. That suicide was staged. He had had the plan in mind for a long time. He had kept ten million dollars of the Whitfield forgery for this. We needed someone to help us. Someone who could not be connected with Bjorn in any way. There was only one such person: Regan.

STEVENS: What made you believe that Mr. Regan would be willing to help in so dangerous an undertaking?

KAREN: He loved me.

STEVENS: And he agreed to help you in spite of that?

KAREN: He agreed *because* of that.

STEVENS: What was the plan, Miss Andre?

KAREN: Regan was to get a corpse. But he wasn't to kill anyone for the purpose. We waited. On the night of January sixteenth, "Lefty" O'Toole, a gunman, was killed by rival gangsters. His murderers have since been arrested and have confessed, so you can be sure that Regan had nothing to do with the murder. But you may remember reading in the papers that O'Toole's body disappeared mysteriously from his mother's house. *That* was Regan's work. O'Toole's height, measurements and hair were the same as Bjorn's. He was the man I threw off the penthouse.

STEVENS: Was that the extent of Mr. Regan's help?

KAREN: No. He was to get an airplane and take Bjorn to South America. Bjorn had never learned to operate a plane. Regan used to be a transport pilot . . . That day, January sixteenth, Bjorn transferred the ten million dollars to three banks in Buenos Aires, in the name of Ragnar Hedin. A month later, I was to meet him at the Hotel Continental in Buenos Aires. Until then—the three of us were not to communicate with each other. No matter what happened, we were not to reveal the secret.

STEVENS: Tell us what happened on January sixteenth, Miss Andre.

KAREN: Bjorn came to my house, that night. I'll never forget his smile when he stepped out of the elevator: he loved danger. We had dinner together. At nine thirty we went to Regan's. He had O'Toole's body dressed in traveling clothes. We drove back to my house. Bjorn wanted to be seen entering the building. So I didn't use my key. I rang the door bell. We were dressed formally, to make it look like a gay party. Bjorn and Regan supported the body as if he were a drunken friend. The night watchman opened the door. Then we went up in the elevator.

STEVENS: And then what happened?

KAREN: Bjorn exchanged clothes with the corpse. He wrote the letter. Then they carried the body out and left it leaning against the parapet. Then . . . then, we said goodbye.

[KAREN'S *voice is not trembling; she is not playing for sympathy; only the slightest effort in her words betrays the pain of these memories*]

Bjorn was to go first. He went down in the elevator. I stood and watched the needle of the indicator moving down, fifty floors down. Then it stopped. He was gone.

STEVENS: And then?

KAREN: Regan followed him a few minutes later. They were to meet ten miles out of the city where Regan had left his plane. I stayed alone for an hour. The penthouse was so silent. I didn't want to wait out in the garden— with the corpse . . . the dead man that was supposed to be Bjorn. I lay on the bed in my bedroom. I took Bjorn's robe and buried my face in it. I could almost feel the warmth of his body. There was a clock by the bed and it ticked in the darkness. I waited. When an hour passed, I knew that the plane had taken off. I got up. I tore my dress—to make it look like a struggle. Then, I went to the garden—to the parapet. I looked down; there were so many lights . . . the world seemed so small, so far away . . . Then, I threw the body over. I watched it fall. I thought all of Bjorn's troubles went with it . . . I didn't know that . . . his life went, too.

STEVENS: That is all, Miss Andre.

FLINT: I must confess, Miss Andre, that there is not much left for me to do: you've done all my work yourself . . .

Now, tell us, didn't Mr. Faulkner have a clear conception of the difference between right and wrong?

KAREN: Bjorn never thought of things as right or wrong. To him, it was only: you can or you can't. He always could.

FLINT: And yourself? Didn't you object to helping him in all those crimes?

KAREN: To me, it was only: he wants or he doesn't.

FLINT: You said that Bjorn Faulkner loved you?

KAREN: Yes.

FLINT: Did he ever ask you to marry him?

KAREN: No. What for?

FLINT: Don't you know that there are laws made for situations such as these?

KAREN: Laws made *by* whom, Mr. Flint? And *for* whom?

FLINT: Miss Andre, did your attorney warn you that anything you say here may be held against you?

KAREN: I am here to tell the truth.

FLINT: You loved Bjorn Faulkner?

KAREN: Yes.

FLINT: Such as he was?

KAREN: *Because* he was such as he was.

FLINT: *Exactly,* Miss Andre. Now what would you do if a woman were to take away from you the man you worshipped so insanely? If she appealed to his soul, not to his animal desires as you seem to have done so successfully? If she changed the ruthless scoundrel you loved into her own ideal of an upright man? Would you still love him?

STEVENS: Your Honor! We object!

JUDGE HEATH: Objection sustained.

KAREN: But I want to answer. I want the District Attorney to know that he is insulting Bjorn Faulkner's memory.

FLINT: You do? But you thought nothing of insulting him while he lived, by an affair with a gangster?

REGAN: [*Jumping up*] You damn—

KAREN: [*Calmly*] Don't, Larry.

[REGAN *sits down reluctantly*]

You're mistaken, Mr. Flint. Regan loved me. I didn't love him.

FLINT: And he didn't demand the usual . . . price, for his help?

KAREN: He demanded nothing.

FLINT: You were the only one who knew all the details of Faulkner's criminal activities?

KAREN: Yes.

FLINT: You had enough information to send him to jail at any time?

KAREN: I'd never do that!

FLINT: But you *could,* if you'd wanted to?

KAREN: I suppose so.

FLINT: Well, Miss Andre, isn't that the explanation of Faulkner's visits to you after his marriage? He had re-formed, he wanted to avoid a crash. But *you* held it over his head. You could ruin his plans and expose him before he had made good for his crimes. Wasn't it fear, not love, that held him in your hands?

KAREN: Bjorn never knew the meaning of the word fear.

FLINT: Miss Andre, who knew about that transfer of ten million dollars to Buenos Aires?

KAREN: Only Bjorn, myself and Regan.

FLINT: *And* Regan! Now, Faulkner could have had perfectly legitimate business reasons for that transfer?

KAREN: I don't know of any.

FLINT: You mean, you *won't tell* of any. Now, Miss Andre, Bjorn Faulkner kept you in extravagant luxury for ten years. You enjoyed platinum gowns and other little things like that. You hated to change your mode of living. You hated to see him turn his fortune over to his investors—to see him poor—didn't you?

KAREN: I was never to see him poor.

FLINT: No! Of course not! Because you and your gangster lover were going to murder him and get the ten million no one knew about!

STEVENS: Your Honor! We object!

JUDGE HEATH: Sustained.

FLINT: You've heard it testified that Faulkner had no reason to commit suicide. He had no more reason to escape from the first happiness he'd ever known. And you hated him for that happiness! Didn't you?

KAREN: You don't understand Bjorn Faulkner.

FLINT: Maybe I don't. But let's see if I understand *you* correctly. You were raped by a man the first day you saw him. You lived with him for ten years in a brazenly illicit relationship. You defrauded thousands of investors the world over. You cultivated a friendship with a notorious gangster. You helped in a twenty-five million dollar forgery. You told us all this proudly, flaunting your defiance of all decency. And you don't expect us to believe you capable of murder?

KAREN: [*Very calmly*] You're wrong, Mr. Flint. I *am* capable of murder—*for Bjorn Faulkner's sake.*

FLINT: That is all, Miss Andre.

[KAREN *walks back to her seat at the defense table, calmly, indifferently*]

STEVENS: Lawrence Regan!
CLERK: Lawrence Regan!

[REGAN *takes the stand*]

You solemnly swear to tell the truth, the whole truth and nothing but the truth so help you God?

REGAN: I do.

STEVENS: What is your name?

REGAN: Lawrence Regan.

STEVENS: [*A little hesitantly*] What is your occupation?

REGAN: [*Calmly, with a faint trace of irony*] Unemployed.

STEVENS: How long have you known Karen Andre?

REGAN: Five months.

STEVENS: Where did you meet her?

REGAN: In Faulkner's office. I went there to . . . to do some business with him. I gave up the business, because I met his secretary.

STEVENS: How did you happen to become friendly with Miss Andre?

REGAN: Well, that first meeting wasn't exactly friendly. She wouldn't let me in to see Faulkner. She said I had enough money to buy orchids by the pound—and I had no business with her boss. I said I'd think it over—and went. I thought it over. Only, I didn't think of the business. I thought of her. The next day I sent her a pound of orchids. Ever see how many that makes? That's how it started.

STEVENS: Did you know of Miss Andre's relations with Mr. Faulkner?

REGAN: I knew it before I ever saw her. What of it? I knew it was hopeless. But I couldn't help it.

STEVENS: You never expected Miss Andre to share your feeling?

REGAN: No.

STEVENS: You never made any attempt to force it upon her?

REGAN: Do you have to know all that?

STEVENS: I'm afraid we do.

REGAN: I kissed her—once. By force. It was the night of Faulkner's wedding. She was alone. She was so unhappy. And I was so crazy about her. She told me it was no use. I never wanted her to know. But she knew. We never mentioned it since.

STEVENS: When did Miss Andre first tell you of Faulkner's planned escape?

REGAN: About two weeks before we pulled it.

STEVENS: Was "Lefty" O'Toole one of your men?

REGAN: No.

STEVENS: Were you connected with his murderers in any way?

REGAN: No.

STEVENS: [*With a little hesitation*] You actually had no definite knowledge of his planned murder?

REGAN: [*With the same faint irony*] No. I just had a way of guessing.

STEVENS: What happened on the night of January sixteenth?

REGAN: It all worked as Miss Andre has told you. But she knows only half the story. I know the rest.

STEVENS: Tell us what happened after you left the penthouse.

REGAN: I left ten minutes after Faulkner. He had taken my car. I had one of my men leave another car for me at the door. I stepped on it—full speed.

STEVENS: Where did you go?

REGAN: To Meadow Lane. Ten miles out, in Kings County. I had left my plane there earlier in the evening. Faulkner was to get there first and wait for me.

STEVENS: What time did you get there?

REGAN: About midnight. There was a bright moon. I turned off the road and I could see tire tracks in the mud—where Faulkner's car had passed. I drove out into the lane. Then, I thought I'd lost my mind: the plane was gone.

STEVENS: What did you do?

REGAN: I searched around that lane for two hours. Faulkner's car was there—where we had agreed to hide it. It was empty, lights turned off, the key in the switch. I saw tracks on the ground—where the plane had taken off. But Faulkner couldn't fly it himself.

STEVENS: Did you search for any clues to this mystery?

REGAN: I searched like a bloodhound.

STEVENS: Did you find anything?

REGAN: I did. One thing. A car.

STEVENS: What kind of a car?

REGAN: It was hidden deep in the bushes on the other side of the lane. It was a big black sedan.

STEVENS: What did you do?

REGAN: I wanted to know whose car it was, so I smashed a window, crawled to the back seat and settled down to wait.

STEVENS: How long did you have to wait?

REGAN: The rest of that night.

STEVENS: And then?

REGAN: Then, the owner came back. I saw him coming. His face looked strange. He had no hat. His clothes were wrinkled and grease-spotted.

STEVENS: What did you do?

REGAN: I pretended to be asleep in the back seat. I watched

him. He approached; opened the door. Then, he saw me. He gave a start and a yell as if he'd been struck in the heart. His nerves must have been jittery.

STEVENS: Then, what did you do?

REGAN: I awakened with a start, stretched, rubbed my eyes, and said: "Oh, it's you? Fancy, such a meeting!" I don't think he liked it. He asked: "Who are you? What are you doing here?" I said: "My name's Guts Regan— you may have heard it. I was in a little trouble and had to hide for a while. And finding this car here was quite a convenience." He said: "That's too bad, but I'll have to ask you to get out. I'm in a hurry."

STEVENS: Did you get out?

REGAN: No. I stretched and asked: "What's the hurry?" He said: "None of your business." I smiled and explained: "It's not for me. You see, it happens that a certain columnist is a friend of mine. He'll appreciate the story about a gentleman of your prominence found wandering in the wilderness at milkman time. But I'm sure he would like to have the whole story."

STEVENS: What did the man say?

REGAN: He said nothing. He took out a check book and looked at me. I shrugged and looked at him. Then, he said: "Would ten thousand dollars be a suitable token of appreciation to keep your mouth shut?" I said: "It'll do. Lawrence Regan's the name." He wrote out the check. Here it is.

[REGAN *produces a check and hands it to* STEVENS. *Reaction in the courtroom*]

STEVENS: [*His voice is tensely ominous*] I offer this check in evidence.

[*He passes the check to the* CLERK. CLERK *glances at it and gives a start*]

FLINT: [*Jumping up*] What's all this nonsense? Who was the man?

STEVENS: [*Solemnly*] Who was the man, Mr. Regan?

REGAN: Let the clerk read that check to you.

STEVENS: [*To* CLERK] Kindly read the check.

CLERK: [*Reading*] January seventeenth . . . Pay to the order of Lawrence Regan the sum of ten thousand dollars." Signed: "John Graham Whitfield."

[*Uproar in the courtroom.* WHITFIELD *jumps to his feet*]

WHITFIELD: It's an outrage!

FLINT: I demand to see that check!

JUDGE HEATH: [*Striking his gavel*] Silence! If there are any more interruptions of this kind, I shall order the courtroom cleared!

STEVENS: We offer this check in evidence!

FLINT: Objection!

JUDGE HEATH: Objection overruled. Admitted in evidence.

STEVENS: What did you do after you received this check, Mr. Regan?

REGAN: I put it in my pocket and thanked him. Then—I drew my gun and stuck it in his ribs, and asked: "Now, you lousy bastard, what did you do with Faulkner?" He opened his mouth like a fish choking and couldn't make a sound.

WHITFIELD: Your Honor! Is this man to be allowed to make such statements in public in my presence?

JUDGE HEATH: The witness is allowed to testify. If it is proved to be perjury, he will suffer the consequences. Proceed, Mr. Stevens.

STEVENS: What did he answer, Mr. Regan?

REGAN: At first, he muttered: "I don't know what you're talking about." But I jammed the gun harder and I said: "Cut it out! I've no time to waste. I'm in on it and so are you. Where did you take him?" He said: "If you kill me, you'll never find out."

STEVENS: Did you get any information out of him?

REGAN: Not a word. I didn't want to kill him—yet. He said: "If you expose me—you'll expose the fake suicide and Faulkner will be found." I asked: "Is he alive?" He said: "Go and ask him." I talked and threatened. It was no use. I let him go. I thought I could always get him.

STEVENS: Then, did you try to find Faulkner?

REGAN: I didn't lose a second. I rushed home, changed my clothes, grabbed a sandwich and an airplane—and flew to Buenos Aires. I searched. I advertised in the papers. I got no answer. No one called at the banks for Ragnar Hedin's millions.

STEVENS: Did you try to communicate about this with Miss Andre?

REGAN: No. We had promised to stay away from each other for a month. And she had been arrested—for Faulkner's murder. I laughed when I read that. I couldn't say a word—not to betray him if he were still alive. I waited.

STEVENS: What were you waiting for?

REGAN: February sixteenth—at the Hotel Continental in Buenos Aires. I set my teeth and waited every minute of every hour of that day. He didn't come.

STEVENS: Then?

REGAN: Then I knew he was dead. I came back to New York. I started a search for my plane. We found it. Yesterday.

STEVENS: Where did you find it?

REGAN: In a deserted valley in New Jersey, a hundred miles from Meadow Lane. I recognized the plane by the engine number. It had been landed and fire set to it.

STEVENS: Was the plane . . . empty?

REGAN: No. I found the body of a man in it.

STEVENS: Could you identify him?

REGAN: No one could. It was nothing but a burned skeleton. But the height was the same. It was Faulkner . . . I examined the body—or what was left of it. I found two bullet holes. One—in a rib, over the heart. The other—straight through the right hand. He didn't die without putting up a fight. He must have been disarmed first, shot through the hand; then, murdered, defenseless, straight through the heart.

STEVENS: [*After a pause*] That's all, Mr. Regan.

FLINT: Just what is your . . . *business,* Mr. Regan?

REGAN: You'd like me to answer, wouldn't you?

STEVENS: We object, your Honor. The witness has a right not to answer that question.

JUDGE HEATH: Sustained.

FLINT: Mr. Regan, what do you do when prospective clients refuse to pay you protection?

REGAN: I'm legally allowed not to understand what you're talking about.

FLINT: Very well. You don't have to understand. May I question you as to whether you read the newspapers?

REGAN: You may.

FLINT: Well?

REGAN: Question me.

FLINT: Will you kindly state whether you read newspapers?

REGAN: Occasionally.

FLINT: Then did you happen to read that when Mr. James Sutton Vance, Jr., refused to pay protection to . . . a certain gangster, his magnificent country house in Westchester was destroyed by an explosion, just after the guests left, barely missing a wholesale slaughter? What was that, Mr. Regan, a coincidence?

REGAN: A remarkable coincidence, Mr. Flint: *just after the guests left.*

FLINT: Did you read that when Mr. Van Dorn refused to—

STEVENS: We object, your Honor! Such questions are irrelevant!

JUDGE HEATH: Sustained.

FLINT: So you had no ill feeling toward Mr. Faulkner for the . . . failure of your business with him?

REGAN: No.

FLINT: Now, Mr. "Guts"—I beg your pardon—Mr. *Lawrence* Regan, what would you do if someone were to take this woman you love so much—and rape her?

REGAN: I'd cut his throat with a dull saw.

FLINT: You would? And you expect us to believe that you, "Guts" Regan, gangster, outlaw, scum of the underworld, would step aside with a grand gesture and throw the woman you wanted into another man's arms?

STEVENS: Your Honor! We—

[STEVENS *is near the witness stand. Calmly and force-fully* REGAN *pushes him aside. Then, turns to* FLINT *and says very calmly, very earnestly*]

REGAN: I loved her.

FLINT: You did? Why did you allow Faulkner to visit her after his marriage?

REGAN: I had nothing to say about that.

FLINT: No? You two didn't hold a blackmail plot over his head?

REGAN: Got any proof of that?

FLINT: Her association with you is the best proof!

STEVENS: Objection!

JUDGE HEATH: Sustained.

FLINT: How did you kill Faulkner in the penthouse that night?

STEVENS: Objection!

JUDGE HEATH: Sustained.

FLINT: Where is your other accomplice, the man who played the drunk?

REGAN: I can give you his exact address: Evergreen Cemetery, Whitfield Family Memorial; which is the swankiest place poor Lefty's ever been.

FLINT: Now, let me get this clear: you claim that the man buried in Evergreen Cemetery is "Lefty" O'Toole, and the man you found in the burned plane is Bjorn Faulkner?

REGAN: Yes.

FLINT: And what is to prove that it isn't the other way around? Supposing you did steal O'Toole's body? What's to prove that you didn't stage that fantastic thing yourself? That you didn't plant the airplane and the body in New Jersey and then appear with that wild story, in a desperate attempt to save your mistress? You've heard her tell us that you'd do anything for her; that you'd lie for her.

STEVENS: We object, your Honor!

JUDGE HEATH: Objection sustained.

FLINT: Where's your real proof, Mr. Regan?

REGAN: [*He looks straight at* FLINT *for a second. When he speaks, his manner is a startling contrast to his former arrogance and irony; it is simple, sincere; it is almost solemn in its earnestness*] Mr. Flint, you're a district attorney and I . . . well, you know what I am. We both have a lot of dirty work to do. Such happens to be life—or most of it. But do you think we're both so low that if something passes us to which one kneels, we no longer have eyes to see it? I loved her; she loved Faulkner. That's our only proof.

FLINT: That's all, Mr. Regan.

[REGAN *returns to the defense table*]

STEVENS: John Graham Whitfield!

[WHITFIELD *walks to the stand hurriedly, resolutely*]

Mr. Whitfield, would you object if I asked for an order to exhume the body buried in Evergreen Cemetery?

WHITFIELD: I would have no objection—but that body has been cremated.

STEVENS: [*Slight emphasis*] I see. Mr. Whitfield, where were you on the night of January sixteenth?

WHITFIELD: I believe I was in New York, on business, that night.

STEVENS: Do you have any witnesses who can prove it?

WHITFIELD: Mr. Stevens, you must realize that I am not in the habit of providing myself with alibis. I've never had reason to keep track of my activities and to secure any witnesses. I would not be able to find them now.

STEVENS: How many cars do you own, Mr. Whitfield?

WHITFIELD: Four.

STEVENS: What are they?

WHITFIELD: One of them is a black sedan, as you are evidently anxious to learn. I may remind you that it is *not* the only black sedan in New York City.

STEVENS: [*Casually*] You have just returned from California by plane?

WHITFIELD: Yes.

STEVENS: You flew it yourself?

WHITFIELD: Yes.

STEVENS: You're a licensed pilot, then?

WHITFIELD: I am.

STEVENS: Now, that story of Mr. Regan's is nothing but a lie in your opinion, isn't it?

WHITFIELD: It is.

STEVENS: [*Changing his manner, fiercely*] Then, who wrote that ten thousand dollar check?

WHITFIELD: [*Very calmly*] I did.

STEVENS: Will you kindly explain it?

WHITFIELD: It is very simple. We all know Mr. Regan's profession. He had threatened to kidnap my daughter. I preferred to pay him off, rather than to take any chances on her life.

STEVENS: The check is dated January seventeenth. On that same day, you announced your offer of a reward for Regan's arrest, didn't you?

WHITFIELD: Yes. You realize that besides my civic duty, I also had my daughter's safety in mind and I wanted prompt action.

STEVENS: Mr. Whitfield, your daughter and your fortune are your most cherished possessions, aren't they?

WHITFIELD: They are.

STEVENS: Then what would you do to the man who took your money and deserted your daughter for another woman?

FLINT: We object, your Honor!

JUDGE HEATH: Objection sustained.

STEVENS: You hated Faulkner. You wanted to break him. You suspected his intention of staging suicide, didn't you? The words Mr. Jungquist heard you say prove it.

WHITFIELD: I suspected nothing of the kind!

STEVENS: And on January sixteenth, didn't you spend the day watching Faulkner?

WHITFIELD: Certainly not!

STEVENS: Weren't you trailing Faulkner in your black sedan? Didn't you follow him as soon as he left his penthouse, that night?

WHITFIELD: Fantastic! How could I have recognized him—supposing it were Faulkner leaving? Van Fleet, the detective, didn't.

STEVENS: Van Fleet wasn't watching for a trick. He had no suspicion of the plot. You had.

WHITFIELD: [*With magnificent calm*] My dear Mr. Stevens, how could I have known about the plot for *that night*?

STEVENS: Didn't you have any particular information about Faulkner's activities at the time?

WHITFIELD: None.

STEVENS: You heard of nothing unusual, that day?

WHITFIELD: Not a thing.

STEVENS: For instance, you did not hear that he transferred ten million dollars to Buenos Aires?

WHITFIELD: I never heard of it.

[*There is a scream, a terrifying cry, as of one mortally wounded.* JUNGQUIST *stands clutching his head, moaning wildly*]

JUNGQUIST: I killed him! I killed Bjorn Faulkner, God help me! I helped *that man* to kill him!

[*He points at* WHITFIELD, *then leaps to the* CLERK'S *desk, seizes the Bible and, raising it frantically over his head in a shaking hand, cries as if taking a solemn, hysterical oath*]

The whole truth, so help me God! . . . I didn't know! But I see it now! [*He points at* WHITFIELD] He killed Faulkner! Because he lied! He knew about the ten million dollars! Because I told him!

[STEVENS *rushes to him*]

FLINT: Now, look here, my man, you can't—

STEVENS: [*Hurriedly*] That's all, Mr. Whitfield.

FLINT: No questions.

[WHITFIELD *leaves the stand*]

STEVENS: Kindly take the stand, Mr. Jungquist.

[JUNGQUIST *obeys*]

You told Mr. Whitfield about that transfer?

JUNGQUIST: [*Hysterically*] He asked me many times about the ten million—where it was spent. I did not know it was a secret. That day—I told him—about Buenos Aires. That day—at noon—January sixteenth!

WHITFIELD: What kind of a frame-up is this?

STEVENS: You told Whitfield? At *noon*?

JUNGQUIST: I did, God have pity on me! I didn't know! I would give my life for Herr Faulkner! And I helped to kill him!

STEVENS: That's all.

FLINT: Were you alone with Mr. Whitfield when you told him?

JUNGQUIST: [*Astonished*] Yes.

FLINT: Then it's *your* word against Mr. *Whitfield's*?

JUNGQUIST: [*Stunned by the sudden thought, feebly*] Yes . . .

FLINT: That's all.

[JUNGQUIST *leaves the stand*]

STEVENS: The defense rests.

JUDGE HEATH: Any other witnesses?

FLINT: No, your Honor.

JUDGE HEATH: The defense may proceed with the closing argument.

STEVENS: Your Honor! Ladies and gentlemen of the jury! You are here to decide the fate of a woman. But much more than one woman is here on trial. Before you pronounce your verdict on Karen Andre, think of your verdict on Bjorn Faulkner. Do you believe that he was the kind of man who would bow, renounce and repent? If you do—she's guilty. But if you believe that in this sad, halfhearted world of ours a man can still be born with life singing in his veins; a scoundrel, a swindler, a criminal, call him anything, but still a conqueror—if you value a strength that is its own motor, an audacity that is its own law, a spirit that is its own vindication—if you are able to admire a man who, no matter what mistakes he may have made in form, had never betrayed his essence: his self-esteem—if, deep in your hearts, you've felt a longing for greatness and for a sense of life beyond the lives around you, if you have known a hunger which gray timidity can't satisfy—you'll understand Bjorn Faulkner. If you do—you'll understand the woman who was his priestess . . . Who is on trial in this case? Karen Andre? No! It's you, ladies and gentlemen of the jury, who are here on trial. It is your own souls that will be brought to light when your decision is rendered!

JUDGE HEATH: The District Attorney may now conclude the case.

FLINT: Your Honor! Ladies and gentlemen of the jury! For once, I agree with the defense counsel. Two different types of humanity are opposed in this case—and your verdict will have to depend on which side you choose to believe. You are asked—by the defense—to take the side of a swindler, a harlot and a gangster against a man who is a model of social responsibility and a woman who is everything the ideal of womanhood has been for centuries. On one side, you see a life of service, duty and unselfishness; on the other—a steamroller of sensual indulgence and egoistic ambition. I agree with the defense counsel that the judgment on this case will be passed deep within your own souls. If you believe that man is placed on earth for a purpose higher than his own enjoyment—if you believe that love is more than sexual indulgence, that love is not confined to your bedroom, but extends to your family and your fellow-men—if you believe that selfless service to others is still the most sacred ideal a man can aspire to—you will believe that simple virtue is more powerful than arrogance and that a man like Bjorn Faulkner would be brought to bow before it. Let your verdict tell us that none shall raise his head too high in defiance of our common standards!

JUDGE HEATH: Ladies and gentlemen of the jury, the Bailiff will now escort you to the jury room. I shall ask you to consider your verdict carefully. You are to determine whether Karen Andre is guilty or not guilty of the murder of Bjorn Faulkner.

[*The* BAILIFF *escorts the* JURY *out of the courtroom. Then the stage is blacked out. Then, one by one, a spotlight picks out of the darkness the different* WITNESSES, *who repeat the most significant lines of their testimony— a quick succession of contradicting statements, presenting both sides of the case, reviewing the case for the audience, giving it swift flashes of what the jury is considering.*

The pin spot illuminates only the faces of the witnesses, one after the other, in the following order]

DR. KIRKLAND: I was called to examine the body of Bjorn Faulkner. I found a body mangled to an extreme degree.

HUTCHINS: Well, he was a bit tight. He wasn't very steady on his feet. Mr. Faulkner and the other gentleman had to help him. They almost dragged him into the elevator.

VAN FLEET: She is hoisting a man's body up on the parapet. A man in evening clothes. Faulkner. He's unconscious. No resistance. She pushes him with all her strength. He goes over the parapet. Down. Into space.

SWEENEY: [*Reading*] "I found only two enjoyable things on this earth whose every door was open to me: my whip over the world and Karen Andre."

MAGDA: He had a platinum gown made for her . . . She wore it on her naked body . . . And if it burned her shameless skin, she laughed like the pagan she is, and he kissed the burn, wild like tiger!

NANCY LEE: We had renounced material concerns, with all their consequences: pride, selfishness, ambition, the desire to rise above our fellow-men. We wanted to devote our life to spiritual values. We were planning to leave the city, to be part of some modest community, to be like everyone else.

WHITFIELD: I had full confidence that my business acumen would have prevented the crash—had Faulkner lived.

CHANDLER: It is not probable that the letter was forged; but it is possible.

JUNGQUIST: Herr Faulkner shrugged and said lightly: "Oh, commit suicide." Herr Whitfield looked at him and said, very slowly: "If you do, be sure you make a good job of it!"

KAREN: Bjorn Faulkner never thought of things as right or wrong. To him it was only: you can or you can't. He always could. To me it was only: he wants or he doesn't.

REGAN: But do you think we're both so low that if something passes us to which one kneels, we no longer have eyes to see it? I loved her; she loved Faulkner. That's our only proof.

[*After the last flash, the stage remains dark for a few seconds. Then the lights come on and the* JURY *returns into the courtroom*]

BAILIFF: Attention of the Court!

CLERK: The prisoner will rise and face the jury.

[KAREN *rises, head high*]

The jury will rise and face the prisoner. Mr. Foreman, have you reached a verdict?

FOREMAN: We have.

CLERK: What say you?

ENDING OF PLAY IF VERDICT IS "NOT GUILTY":

FOREMAN: Not guilty!

[KAREN *receives the verdict calmly. She raises her head a little higher and says slowly, solemnly*]

KAREN: Ladies and gentlemen, I thank you—in the name of Bjorn Faulkner.

CURTAIN

ENDING OF PLAY IF VERDICT IS "GUILTY":

FOREMAN: Guilty!

[KAREN *shows no reaction; she stands motionless.* STEVENS *jumps to his feet*]

STEVENS: We shall appeal the case!
KAREN: [*Calmly, firmly*] There will be no appeal. Ladies and gentlemen, I will not be here to serve the sentence. I have nothing to seek in your world.

CURTAIN

Ideal

PREFACE

Ideal was written in 1934, at a time when Ayn Rand had cause to be unhappy with the world. *We the Living* was being rejected by a succession of publishers for being "too intellectual" and too opposed to Soviet Russia (this was the time of America's Red Decade); *Night of January 16th* had not yet found a producer; and Miss Rand's meager savings were running out. The story was written originally as a novelette and then, probably within a year or two, was extensively revised and turned into a stage play. It has never been produced.

After the political themes of her first professional work, Ayn Rand now returns to the subject matter of her early stories: the role of values in men's lives. The focus in this case, is negative, but this time the treatment is not jovial; dominantly, it is sober and heartfelt. The issue now is men's lack of integrity, their failure to act according to the ideals they espouse. The theme is the evil of divorcing ideals from life.

An acquaintance of Miss Rand's, a conventional middle-aged woman, told her once that she worshiped a certain famous actress and would give her life to meet her. Miss Rand was dubious about the authenticity of the woman's emotion, and this suggested a dramatic idea: a story in which a famous actress, so beautiful that she comes to represent to men the embodiment of their deepest ideals, actually enters the lives of her admirers. She comes in a context suggesting that she is in grave danger. Until this point, her worshipers have professed their reverence for her—in words, which cost them nothing. Now, however, she is no longer a distant dream, but a reality demanding action on their part, or betrayal.

"What do you dream of?" Kay Gonda, the actress, asks one of the characters, in the play's thematic statement.

"Nothing," he answers. "Of what account are dreams?"

"Of what account is life?"

"None. But who made it so?"

"Those who cannot dream."

"No. Those who can *only* dream."

In a journal entry written at the time (dated April 9, 1934), Miss Rand elaborates this viewpoint:

> I believe—and I want to gather all the facts to illustrate this—that the worst curse on mankind is the ability to consider ideals as something quite abstract and detached from one's everyday life. The ability of *living* and *thinking* quite differently, in other words eliminating thinking from your actual life. This applied not to deliberate and conscious hypocrites, but to those more dangerous and hopeless ones who, alone with themselves and to themselves, tolerate a complete break between their convictions and their lives, and still believe that they have convictions. To them—either their ideals or their lives are worthless—and usually both.

Such "dangerous and hopeless ones" may betray their ideal in the name of "social respectability" (the small businessman in this story) or in the name of the welfare of the masses (the Communist) or the will of God (the evangelist) or the pleasure of the moment (the playboy Count)—or they may do it for the license of claiming that the good is impossible and therefore the struggle for it unnecessary (the painter). *Ideal* captures eloquently the essence of each of these diverse types and demonstrates their common denominator. In this regard, it is an intellectual tour de force. It is a philosophical guide to hypocrisy, a dramatized inventory of the kinds of ideas and attitudes that lead to the impotence of ideals—that is, to their detachment from life.

(The inventory, however, is not offered in the form of a developed plot structure. In the body of the play, there is no progression of events, no necessary connection between one encounter and the next. It is a series of evocative vignettes, often illuminating and ingenious, but as theater, I think, unavoidably somewhat static.)

Dwight Langley, the painter, is the pure exponent of the evil the play is attacking; he is, in effect, the spokesman for Platonism, who explicitly preaches that beauty is unreachable in this world and perfection unattainable. Since he insists that ideals are impossible on earth, he cannot, logically enough, believe in the reality of any ideal, even when it actually confronts him. Thus, although he knows every facet of Kay Gonda's face, he (alone among the characters) does not recognize her when she appears in his life. This philosophically induced blindness, which motivates his betrayal of her, is a particularly brilliant concretization of the play's theme, and makes a dramatic Act I curtain.

In her journal of the period, Miss Rand singles out religion as the main cause of men's lack of integrity. The worst of the characters, accordingly, the one who evokes her greatest indignation, is Hix, the evangelist, who preaches earthly suffering as a means to heavenly happiness. In an excellently worked-out scene, we see that it is not his vices, but his religion, including his definition of virtue, that brings him to demand the betrayal of Kay Gonda, her deliberate sacrifice to the lowest of creatures. By gaining a stranglehold on ethics, then preaching sacrifice as an ideal, religion, no matter what its intentions, systematically inculcates hypocrisy: it teaches men that achieving values is low ("selfish"), but that giving them up is noble. "Giving them up," in practice, means betraying them.

"None of us," one of the characters complains, "ever chooses the bleak, hopeless life he is forced to lead." Yet, as the play demonstrates, all these men do choose the lives they lead. When confronted by the ideal they profess to desire, they do not want it. Their vaunted "idealism" is largely a form of self-deception, enabling them to pretend to themselves and others that they aspire to something higher. In fact and in reality, however, they don't.

Kay Gonda, by contrast, is a passionate valuer; she cannot accept anything less than the ideal. Her exalted sense of life cannot accept the ugliness, the pain, the "dismal little pleasures" that she sees all around her, and she feels a desperate need to know that she is not alone in this regard. There is no doubt that Ayn Rand herself shared Kay Gonda's sense of life, and often her loneliness, too—and that Kay's cry in the play is her own:

> I want to see, real, living, and in the hours of my own days, that glory I create as an illusion! I want it real! I want to know that there is someone, somewhere, who wants it, too! Or else what is the use of seeing it, and working, and burning oneself for an impossible vision? A spirit, too, needs fuel. It can run dry.

Emotionally, *Ideal* is unique among Ayn Rand's works. But *Ideal* focuses almost exclusively on evil or mediocrity; it is pervaded by Kay Gonda's feeling of alienation from mankind, the feeling, tinged by bitterness, that the true idealist is in a minuscule minority amid an earthful of value-betrayers with whom no communication is possible. In accordance with this perspective, the hero, Johnnie Dawes, is not a characteristic Ayn Rand figure, but a misfit utterly estranged from the world, a man whose virtue is that he does not know how to live today (and has often wanted to die). If Leo feels this in Soviet Russia, the explanation is political, not metaphysical. But Johnnie feels it in the United States.

In her other works, Ayn Rand herself gave the answer to such a "malevolent universe" viewpoint, as she called it. Dominique Francon in *The Fountainhead*, for instance, strikingly resembles Kay and Johnnie in her idealistic alienation from the world, yet she eventually discovers how to reconcile evil with the "benevolent universe" approach. "You must learn," Roark tells her, "not to be afraid of the world. Not to be held by it as you are now. Never to be hurt by it as you were in that courtroom." Dominique does learn it; but Kay and Johnnie do not, or at least not fully. The effect is untypical Ayn Rand: a story written *approvingly* from Dominique's initial viewpoint.

Undoubtedly, the intensity of Miss Rand's personal struggle at the time—her intellectual and professional struggle against a seemingly deaf, even hostile culture—helps to account for the play's approach. Dominique, Miss Rand has said, is "myself in a bad mood." The same may be said of this aspect of *Ideal*.

Despite its somber essence, however, *Ideal* is not entirely a malevolent story. The play does have its lighter, even humorous side, such as its witty satire of Chuck Fink, the "selfless" radical, and of the Elmer Gantry-like Sister Essie Twomey, with her Service Station of the Spirit. The ending, moreover, however unhappy, is certainly not intended as tragedy or defeat. Johnnie's final action is *action*—that is the whole point—action to protect the ideal, as against empty words or dreams. *His* idealism, therefore, is genuine, and Kay Gonda's search ends on a positive note. In this respect, even *Ideal* may be regarded as an affirmation (albeit in an unusual form) of the benevolent universe.

—Leonard Peikoff

CHARACTERS

BILL McNITT, screen director
CLAIRE PEEMOLLER, scenario writer
SOL SALZER, associate producer
ANTHONY FARROW, president of the Farrow Film Studios
FREDERICA SAYERS
MICK WATTS, press agent
MISS TERRENCE, Kay Gonda's secretary
GEORGE S. PERKINS, assistant manager of the Daffodil
Canning Co.
MRS. PERKINS, his wife
MRS. SHLY, her mother
KAY GONDA
CHUCK FINK, sociologist
JIMMY, Chuck's friend
FANNY FINK, Chuck's wife
DWIGHT LANGLEY, artist
EUNICE HAMMOND
CLAUDE IGNATIUS HIX, evangelist
SISTER ESSIE TWOMEY, evangelist
EZRY
COUNT DIETRICH VON ESTERHAZY
LALO JANS
MRS. MONAGHAN
JOHNNIE DAWES

SECRETARIES, LANGLEY'S GUESTS, POLICEMEN

Place   Los Angeles, California

Time   Present; from afternoon to early evening of the following day

Synopsis of scenes

Ideal

PROLOGUE

Late afternoon. Office of ANTHONY FARROW *in the Far-row Film Studios. A spacious, luxurious room in an overdone modernistic style, which looks like the dream of a second-rate interior decorator with no limits set to the bill.*

Entrance door is set diagonally in the upstage Right corner. Small private door downstage in wall Right. Window in wall Left. A poster of KAY GONDA, *on wall Center; she stands erect, full figure, her arms at her sides, palms up, a strange woman, tall, very slender, very pale; her whole body is stretched up in such a line of reverent, desperate aspiration that the poster gives a strange air to the room, an air that does not belong in it. The words "KAY GONDA IN* FORBIDDEN EC-STASY" *stand out on the poster.*

The curtain rises to disclose CLAIRE PEEMOLLER, SOL SALZER, *and* BILL McNITT. SALZER, *forty, short, stocky, stands with his back to the room, looking hopelessly out of the window, his fingers beating nervously, monoto-nously, against the glass pane.* CLAIRE PEEMOLLER, *in her early forties, tall, slender, with a sleek masculine haircut and an exotically tailored outfit, reclines in her chair, smoking a cigarette in a lengthy holder.* McNITT, *who looks like a brute of a man and acts it, lies rather than sits in a deep armchair, his legs stretched out, picking his teeth with a match. No one moves. No one speaks. No one looks at the others. The silence is tense,*

anxious, broken only by the sound of SALZER's *fingers
on the glass.*

McNITT: [*Exploding suddenly*] Stop it, for Christ's sake!

[SALZER *turns slowly to look at him and turns away
again, but stops the beating. Silence*]

CLAIRE: [*Shrugging*] Well? [*No one answers*] Hasn't anyone here a suggestion to offer?

SALZER: [*Wearily*] Aw, shut up!

CLAIRE: I see absolutely no sense in behaving like this. We
can talk about something *else,* can't we?

McNITT: Well, talk about something else.

CLAIRE: [*With unconvincing lightness*] I saw the rushes
of *Love Nest* yesterday. It's a smash, *but* a smash!
You should see Eric in that scene where he kills the old
man and . . . [*A sudden jerk from the others. She stops
short*] Oh, I see. I beg your pardon. [*Silence. She resumes uneasily*] Well, I'll tell you about my new car.
The gorgeous thing is so chic! It's simply dripping, *but*
dripping with chromium! I was doing eighty yesterday
and not a bump! They say this new Sayers Gas is . . .
[*There is a stunned, involuntary gasp from the others.
She looks at two tense faces*] Well, what on earth is the
matter?

SALZER: Listen, Peemoller, for God's sake, Peemoller,
don't mention it!

CLAIRE: What?

McNITT: The name!

CLAIRE: What name?

SALZER: *Sayers,* for God's sake!

CLAIRE: Oh! [*Shrugs with resignation*] I'm sorry.

[*Silence.* McNITT *breaks the match in his teeth, spits it
out, produces a match folder, tears off another match,
and continues with his dental work. A man's voice is
heard in the next room. They all whirl toward the entrance door*]

SALZER: [*Eagerly*] There's Tony! He'll tell us! He must know something!

[ANTHONY FARROW *opens the door, but turns to speak to someone offstage before entering. He is tall, stately, middle-aged, handsomely tailored and offensively distinguished*]

FARROW: [*Speaking into the next room*] Try Santa Barbara again. Don't hang up until you get her personally. [*Enters, closing the door. The three look at him anxiously, expectantly*] My friends, has any of you seen Kay Gonda today? [*A great sigh, a moan of disappointment, rises from the others*]

SALZER: Well, that's that. You, too. And I thought you knew something!

FARROW: Discipline, my friends. Let us keep our heads. The Farrow Studios expect each man to do his duty.

SALZER: Skip it, Tony! What's the latest?

CLAIRE: It's preposterous! *But* preposterous!

McNITT: I've always expected something like this from Gonda!

FARROW: No panic, please. There is no occasion for panic. I have called you here in order to formulate our policy in this emergency, coolly and calmly and . . . [*The interoffice communicator on his desk buzzes sharply. He leaps forward, his great calm forgotten, clicks the switch, speaks anxiously*] Yes? . . . You did? Santa Barbara? . . . Give it to me! . . . *What?!* Miss Sayers won't speak to *me*?! . . . She *can't* be out, it's an evasion! Did you tell them it was Anthony Farrow? Of the Farrow Films? . . . Are you sure you made it clear? *President* of the Farrow Films? . . . [*His voice falling dejectedly*] I see. . . . When did Miss Sayers leave? . . . It's an evasion. Try again in half-an-hour. . . . And try again to get the chief of police.

SALZER: [*Desperately*] That I could have told you! The Sayers dame won't talk. If the papers could get nothing out of her—we can't!

FARROW: Let us be systematic. We cannot face a crisis

without a system. Let us have discipline, calm. Am I understood? . . . [*Breaks in two a pencil he has been playing with nervously*] . . . *Calm!*

SALZER: Calm he wants at a time like this!

FARROW: Let us . . . [*The intercom buzzes. He leaps to it*] Yes? . . . Fine! Put him on! . . . [*Very jovially*] Hel-lo, Chief! How are you? I . . . [*Sharply*] What do you mean you have nothing to say? This is *Anthony Farrow* speaking! . . . Well, it usually *does* make a difference. Hel . . . I mean, Chief, there's only one question I have to ask you, and I think I'm entitled to an answer. Have there or have there not been any charges filed in Santa Barbara? [*Through his teeth*] Very well. . . . Thank you. [*Switches off, trying to control himself*]

SALZER: [*Anxiously*] Well?

FARROW: [*Hopelessly*] He won't talk. No one will talk. [*Turns to the intercom again*] Miss Drake? . . . Have you tried Miss Gonda's home once more? . . . Have you tried all her friends? . . . I know she hasn't any, but try them anyway! [*Is about to switch off, then adds*] And get Mick Watts, if you can find the bast—if you can find him. If anyone knows, *he* knows!

McNITT: That one won't talk either.

FARROW: And that is precisely the thing for us to do. Silence. Am I understood? *Silence.* Do not answer any questions on the lot or outside. Avoid all references to this morning's papers.

SALZER: *Us* the papers should avoid!

FARROW: They haven't said much so far. It's only rumors. Idle gossip.

CLAIRE: But it's all over town! Hints, whispers, questions. If I could see any point in it, I'd say someone was spreading it intentionally.

FARROW: Personally, I do not believe the story for a minute. However, I want all the information you can give me. I take it that none of you has seen Miss Gonda since yesterday?

[*The others shrug hopelessly, shaking their heads*]

SALZER: If the papers couldn't find her—we can't.

FARROW: Had she mentioned to any of you that she was going to have dinner with Granton Sayers last night?

CLAIRE: When has she ever told anyone anything?

FARROW: Did you notice anything suspicious in her behavior when you saw her last?

CLAIRE: I . . .

McNITT: I should say I did! I thought at the time it was damn funny. Yesterday morning, it was. I drove up to her beach home and there she was, out at sea, tearing through the rocks in a motorboat till I thought I'd have heart failure watching it.

SALZER: My God! That's against our contracts!

McNITT: What? My having heart failure?

SALZER: To hell with you! Gonda driving her motorboat!

McNITT: Try and stop her! So she climbs up to the road, finally, wet all over. "You'll get killed someday," I say to her, and she looks straight at me and she says, "That won't make any difference to me," she says, "nor to anyone else anywhere."

FARROW: She said that?

McNITT: She did. "Listen," I said, "I don't give a damn if you break your neck, but you'll get pneumonia in the middle of my next picture!" She looks at me in that damnable way of hers and she says, "Maybe there won't be any next picture." And she walks straight back to the house and her damn flunkey wouldn't let me in!

FARROW: She actually said that? Yesterday?

McNITT: She did—damn the slut! I never wanted to direct her anyway. I . . .

[*Intercom buzzes*]

FARROW: [*Clicking the switch*] Yes? . . . *Who?* Who is Goldstein and Goldstein? . . . [*Exploding*] Tell them to go to hell! . . . Wait! Tell them Miss Gonda does *not* need any attorneys! Tell them you don't know what on earth made them think she did! [*Switches off furiously*]

SALZER: God! I wish we'd never signed her! A headache we should have ever since she came on the lot!

FARROW: Sol! You're forgetting yourself! After all! Our greatest star!

SALZER: Where did we find her? In the gutter we found her! In the gutter in Vienna! What do we get for our pains? Gratitude we get?

CLAIRE: Down-to-earthiness, that's what she lacks. You know. No finer feelings. *But* none! No sense of human brotherhood. Honestly, I don't understand what they all see in her, anyway!

SALZER: Five million bucks net per each picture—that's what *I* see!

CLAIRE: I don't know why she draws them like that. She's completely heartless. I went down to her house yesterday afternoon—to discuss her next script. And what's the use? She wouldn't let me put in a baby or a dog, as I wanted to. Dogs have such human appeal. You know, we're all brothers under the skin, and . . .

SALZER: Peemoller's right. She's got something there.

CLAIRE: And furthermore . . . [*Stops suddenly*] Wait! That's funny! I haven't thought of this before. She did mention the dinner.

FARROW: [*Eagerly*] What did she say?

CLAIRE: She got up and left me flat, saying she had to dress. "I'm going to Santa Barbara tonight," she said. Then she added, "I do not like missions of charity."

SALZER: My God, what did she mean by that?

CLAIRE: What does she mean by anything? So then I just couldn't resist it, *but* couldn't! I said, "Miss Gonda, do you really think you're so much better than everybody else?" And what did she have the nerve to answer? "Yes," she said, "I do. I wish I didn't have to."

FARROW: Why didn't you tell me this sooner?

CLAIRE: I had forgotten. I really didn't know there was anything between Gonda and Granton Sayers.

McNITT: An old story. I thought she was through with him long ago.

CLAIRE: What did *he* want with her?

FARROW: Well, Granton Sayers—you know Granton Sayers. A reckless fool. Fifty million dollars, three years ago. Today—who knows? Perhaps, fifty thousand. Perhaps, fifty cents. But cut-crystal swimming pools and Greek temples in his garden, and . . .

CLAIRE: . . . And Kay Gonda.

FARROW: Ah, yes, and Kay Gonda. An expensive little plaything or art work, depending on how you want to look at it. Kay Gonda, that is, two years ago. Not today. I know that she had not seen Sayers for over a year, previous to that dinner in Santa Barbara last night.

CLAIRE: Had there been any quarrel between them?

FARROW: None. Never. That fool had proposed to her three times, to my knowledge. She could have had him, Greek temples and oil wells and all, anytime she winked an eyelash.

CLAIRE: Has she had any trouble of any kind lately?

FARROW: None. None whatever. In fact, you know, she was to sign her new contract with us today. She promised me faithfully to be here at five, and . . .

SALZER: [*Clutching his head suddenly*] Tony! It's the contract!

FARROW: What about the contract?

SALZER: Maybe she's changed her mind again, and quit for good.

CLAIRE: A pose, Mr. Salzer, just a pose. She's said that after every picture.

SALZER: Yeah? You should laugh if you had to crawl after her on your knees like we've done for two months. "I'm through," she says. "Does it really mean anything?" Five million net per each picture—does it mean anything! "Is it really worth doing?" Ha! Twenty thousand a week we offer her and she asks is it worth doing!

FARROW: Now, now, Sol. Control your subconscious. You know, I have an idea that she will come here at five. It would be just like her. She is so utterly unpredictable. We cannot judge her actions by the usual standards. With her—anything is possible.

SALZER: Say, Tony, how about the contract? Did she insist again . . . is there anything in it again about Mick Watts?

FARROW: [*Sighing*] There is, unfortunately. We had to write it in again. So long as she is with us, Mick Watts will be her personal press agent. Most unfortunate.

CLAIRE: That's the kind of trash she gathers around her. But the rest of us aren't good enough for her! Well, if she's got herself into a mess now—I'm glad. Yes, glad! I don't see why we should all worry ourselves sick over it.

McNITT: I don't give a damn myself! I'd much rather direct Joan Tudor anyway.

CLAIRE: And I'd just as soon write for Sally Sweeney. She's such a sweet kid. And . . .

[*The entrance door flies open.* MISS DRAKE *rushes in, slamming it behind her, as if holding the door against someone*]

MISS DRAKE: She's here!

FARROW: [*Leaping to his feet*] Who? Gonda?!

MISS DRAKE: No! Miss Sayers! Miss Frederica Sayers!

[*They all gasp*]

FARROW: What?! Here?!

MISS DRAKE: [*Pointing at the door foolishly*] In there! Right in there!

FARROW: Good Lord!

MISS DRAKE: She wants to see you, Mr. Farrow. She *demands* to see you!

FARROW: Well, let her in! Let her right in, for God's sake! [*As* MISS DRAKE *is about to rush out*] Wait! [*To the others*] You'd better get out of here! It may be confidential. [*Rushes them to private door Right*]

SALZER: [*On his way out*] Make her talk, Tony! For God's sake, make her talk!

FARROW: Don't worry!

[SALZER, CLAIRE, *and* McNITT *exit Right.* FARROW *whirls on* MISS DRAKE]

FARROW: Don't stand there shaking! Bring her right in!

[MISS DRAKE *exits hurriedly.* FARROW *flops down behind his desk and attempts a nonchalant attitude. The entrance door is thrown open as* FREDERICA SAYERS *enters. She is a tall, sparse, stern lady of middle age, gray-haired, erect in her black clothes of mourning.* MISS DRAKE *hovers anxiously behind her.* FARROW *jumps to his feet*]

MISS DRAKE: Miss Frederica Sayers, Mr. Far—

MISS SAYERS: [*Brushing her aside*] Abominable discipline in your studio, Farrow! That's no way to run the place. [MISS DRAKE *slips out, closing the door*] Five reporters pounced on me at the gate and trailed me to your office. I suppose it will all appear in the evening papers, the color of my underwear included.

FARROW: My *dear* Miss Sayers! How do you do? So kind of you to come here! Rest assured that I . . .

MISS SAYERS: Where's Kay Gonda? I must see her. At once.

FARROW: [*Looks at her, startled. Then:*] Do sit down, Miss Sayers. Please allow me to express my deepest sympathy for your grief at the untimely loss of your brother, who . . .

MISS SAYERS: My brother was a fool. [*Sits down*] I've always known he'd end up like this.

FARROW: [*Cautiously*] I must admit I have not been able to learn all the unfortunate details. How *did* Mr. Sayers meet his death?

MISS SAYERS: [*Glancing at him sharply*] Mr. Farrow, your time is valuable. So is mine. I did not come here to answer questions. In fact, I did not come here to speak to you at all. I came to find Miss Gonda. It is most urgent.

FARROW: Miss Sayers, let us get this clear. I have been trying to get in touch with you since early this morning. You must know who started these rumors. And you must realize how utterly preposterous it is. Miss Gonda happens to have dinner with your brother last night. He is found dead, this morning, with a bullet through him. . . . Most unfortunate and I do sympathize, believe me, but is this ground enough for a suspicion of murder against a lady of Miss Gonda's standing? Merely the fact that she happened to be the last one seen with him?

MISS SAYERS: And the fact that nobody has seen her since.

FARROW: Did she . . . did she really do it?

MISS SAYERS: I have nothing to say about that.

FARROW: Was there anyone else at your house last night?

MISS SAYERS: I have nothing to say about that.

FARROW: But good God! [*Controlling himself*] Look here, Miss Sayers, I can well understand that you may not wish to give it out to the press, but you can tell me, in strict confidence, can't you? What were the exact circumstances of your brother's death?

MISS SAYERS: I have given my statement to the police.

FARROW: The police refuse to disclose anything!

MISS SAYERS: They must have their reasons.

FARROW: Miss Sayers! Please try to understand the position I'm in! I'm entitled to know. What actually happened at that dinner?

MISS SAYERS: I have never spied on Granton and his mistresses.

FARROW: But . . .

MISS SAYERS: Have you asked Miss Gonda? What did she say?

FARROW: Look here, if you don't talk—I don't talk, either.

MISS SAYERS: I have not asked you to talk. In fact, I haven't the slightest interest in anything you may say. I want to see Miss Gonda. It is to her own advantage. To yours also, I suppose.

FARROW: May I give her the message?

MISS SAYERS: Your technique is childish, my good man.

FARROW: But in heaven's name, what is it all about? If you've accused her of murder, you have no right to come here demanding to see her! If she's hiding, wouldn't she be hiding from you above all people?

MISS SAYERS: Most unfortunate, if she is. Highly ill advised. Highly.

FARROW: Look here, I'll offer you a bargain. You tell me everything and I'll take you to Miss Gonda. Not otherwise.

MISS SAYERS: [*Rising*] I have always been told that picture people had abominable manners. Most regrettable. Please tell Miss Gonda that I have tried. I shall not be responsible for the consequences now.

FARROW: [*Rushing after her*] Wait! Miss Sayers! Wait a moment! [*She turns to him*] I'm so sorry! Please forgive me! I'm . . . I'm quite upset, as you can well understand. I beg of you, Miss Sayers, consider what it means! The greatest star of the screen! The dream woman of the world! They worship her, millions of them. It's practically a cult.

MISS SAYERS: I have never approved of motion pictures. Never saw one. The pastime of morons.

FARROW: You wouldn't say that if you read her fan mail. Do you think it comes from shopgirls and school kids, like the usual kind of trash? No. Not Kay Gonda's mail. From college professors and authors and judges and ministers! Everybody! Dirt farmers and international names! It's extraordinary! I've never seen anything like it in my whole career.

MISS SAYERS: Indeed?

FARROW: I don't know what she does to them all—but she does something. She's not a movie star to them— she's a goddess. [*Correcting himself hastily*] Oh, forgive me. I understand how you must feel about her. Of course, you and I know that Miss Gonda is not exactly above reproach. She is, in fact, a very objectionable person who . . .

MISS SAYERS: I thought she was a rather charming young woman. A bit anemic. A vitamin deficiency in her diet, no doubt. [*Turning to him suddenly*] Was she happy?

FARROW: [*Looking at her*] Why do you ask that?

MISS SAYERS: I don't think she was.

FARROW: That, Miss Sayers, is a question I've been asking myself for years. She's a strange woman.

MISS SAYERS: She is.

FARROW: But surely you can't hate her so much as to want to ruin her!

MISS SAYERS: I do not hate her at all.

FARROW: Then for heaven's sake, help me to save her

name! Tell me what happened. One way or the other,
only let's stop these rumors! Let's stop these rumors!

MISS SAYERS: This is getting tiresome, my good man. For
the last time, will you let me see Miss Gonda or
won't you?

FARROW: I'm so sorry, but it is impossible, and . . .

MISS SAYERS: Either you are a fool or you don't know
where she is yourself. Regrettable, in either case. I wish
you a good day.

[*She is at the entrance door when the private door Right
is thrown open violently.* SALZER *and* McNITT *enter,
dragging and pushing* MICK WATTS *between them.* MICK
WATTS *is tall, about thirty-five, with disheveled plati-
num-blond hair, the ferocious face of a thug, and the
blue eyes of a baby. He is obviously, unquestionably
drunk*]

McNITT: There's your precious Mick Watts for you!

SALZER: Where do you think we found him? He was . . .
[*Stops short seeing* MISS SAYERS] Oh, I beg your pardon!
We thought Miss Sayers had left!

MICK WATTS: [*Tearing himself loose from them*] Miss
Sayers?! [*Reels ferociously toward her*] What did you
tell them?

MISS SAYERS: [*Looking at him coolly*] And who are you,
young man?

MICK WATTS: *What did you tell them?*

MISS SAYERS: [*Haughtily*] I have told them nothing.

MICK WATTS: Well, keep your mouth shut! Keep your
mouth shut!

MISS SAYERS: That, young man, is precisely what I am doing. [*Exits*]

McNITT: [*Lurching furiously at* MICK WATTS] Why, you
drunken fool!

FARROW: [*Interfering*] Wait a moment! What happened?
Where did you find him?

SALZER: Down in the publicity department! Just think
of that! He walked right in and there's a mob of re-

porters pounced on him and started filling him up with liquor and—

FARROW: Oh, my Lord!

SALZER:—and here's what he was handing out for a press release! [*Straightens out a slip of paper he has crumpled in his hand, reads:*] "Kay Gonda does not cook her own meals or knit her own underwear. She does not play golf, adopt babies, or endow hospitals for homeless horses. She is not kind to her dear old mother—she *has* no dear old mother. She is not just like you and me. She never was like you and me. She's like nothing you bastards ever dreamed of!"

FARROW: [*Clutching his head*] Did they get it?

SALZER: A fool you should think I am? We dragged him out of there just in time!

FARROW: [*Approaching* MICK WATTS, *ingratiatingly*] Sit down, Mick, do sit down. There's a good boy.

[MICK WATTS *flops down on a chair and sits motionless, staring into space*]

McNITT: If you let me punch the bastard just once, he'll talk all right.

[SALZER *nudges him frantically to keep quiet.* FARROW *hurries to a cabinet, produces a glass and a decanter, pours*]

FARROW: [*Bending over* MICK WATTS, *solicitously, offering him the glass*] A drink, Mick? [MICK WATTS *does not move or answer*] Nice weather we're having, Mick. Nice, but hot. Awfully hot. Supposing you and I have a drink together?

MICK WATTS: [*In a dull monotone*] I don't know a thing. Save your liquor. Go to hell.

FARROW: What *are* you talking about?

MICK WATTS: I'm talking about nothing—and that goes for everything.

FARROW: You could stand a drink once in a while, couldn't you? You look thirsty to me.

MICK WATTS: I don't know a thing about Kay Gonda. Never heard of her. . . . Kay Gonda. It's a funny name, isn't it? I went to confession once, long ago—and they talked about the redemption of all sins. It's useless to yell "Kay Gonda" and to think that all your sins are washed away. Just pay two bits in the balcony—and come out pure as snow.

[*The others exchange glances and shrug hopelessly*]

FARROW: On second thought, Mick, I won't offer you another drink. You'd better have something to eat.

MICK WATTS: I'm not hungry. I stopped being hungry many years ago. But she is.

FARROW: Who?

MICK WATTS: Kay Gonda.

FARROW: [*Eagerly*] Any idea where she's having her next meal?

MICK WATTS: In heaven. [FARROW *shakes his head helplessly*] In a blue heaven with white lilies. Very white lilies. Only she'll never find it.

FARROW: I don't understand you, Mick.

MICK WATTS: [*Looking at him slowly for the first time*] You don't understand? She doesn't either. Only it's no use. It's no use trying to unravel, because if you try, you end up with more dirt on your hands than you care to wipe off. There are not enough towels in the world to wipe it off. Not enough towels. That's the trouble.

SALZER: [*Impatiently*] Look here, Watts, you must know something. You'd better play ball with us. Remember, you've been fired from every newspaper on both coasts—

MICK WATTS:—and from many others in between.

SALZER:—so that if anything should happen to Gonda, you won't have a job here unless you help us now and . . .

MICK WATTS: [*His voice emotionless*] Do you think I'd want to stay with the lousy bunch of you if it weren't for her?

McNITT: Jesus, it beats me what they all see in that bitch!

[MICK WATTS *turns and looks at* McNITT *fixedly, ominously*]

SALZER: [*Placatingly*] Now, now, Mick, he doesn't mean it, he's kidding, he's—

[MICK WATTS *rises slowly, deliberately, walks up to* McNITT *without hurry, then strikes him flat on the face, a blow that sends him sprawling on the floor.* FARROW *rushes to help the stunned* McNITT. MICK WATTS *stands motionless, with perfect indifference, his arms limp*]

McNITT: [*Raising his head slowly*] The damn . . .
FARROW: [*Restraining him*] Discipline, Bill, discipline, control your . . .

[*The door is flung open as* CLAIRE PEEMOLLER *rushes in breathlessly*]

CLAIRE: She's coming! She's coming!
FARROW: Who?!
CLAIRE: Kay Gonda! I just saw her car turning the corner!
SALZER: [*Looking at his wristwatch*] By God! It's five o'clock! Can you beat that!
FARROW: I knew she would! I knew it! [*Rushes to intercom, shouts:*] Miss Drake! Bring in the contract!
CLAIRE: [*Tugging at* FARROW'S *sleeve*] Tony, you won't tell her what I said, will you, Tony? I've always been her best friend! I'll do anything to please her! I've always . . .
SALZER: [*Grabbing a telephone*] Get the publicity department! Quick!
McNITT: [*Rushing to* MICK WATTS] I was only kidding, Mick! You know I was only kidding. No hard feelings, eh, pal?

[MICK WATTS *does not move or look at him.* WATTS *is the only one motionless amid the frantic activity*]

SALZER: [*Shouting into the phone*] Hello, Meagley? . . .
Call all the papers! Reserve the front pages! Tell you
later! [*Hangs up*]

[MISS DRAKE *enters, carrying a batch of legal documents*]

FARROW: [*At his desk*] Put it right here, Miss Drake! Thank
you! [*Steps are heard approaching*] Smile, all of you!
Smile! Don't let her think that we thought for a minute
that she . . .

[*Everyone obeys, save* MICK WATTS, *all eyes turned to
the door. The door opens.* MISS TERRENCE *enters and
steps on the threshold. She is a prim, ugly little shrimp
of a woman*]

MISS TERRENCE: Is Miss Gonda here?

[*A moan rises from the others*]

SALZER: Oh, God!

MISS TERRENCE: [*Looking at the stunned group*] Well,
what is the matter?

CLAIRE: [*Choking*] Did you . . . did *you* drive up in Miss
Gonda's car?

MISS TERRENCE: [*With hurt dignity*] Why, certainly. Miss
Gonda had an appointment here at five o'clock, and I
thought it a secretary's duty to come and tell Mr. Farrow
that it looks as if Miss Gonda will not be able to keep it.

FARROW: [*Dully*] So it does.

MISS TERRENCE: There is also something rather peculiar I
wanted to check on. Has anyone from the studio been at
Miss Gonda's home last night?

FARROW: [*Perking up*] No. Why, Miss Terrence?

MISS TERRENCE: This is *most* peculiar.

SALZER: *What* is?

MISS TERRENCE: I'm sure I can't understand it. I've questioned the servants, but they have not taken them.

FARROW: Taken what?

MISS TERRENCE: If no one else took them, then Miss Gonda must have been back at home late last night.

FARROW: [*Eagerly*] Why, Miss Terrence?

MISS TERRENCE: Because I saw them on her desk yesterday after she left for Santa Barbara. And when I entered her room this morning, they were gone.

FARROW: What was gone?

MISS TERRENCE: Six letters from among Miss Gonda's fan mail.

[*A great sigh of disappointment rises from all*]

SALZER: Aw, nuts!

McNITT: And I thought it was something!

[MICK WATTS *bursts out laughing suddenly, for no apparent reason*]

FARROW: [*Angrily*] What are you laughing at?

MICK WATTS: [*Quietly*] Kay Gonda.

McNITT: Oh, throw the drunken fool out!

MICK WATTS: [*Without looking at anyone*] A great quest. The quest of the hopeless. Why do we hope? Why do we seek it, when we'd be luckier if we didn't think that it could exist? Why does she? Why does she have to be hurt? [*Whirls suddenly upon the others with ferocious hatred*] God damn you all! [*Rushes out, slamming the door*]

CURTAIN

ACT I

When the curtain rises, a motion-picture screen is disclosed and a letter is flashed on the screen, unrolling slowly. It is written in a neat, precise, respectable handwriting:

Dear Miss Gonda,

I am not a regular movie fan, but I have never missed a picture of yours. There is something about you which I can't give a name to, something I had and lost, but I feel as if you're keeping it for me, for all of us. I had it long ago, when I was very young. You know how it is: when you're very young, there's something ahead of you, so big that you're afraid of it, but you wait for it and you're so happy waiting. Then the years pass and it never comes. And then you find, one day, that you're not waiting any longer. It seems foolish, because you didn't even know what it was you were waiting for. I look at myself and I don't know. But when I look at you—I do.

And if ever, by some miracle, you were to enter my life, I'd drop everything, and follow you, and gladly lay down my life for you, because, you see, I'm still a human being.

Very truly yours,

George S. Perkins
. . . S. Hoover Street
Los Angeles, California

When the letter ends, all lights go out, and when they come on again, the screen has disappeared and the stage reveals the living room of GEORGE S. PERKINS.

It is a room such as thousands of other rooms in thousands of other homes whose owners have a respectable little income and a respectable little character.

Center back, a wide glass door opening on the street. Door into the rest of the house in wall Left.

When the curtain rises, it is evening. The street outside is dark. MRS. PERKINS *stands in the middle of the room, tense, erect, indignant, watching with smoldering emotion the entrance door where* GEORGE S. PERKINS *is seen outside turning the key in the lock.* MRS. PERKINS *looks like a dried-out bird of prey that has never been young.* GEORGE S. PERKINS *is short, blond, heavy, helpless, and over forty. He is whistling a gay tune as he enters. He is in a very cheerful mood.*

MRS. PERKINS: [*Without moving, ominously*] You're late.

PERKINS: [*Cheerfully*] Well, dovey, I have a good excuse for being late.

MRS. PERKINS: [*Speaking very fast*] I have no doubt about that. But listen to me, George Perkins, you'll have to do something about Junior. That boy of yours got D again in arithmetic. If a father don't take the proper interest in his children, what can you expect from a boy who . . .

PERKINS: Aw, honeybunch, we'll excuse the kid for once—just to celebrate.

MRS. PERKINS: Celebrate what?

PERKINS: How would you like to be Mrs. Assistant Manager of the Daffodil Canning Company?

MRS. PERKINS: I would like it very much. Not that I have any hopes of ever being.

PERKINS: Well, dovey, you are. As of today.

MRS. PERKINS: [*Noncommittally*] Oh. [*Calls into house*] Mama! Come here!

[MRS. SHLY *waddles in from door Left. She is fat and looks chronically dissatisfied with the whole world.* MRS. PERKINS *speaks, half-boasting, half-bitter*]

Mama, Georgie's got a promotion.

MRS. SHLY: [*Dryly*] Well, we've waited for it long enough.

PERKINS: But you don't understand. I've been made *Assistant Manager*—[*Looks for the effect on her face, finds none, adds lamely*]—of the Daffodil Canning Company.

MRS. SHLY: Well?

PERKINS: [*Spreading his hands helplessly*] Well . . .

MRS. SHLY: All I gotta say is it's a fine way to start off on your promotion, coming home at such an hour, keeping us waiting with dinner and . . .

PERKINS: Oh, I . . .

MRS. SHLY: Oh, we ate all right, don't you worry! Never seen a man that cared two hoops about his family, not two hoops!

PERKINS: I'm sorry. I had dinner with the boss. I should've phoned, only I couldn't keep him waiting, you know, the boss asking me to dinner, in person.

MRS. PERKINS: And here I was waiting for you, I had something to tell you, a nice surprise for you, and . . .

MRS. SHLY: Don't you tell him, Rosie. Don't you tell him now. Serves him right.

PERKINS: But I figured you'd understand. I figured you'd be happy—[*Corrects his presumption hastily*]—well, *glad* that I've been made—

MRS. PERKINS:—Assistant Manager! Lord, do we have to hear it for the rest of our lives?

PERKINS: [*Softly*] Rosie, it's twenty years I've waited for it.

MRS. SHLY: That, my boy, is nothing to brag about!

PERKINS: It's a long time, twenty years. One gets sort of tired. But now we can take it easy . . . light . . . [*With sudden eagerness*] . . . you know, *light* . . . [*Coming down to earth, apologetically*] . . . easy, I mean.

MRS. SHLY: Listen to him! How much you got, Mr. Rockafeller?

PERKINS: [*With quiet pride*] One hundred and sixty-five dollars.

MRS. PERKINS: A *week*?

PERKINS: Yes, dovey, a week. Every single week.

MRS. SHLY: [*Impressed*] Well! [*Gruffly*] Well, what're you standing there for? Sit down. You must be all tired out.

PERKINS: [*Removing his coat*] Mind if I slip my coat off? Sort of stuffy tonight.

MRS. PERKINS: I'll fetch your bathrobe. Don't you go catching a cold. [*Exits Left*]

MRS. SHLY: We gotta think it over careful. There's lots a man can do with one-sixty-five a week. Not that there ain't some men what get around two hundred. Still, one-sixty-five ain't to be sneezed at.

PERKINS: I've been thinking . . .

MRS. PERKINS: [*Returning with a flashy striped flannel bathrobe*] Now put it on like a good boy, nice and comfy.

PERKINS: [*Obeying*] Thanks. . . . Dovey, I was sort of planning . . . I've been thinking of it for a long time, nights, you know . . . making plans . . .

MRS. PERKINS: Plans? But your wife's not let in on it?

PERKINS: Oh, it was only sort of like dreaming . . . I wanted to . . .

[*There is a thunderous crash upstairs, the violent scuffle of a battle and a child's shrill scream*]

BOY'S VOICE: [*Offstage*] No, ya don't! No, ya don't! Ya dirty snot!

GIRL'S VOICE: Ma-a-a!

BOY'S VOICE: I'll learn ya! I'll . . .

GIRL'S VOICE: Ma-a! He bit me on the pratt!

MRS. PERKINS: [*Throws the door Left open, yells upstairs*] Keep quiet up there and march straight to bed, or I'll beat the living Jesus out of the both of you! [*Slams the door. The noise upstairs subsides to thin whimpers*] For the life of me, I don't see why of all the children in the world I had to get these!

PERKINS: Please, dovey, not tonight. I'm tired. I wanted to talk about . . . the plans.

MRS. PERKINS: What plans?

PERKINS: I was thinking . . . if we're very careful, we could take a vacation maybe . . . in a year or two . . . and go to Europe, you know, like Switzerland or Italy . . . [*Looks at her hopefully, sees no reaction, adds*] . . . It's where they have mountains, you know.

MRS. PERKINS: Well?

PERKINS: Well, and lakes. And snow high up on the peaks. And sunsets.

MRS. PERKINS: And what would we do?

PERKINS: Oh . . . well . . . just rest, I guess. And look around, sort of. You know, at the swans and the sailboats. Just the two of us.

MRS. SHLY: Uh-huh. Just the *two* of you.

MRS. PERKINS: Yes, you were always a great one for making up ways of wasting good money, George Perkins. And me slaving and skimping and saving every little penny. Swans, indeed! Well, before you go thinking of any swans, you'd better get us a new Frigidaire, that's all I've got to say.

MRS. SHLY: And a mayonnaise mixer. And a 'lectric washing machine. And it's about time to be thinking of a new car, too. The old one's a sight. And . . .

PERKINS: Look, you don't understand. I don't want anything that we need.

MRS. PERKINS: What?

PERKINS: I want something I don't need at all.

MRS. PERKINS: George Perkins! Have you been drinking?

PERKINS: Rosie, I . . .

MRS. SHLY: [*Resolutely*] Now I've had just about enough of this nonsense! Now you come down to earth, George Perkins. There's something bigger to think about. Rosie has a surprise for you. A pretty surprise. Tell him, Rosie.

MRS. PERKINS: I just found it out today, Georgie. You'll be glad to hear it.

MRS. SHLY: He'll be tickled pink. Go on.

MRS. PERKINS: Well, I . . . I've been to the doctor's this morning. We have a baby coming.

[*Silence. The two women look, with bright smiles, at* PERKINS' *face, a face that distorts slowly before their eyes into an expression of stunned horror*]

PERKINS: [*In a choked voice*] Another one?

MRS. PERKINS: [*Brightly*] Uh-huh. A brand-new little baby. [*He stares at her silently*] Well? [*He stares without moving*] Well, what's the matter with you? [*He does not move*] Aren't you glad?

PERKINS: [*In a slow, heavy voice*] You're not going to have it.

MRS. PERKINS: Mama! What's he saying?

PERKINS: [*In a dull, persistent monotone*] You know what I'm saying. You can't have it. You won't.

MRS. SHLY: Have you gone plumb outta your mind? Are you thinking of . . . of . . .

PERKINS: [*Dully*] Yes.

MRS. PERKINS: Mama!!

MRS. SHLY: [*Ferociously*] D'you know who you're talking to? It's my daughter you're talking to, not a street woman! To come right out with a thing like that . . . to his own wife . . . to his own . . .

MRS. PERKINS: What's happened to you?

PERKINS: Rosie, I didn't mean to insult you. It's not even dangerous nowadays and . . .

MRS. PERKINS: Make him stop, Mama!

MRS. SHLY: Where did you pick that up? Decent people don't even know about such things! You hear about it maybe with gangsters and actresses. But in a respectable married home!

MRS. PERKINS: What's happened to you today?

PERKINS: It's not today, Rosie. It's for a long, long time back. . . . But I'm set with the firm now. I can take good care of you and the children. But the rest—Rosie, I can't throw it away for good.

MRS. PERKINS: What are you talking about? What better use can you find for your extra money than to take care of a baby?

PERKINS: That's just it. Take care of it. The hospital and the doctors. The strained vegetables—at two bits the can.

The school and the measles. All over again. And nothing else.

MRS. PERKINS: So that's how you feel about your duties! There's nothing holier than to raise a family. There's no better blessing. Haven't I spent my life making a home for you? Don't you have everything every decent man struggles for? What else do you want?

PERKINS: Rosie, it's not that I don't like what I've got. I like it fine. Only . . . Well, it's like this bathrobe of mine. I'm glad I have it, it's warm and comfortable, and I like it, just the same as I like the rest of it. Just like that. And no more. There should be more.

MRS. PERKINS: Well, I like that! The swell bathrobe I picked out for your birthday! Well, if you didn't like it, why didn't you exchange it?

PERKINS: Oh, Rosie, it's not that! It's only that a man can't live his whole life for a bathrobe. Or for things that he feels the same way about. Things that do nothing to him—inside, I mean. There should be something that he's afraid of—afraid and happy. Like going to church—only not in a church. Something he can look up to. Something—high, Rosie . . . that's it, *high*.

MRS. PERKINS: Well, if it's culture you want, didn't I subscribe to the Book-of-the-Month Club?

PERKINS: Oh, I know I can't explain it! All I ask is, don't let's have that baby, Rosie. That would be the end of it all for me. I'll be an old man, if I give those things up. I don't want to be old. Not yet. God, not yet! Just leave me a few years, Rosie!

MRS. PERKINS: [*Breaking down into tears*] Never, never, never did I think I'd live to hear this!

MRS. SHLY: [*Rushing to her*] Rosie, sweetheart! Don't cry like that, baby! [*Whirling upon* PERKINS] See what you've done? Now don't let me hear another word out of that filthy mouth of yours! Do you want to kill your wife? Take the Chinese, for instance. They go in for abortions, that's why all the Chinks have rickets.

PERKINS: Now, Mother, who ever told you that?

MRS. SHLY: Well, I suppose I don't know what I'm talking

about? I suppose the big businessman is the only one to tell us what's what?

PERKINS: I didn't mean . . . I only meant that . . .

MRS. PERKINS: [*Through her sobs*] You leave Mama alone, George.

PERKINS: [*Desperately*] But I didn't . . .

MRS. SHLY: I understand. I understand perfectly, George Perkins. An old mother, these days, is no good for anything but to shut up and wait for the graveyard!

PERKINS: [*Resolutely*] Mother, I wish you'd stop trying to . . . [*Bravely*] . . . to make trouble.

MRS. SHLY: So? So that's it? So I'm making trouble? So I'm a burden to you, am I? Well, I'm glad you came out with it, Mr. Perkins! And here I've been, poor fool that I am, slaving in this house like if it was my own! That's the gratitude I get. Well, I won't stand for it another minute. Not one minute. [*Rushes out Left, slamming the door*]

MRS. PERKINS: [*With consternation*] George! . . . George, if you don't apologize, Mama will leave us!

PERKINS: [*With sudden, desperate courage*] Well, let her go.

MRS. PERKINS: [*Stares at him incredulously, then:*] So it's come to that? So that's what it does to you, your big promotion? Coming home, picking a fight with everybody, throwing his wife's old mother out into the gutter! If you think I'm going to stand for . . .

PERKINS: Listen, I've stood about as much of her as I'm going to stand. She'd better go. It was coming to this, sooner or later.

MRS. PERKINS: You just listen to me, George Perkins! If you don't apologize to Mama, if you don't apologize to her before tomorrow morning, I'll never speak to you again as long as I live!

PERKINS: [*Wearily*] How many times have I heard that before?

[MRS. PERKINS *runs to door Left and exits, slamming the door.* PERKINS *sits wearily, without moving. An old-fashioned clock strikes nine. He rises slowly, turns out the lights, pulls the shade down over the glass entrance door. The room is dim but for one lamp burning by the fireplace. He leans against the mantelpiece, his head on his arm, slumped wearily. The doorbell rings. It is a quick, nervous, somehow furtive sound.* PERKINS *starts, looks at the entrance door, surprised, hesitates, then crosses to door and opens it. Before we can see the visitor, his voice a stunned explosion:*] Oh, my God!! [PERKINS *steps aside.* KAY GONDA *stands on the threshold. She wears an exquisitely plain black suit, very modern, austerely severe; a black hat, black shoes, stockings, bag, and gloves. The sole and startling contrast to her clothes is the pale, luminous gold of her hair and the whiteness of her face. It is a strange face with eyes that make one uncomfortable. She is tall and very slender. Her movements are slow, her steps light, soundless. There is a feeling of unreality about her, the feeling of a being that does not belong on this earth. She looks more like a ghost than a woman*]

KAY GONDA: Please keep quiet. And let me in.

PERKINS: [*Stuttering foolishly*] You . . . you are . . .

KAY GONDA: Kay Gonda. [*She enters and closes the door behind her*]

PERKINS: W-why . . .

KAY GONDA: Are you George Perkins?

PERKINS: [*Foolishly*] Yes, ma'am. George Perkins. George S. Perkins. . . . Only how . . .

KAY GONDA: I am in trouble. Have you heard about it?

PERKINS: Y-yes . . . oh my God! . . . Yes. . . .

KAY GONDA: I have to hide. For the night. It is dangerous. Can you let me stay here?

PERKINS: *Here?*

KAY GONDA: Yes. For one night.

PERKINS: But how . . . that is . . . why did you . . .

KAY GONDA: [*Opens her bag and shows him the letter*] I read your letter. And I thought that no one would look for me here. And I thought you would want to help me.

PERKINS: I . . . Miss Gonda, you'll excuse me, please, you know it's enough to make a fellow . . . I mean, if I don't seem to make sense or . . . I mean, if you need help, you can stay here the rest of your life, Miss Gonda.

KAY GONDA: [*Calmly*] Thank you. [*She throws her bag on a table, takes off her hat and gloves, indifferently, as if she were quite at home. He keeps staring at her*]

PERKINS: You mean . . . they're really after you?

KAY GONDA: The police. [*Adds*] For murder.

PERKINS: I won't let them get you. If there's anything I can . . . [*He stops short. Steps are heard approaching, behind the door Left*]

MRS. PERKINS' VOICE: [*Offstage*] George!

PERKINS: Yes . . . dovey?

MRS. PERKINS' VOICE: Who was that who rang the bell?

PERKINS: No . . . no one, dovey. Somebody had the wrong address. [*He listens to the steps moving away, then whispers:*] That was my wife. We'd better keep quiet. She's all right. Only . . . she wouldn't understand.

KAY GONDA: It will be dangerous for you, if they find me here.

PERKINS: I don't care. [*She smiles slowly. He points to the room helplessly*] Just make yourself at home. You can sleep right here, on the davenport, and I'll stay outside and watch to see that no one . . .

KAY GONDA: No. I don't want to sleep. Stay here. You and I, we have so much to talk about.

PERKINS: Oh, yes. Sure . . . that is . . . about what, Miss Gonda?

[*She sits down without answering. He sits down on the edge of a chair, gathering his bathrobe, miserably uncomfortable. She looks at him expectantly, a silent question in her eyes. He blinks, clears his throat, says resolutely:*]

Pretty cold night, this is.

KAY GONDA: Yes.

PERKINS: That's California for you . . . the Golden West . . . Sunshine all day, but cold as the . . . but very cold at night.

KAY GONDA: Give me a cigarette.

[*He leaps to his feet, produces a package of cigarettes, strikes three matches before he can light one. She leans back, the lighted cigarette between her fingers*]

PERKINS: [*He mutters helplessly*] I . . . I smoke this kind. Easier on your throat, they are. [*He looks at her miserably. He has so much to tell her. He fumbles for words. He ends with:*] Now Joe Tucker—that's a friend of mine—Joe Tucker, he smokes cigars. But I never took to them, never did.

KAY GONDA: You have many friends?

PERKINS: Yes, sure. Sure I have. Can't complain.

KAY GONDA: You like them?

PERKINS: Yes, I like them fine.

KAY GONDA: And they like you? They approve of you, and they bow to you on the street?

PERKINS: Why . . . I guess so.

KAY GONDA: How old are you, George Perkins?

PERKINS: I'll be forty-three this coming June.

KAY GONDA: It will be hard to lose your job and to find yourself in the street. In a dark, lonely street, where you'll see your friends passing by and looking past you, as if you did not exist. Where you will want to scream and tell them of the great things you know, but no one will hear and no one will answer. It will be hard, won't it?

PERKINS: [*Bewildered*] Why . . . When should that happen?

KAY GONDA: [*Calmly*] When they find me here.

PERKINS: [*Resolutely*] Don't worry about that. No one will find you here. Not that I'm afraid for myself. Suppose they learn I helped you? Who wouldn't? Who'd hold that against me? Why should they?

KAY GONDA: Because they hate me. And they hate all those who take my side.

PERKINS: Why should they hate you?

KAY GONDA: [*Calmly*] I am a murderess, George Perkins.

PERKINS: Well, if you ask me, I don't believe it. I don't even want to ask you whether you've done it. I just don't believe it.

KAY GONDA: If you mean Granton Sayers . . . no, I do not want to speak about Granton Sayers. Forget that. But I am still a murderess. You see, I came here and, perhaps, I will destroy your life—everything that has been your life for forty-three years.

PERKINS: [*In a low voice*] That's not much, Miss Gonda.

KAY GONDA: Do you always go to see my pictures?

PERKINS: Always.

KAY GONDA: Are you happy when you come out of the theater?

PERKINS: Yes. Sure. . . . No, I guess I'm not. That's funny, I never thought of it that way. . . . Miss Gonda, you won't laugh at me if I tell you something?

KAY GONDA: Of course not.

PERKINS: Miss Gonda, I . . . I cry when I come home after seeing a picture of yours. I just lock myself in the bathroom and I cry, every time. I don't know why.

KAY GONDA: I knew that.

PERKINS: How?

KAY GONDA: I told you I am a murderess. I kill so many things in people. I kill the things they live by. But they come to see me because I am the only one who makes them realize that they want those things to be killed. Or they think they do. And it's their whole pride, that they think and say they do.

PERKINS: I'm afraid I don't follow you, Miss Gonda.

KAY GONDA: You'll understand someday.

PERKINS: Did you really do it?

KAY GONDA: What?

PERKINS: Did you kill Granton Sayers? [*She looks at him, smiles slowly, shrugs*] I was only wondering why you could have done it.

KAY GONDA: Because I could not stand it any longer. There are times when one can't stand it any longer.

PERKINS: Yes. There are.

KAY GONDA: [*Looking straight at him*] Why do you want to help me?

PERKINS: I don't know . . . only that . . .

KAY GONDA: Your letter, it said . . .

PERKINS: Oh! I never thought you'd read the silly thing.

KAY GONDA: It was not silly.

PERKINS: I bet you have plenty of them, fans, I mean, and letters.

KAY GONDA: I like to think that I mean something to people.

PERKINS: You must forgive me if I said anything fresh, you know, or personal.

KAY GONDA: You said you were not happy.

PERKINS: I . . . I didn't mean to complain, Miss Gonda, only . . . I guess I've missed something along the way. I don't know what it is, but I know I've missed it. Only I don't know why.

KAY GONDA: Perhaps it is because you wanted to miss it.

PERKINS: No. [*His voice is suddenly firm*] No. [*He rises and stands looking straight at her*] You see, I'm not unhappy at all. In fact, I'm a very happy man—as happiness goes. Only there's something in me that knows of a life I've never lived, the kind of life no one has ever lived, but should.

KAY GONDA: You know it? Why don't you live it?

PERKINS: Who does? Who can? Who ever gets a chance at the . . . the very best possible to him? We all bargain. We take the second best. That's all there is to be had. But the . . . the God in us, it knows the other . . . the very best . . . which never comes.

KAY GONDA: And . . . if it came?

PERKINS: We'd grab it—because there *is* a God in us.

KAY GONDA: And . . . the God in you, you really want it?

PERKINS: [*Fiercely*] Look, I know this: let them come, the cops, let them come now and try to get you. Let them tear this house down. I built it—took me fifteen years to pay for it. Let them tear it down, before I let them take you. Let them come, whoever it is that's after you . . . [*The door Left is flung open.* MRS. PERKINS *stands on the threshold; she wears a faded corduroy bathrobe and a long nightgown of grayish-pink cotton*]

MRS. PERKINS: [*Gasping*] George! . . .

[KAY GONDA *rises and stands looking at them*]

PERKINS: Dovey, keep quiet! For God's sake, keep quiet . . . come in . . . close the door!

MRS. PERKINS: I thought I heard voices . . . I . . . [*She chokes, unable to continue*]

PERKINS: Dovey . . . this . . . Miss Gonda, may I present— my wife? Dovey, this is Miss Gonda, Miss Kay Gonda! [KAY GONDA *inclines her head, but* MRS. PERKINS *remains motionless, staring at her.* PERKINS *says desperately:*] Don't you understand? Miss Gonda's in trouble, you know, you've heard about it, the papers said . . . [*He stops.* MRS. PERKINS *shows no reaction. Silence. Then:*]

MRS. PERKINS: [*To* KAY GONDA, *her voice unnaturally emotionless*] Why did you come here?

KAY GONDA: [*Calmly*] Mr. Perkins will have to explain that.

PERKINS: Rosie, I . . . [*Stops*]

MRS. PERKINS: Well?

PERKINS: Rosie, there's nothing to get excited about, only that Miss Gonda is wanted by the police and—

MRS. PERKINS: Oh.

PERKINS:—and it's for murder and—

MRS. PERKINS: Oh!

PERKINS:—and she just has to stay here overnight. That's all.

MRS. PERKINS: [*Slowly*] Listen to me, George Perkins: either she goes out of the house this minute, or else I go.

PERKINS: But let me explain . . .

MRS. PERKINS: I don't need any explanations. I'll pack my things, and I'll take the children, too. And I'll pray to God we never see you again. [*She waits. He does not answer*] Tell her to get out.

PERKINS: Rosie . . . I can't.

MRS. PERKINS: We've struggled together pretty hard, haven't we, George? Together. For fifteen years.

PERKINS: Rosie, it's just one night. . . . If you knew . . .

MRS. PERKINS: I don't want to know. I don't want to know why my husband should bring such a thing upon me. A fancy woman or a murderess, or both. I've been a

faithful wife to you, George. I've given you the best
years of my life. I've borne your children.

PERKINS: Yes, Rosie . . .

MRS. PERKINS: It's not just for me. Think of what will
happen to you. Shielding a murderess. Think of the
children. [*He doesn't answer*] And your job, too. You
just got that promotion. We were going to get new
drapes for the living room. The green ones. You always
wanted them.

PERKINS: Yes . . .

MRS. PERKINS: And that golf club you wanted to join. They
have the best of members, solid, respectable members,
not men with their fingerprints in the police files.

PERKINS: [*His voice barely audible*] No . . .

MRS. PERKINS: Have you thought of what will happen
when people learn about this?

PERKINS: [*Looks desperately for a word, a glance from*
KAY GONDA. *He wants her to decide. But* KAY GONDA
*stands motionless, as if the scene did not concern her at
all. Only her eyes are watching him. He speaks to her,
his voice a desperate plea*] What will happen when people learn about this?

[KAY GONDA *does not answer*]

MRS. PERKINS: I'll tell you what will happen. No decent
person will ever want to speak to you again. They'll fire
you, down at the Daffodil Company, they'll throw you
right out in the street!

PERKINS: [*Repeats softly, dazedly, as if from far away*] . . .
in a dark, lonely street where your friends will be passing by and looking straight past you . . . and you'll want
to scream . . . [*He stares at* KAY GONDA, *his eyes wide.
She does not move*]

MRS. PERKINS: That will be the end of everything you've
ever held dear. And in exchange for what? Back roads
and dark alleys, fleeing by night, hunted and cornered,
and forsaken by the whole wide world! . . . [*He does not
answer or turn to her. He is staring at* KAY GONDA *with
a new kind of understanding*] Think of the children,

George. . . . [*He does not move*] We've been pretty happy together, haven't we, George? Fifteen years. . . .

[*Her voice trails off. There is a long silence. Then* PERKINS *turns slowly away from* KAY GONDA *to look at his wife. His shoulders droop, he is suddenly old*]

PERKINS: [*Looking at his wife*] I'm sorry, Miss Gonda, but under the circumstances . . .
KAY GONDA: [*Calmly*] I understand.

[*She puts on her hat, picks up her bag and gloves. Her movements are light, unhurried. She walks to the door Center. When she passes* MRS. PERKINS, *she stops to say calmly:*]

I'm sorry. I had the wrong address.

[*She walks out.* PERKINS *and his wife stand at the open door and watch her go*]

PERKINS: [*Putting his arm around his wife's waist*] Is mother asleep?
MRS. PERKINS: I don't know. Why?
PERKINS: I thought I'd go in and talk to her. Make up, sort of. She knows all about raising babies.

CURTAIN

SCENE 2

When the curtain rises, another letter is projected on the screen. This one is written in a small uneven, temperamental handwriting:

Dear Miss Gonda,
    The determinism of duty has conditioned me to pursue the relief of my fellow men's suffering. I see daily before me the wrecks and victims of an out-

rageous social system. But I gain courage for my
cause when I look at you on the screen and realize of what greatness the human race is capable.
Your art is a symbol of the hidden potentiality
which I see in my derelict brothers. None of them
chose to be what he is. None of us ever chooses the
bleak, hopeless life he is forced to lead. But in our
ability to recognize you and bow to you lies the
hope of mankind.

Sincerely yours,

Chuck Fink
. . . Spring Street
Los Angeles, California

*Lights go out, screen disappears, and stage reveals liv-
ing room in the home of* CHUCK FINK. *It is a miserable
room in a run-down furnished bungalow. Entrance
door upstage in wall Right; large open window next to
it, downstage; door to bedroom in wall Center. Late
evening. Although there are electric fixtures in the
room, it is lighted by a single kerosene lamp smoking in
a corner. The tenants are moving out; two battered
trunks and a number of grocery cartons stand in the
middle of the room; closets and chests gape open, half
emptied; clothes, books, dishes, every conceivable
piece of household junk are piled indiscriminately into
great heaps on the floor.*

At curtain rise, CHUCK FINK *is leaning anxiously out
of the window; he is a young man of about thirty, slight,
anemic, with a rich mane of dark hair, a cadaverous
face, and a neat little mustache. He is watching the
people seen hurrying past the window in great agita-
tion; there is a dim confusion of voices outside. He sees
someone outside and calls:*

FINK: Hey, Jimmy!
JIMMY'S VOICE: [*Offstage*] Yeah?
FINK: Come here a minute!

[JIMMY *appears at the window outside; he is a haggard-looking youth, his clothes torn, his eyes swollen, blood running down the side of his face from a gash on his forehead*]

JIMMY: Oh, that you, Chuck? Thought it was a cop. What d'you want?

FINK: Have you seen Fanny down there?

JIMMY: Huh! Fanny!

FINK: Have you seen her?

JIMMY: Not since it started.

FINK: Is she hurt?

JIMMY: Might be. I seen her when it started. She threw a brick plumb through their window.

FINK: What's happened out there?

JIMMY: Tear gas. They've arrested a bunch of the pickets. So we beat it.

FINK: But hasn't anyone seen Fanny?

JIMMY: Oh, to hell with your Fanny! There's people battered all over the place. Jesus, that was one swell free-for-all!

[JIMMY *disappears down the street.* FINK *leaves the window. Paces nervously, glancing at his watch. The noise subsides in the street.* FINK *tries to continue his packing, throws a few things into cartons halfheartedly. The entrance door flies open.* FANNY FINK *enters. She is a tall, gaunt, angular girl in her late twenties, with a sloppy masculine haircut, flat shoes, a man's coat thrown over her shoulders. Her hair is disheveled, her face white. She leans against the doorjamb for support*]

FINK: Fanny! [*She does not move*] Are you all right? What happened? Where have you been?

FANNY: [*In a flat, husky voice*] Got any Mercurochrome?

FINK: What?

FANNY: Mercurochrome. [*Throws her coat off. Her clothes are torn, her bare arms bruised; there is a bleeding cut on one forearm*]

FINK: Jesus!

FANNY: Oh, don't stand there like an idiot! [*Walks resolutely to a cabinet, rummages through the shelves, produces a tiny bottle*] Stop staring at me! Nothing to get hysterical over!

FINK: Here, let me help.

FANNY: Never mind. I'm all right. [*Dabs her arm with Mercurochrome*]

FINK: Where have you been so late?

FANNY: In jail.

FINK: Huh?!

FANNY: All of us. Pinky Thomlinson, Bud Miller, Mary Phelps, and all the rest. Twelve of us.

FINK: What happened?

FANNY: We tried to stop the night shift from going in.

FINK: And?

FANNY: Bud Miller started it by cracking a scab's skull. But the damn Cossacks were prepared. Biff just sprung us out on bail. Got a cigarette? [*She finds one and lights it; she smokes nervously, continuously throughout the scene*] Trial next week. They don't think the scab will recover. It looks like a long vacation in the cooler for yours truly. [*Bitterly*] You don't mind, do you, sweetheart? It will be a nice, quiet rest for you here without me.

FINK: But it's outrageous! I won't allow it! We have some rights . . .

FANNY: Sure. Rights. C.O.D. rights. Not worth a damn without cash. And where will you get that?

FINK: [*Sinking wearily into a chair*] But it's unthinkable!

FANNY: Well, don't think of it, then. . . . [*Looks around*] You don't seem to have done much packing, have you? How are we going to finish with all this damn junk tonight?

FINK: What's the hurry? I'm too upset.

FANNY: What's the hurry! If we're not out of here by morning, they'll dump it all, right out on the sidewalk.

FINK: If that wasn't enough! And now this trial! Now you had to get into this! What are we going to do?

FANNY: I'm going to pack. [*Starts gathering things, hardly looking at them, and flinging them into the cartons with ferocious hatred*] Shall we move to the Ambassador or the Beverly-Sunset, darling? [*He does not answer. She flings a book into the carton*] The Beverly-Sunset would be nice, I think. . . . We shall need a suite of seven rooms—do you think we could manage in seven rooms? [*He does not move. She flings a pile of underwear into the carton*] Oh, yes, and a private swimming pool. [*Flings a coffee pot into carton viciously*] And a two-car garage! For the Rolls-Royce! [*Flings a vase down; it misses the carton and shatters against a chair leg. She screams suddenly hysterically*] Goddamn them! Why do some people have all of that!

FINK: [*Languidly, without moving*] Childish escapism, my dear.

FANNY: The heroics is all very well, but I'm so damn sick of standing up to make speeches about global problems and worrying all the time whether the comrades can see the runs in my stockings!

FINK: Why don't you mend them?

FANNY: Save it, sweetheart! Save the brilliant sarcasm for the magazine editors—maybe it will sell an article for you someday.

FINK: That was uncalled for, Fanny.

FANNY: Well, it's no use fooling yourself. There's a name for people like us. At least, for one of us, I'm sure. Know it? Does your brilliant vocabulary include it? Failure's the word.

FINK: A relative conception, my love.

FANNY: Sure. What's rent money compared to infinity? [*Flings a pile of clothing into a carton*] Do you know it's number five, by the way?

FINK: Number five what?

FANNY: Eviction number five for us, Socrates! I've counted them. Five times in three years. All we've ever done is paid the first month and waited for the sheriff.

FINK: That's the way most people live in Hollywood.

FANNY: You might *pretend* to be worried—just out of decency.

FINK: My dear, why waste one's emotional reserves in blaming oneself for what is the irrevocable result of an inadequate social system?

FANNY: You could at least refrain from plagiarism.

FINK: Plagiarism?

FANNY: You lifted that out of *my* article.

FINK: Oh, yes. *The* article. I beg your pardon.

FANNY: Well, at least it was published.

FINK: So it was. Six years ago.

FANNY: [*Carrying an armful of old shoes*] Got any acceptance checks to show since then? [*Dumps her load into a carton*] Now what? Where in hell are we going to go tomorrow?

FINK: With thousands homeless and jobless—why worry about an individual case?

FANNY: [*Is about to answer angrily, then shrugs, and turning away stumbles over some boxes in the semidarkness*] Goddamn it! It's enough that they're throwing us out. They didn't have to turn off the electricity!

FINK: [*Shrugging*] Private ownership of utilities.

FANNY: I wish there was a kerosene that didn't stink.

FINK: Kerosene is the commodity of the poor. But I understand they've invented a new, odorless kind in Russia.

FANNY: Sure. Nothing stinks in Russia. [*Takes from a shelf a box full of large brown envelopes*] What do you want to do with these?

FINK: What's in there?

FANNY: [*Reading from the envelopes*] Your files as trustee of the Clark Institute of Social Research . . . Correspondence as Consultant to the Vocational School for Subnormal Children . . . Secretary to the Free Night Classes of Dialectic Materialism . . . Adviser to the Workers' Theater . . .

FINK: Throw the Workers' Theater out. I'm through with them. They wouldn't put my name on their letterheads.

FANNY: [*Flings one envelope aside*] What do you want me to do with the rest? Pack it or will you carry it yourself?

FINK: Certainly I'll carry it myself. It might get lost. Wrap them up for me, will you?

FANNY: [*Picks up some newspapers, starts wrapping the files, stops, attracted by an item in a paper, glances at it*] You know, it's funny, this business about Kay Gonda.

FINK: What business?

FANNY: In this morning's paper. About the murder.

FINK: Oh, that? Rubbish. She had nothing to do with it. Yellow press gossip.

FANNY: [*Wrapping up the files*] That Sayers guy sure had the dough.

FINK: Used to have. Not anymore. I know from that time when I helped to picket Sayers Oil last year that the big shot was going by the board even then.

FANNY: It says here that Sayers Oil was beginning to pick up.

FINK: Oh, well, one plutocrat less. So much the better for the heirs.

FANNY: [*Picks up a pile of books*] Twenty-five copies of *Oppress the Oppressors*—[*Adds with a bow*]—by Chuck Fink! . . . What the hell are we going to do with them?

FINK: [*Sharply*] What do you *think* we're going to do with them?

FANNY: God! Lugging all that extra weight around! Do you think there are twenty-five people in the United States who bought one copy each of your great masterpiece?

FINK: The number of sales is no proof of a book's merit.

FANNY: No, but it sure does help!

FINK: Would you like to see me pandering to the middle-class rabble, like the scribbling lackeys of capitalism? You're weakening, Fanny. You're turning petty bourgeois.

FANNY: [*Furiously*] Who's turning petty bourgeois? I've done more than you'll ever hope to do! I don't go running with manuscripts to third-rate publishers. I've had an article printed in *The Nation*! Yes, in *The Nation*! If I didn't bury myself with you in this mudhole of a . . .

FINK: It's in the mudholes of the slums that the vanguard trenches of social reform are dug, Fanny.

FANNY: Oh, Lord, Chuck, what's the use? Look at the others. Look at Miranda Lumkin. A column in the *Courier* and a villa at Palm Springs! And she couldn't hold a candle to me in college! Everybody always said I was an advanced thinker. [*Points at the room*] This is what one gets for being an advanced thinker.

FINK: [*Softly*] I know, dear. You're tired. You're frightened. I can't blame you. But, you see, in our work one must give up everything. All thought of personal gain or comfort. I've done it. I have no private ego left. All I want is that millions of men hear the name of Chuck Fink and come to regard it as that of their leader!

FANNY: [*Softening*] I know. You mean it all right. You're real, Chuck. There aren't many unselfish men in the world.

FINK: [*Dreamily*] Perhaps, five hundred years from now, someone will write my biography and call it *Chuck Fink the Selfless.*

FANNY: And it will seem so silly, then, that here we were worried about some piddling California landlord!

FINK: Precisely. One must know how to take a long view on things. And . . .

FANNY: [*Listening to some sound outside, suddenly*] Sh-sh! I think there's someone at the door.

FINK: Who? No one'll come here. They've deserted us. They've left us to . . . [*There is a knock at the door. They look at each other.* FINK *walks to the door*] Who's there? [*There is no answer. The knock is repeated. He throws the door open angrily*] What do you . . . [*He stops short as* KAY GONDA *enters; she is dressed as in the preceding scene. He gasps*] Oh! . . . [*He stares at her, half frightened, half incredulous.* FANNY *makes a step forward and stops. They can't make a sound*]

KAY GONDA: Mr. Fink?

FINK: [*Nodding frantically*] Yes. Chuck Fink. In person. . . . But you . . . you're *Kay Gonda,* aren't you?

KAY GONDA: Yes. I am hiding. From the police. I have no place to go. Will you let me stay here for the night?

FINK: Well, I'll be damned! . . .Oh, excuse me!

FANNY: You want us to hide you here?

KAY GONDA: Yes. If you are not afraid of it.

FANNY: But why on earth did you pick . . .

KAY GONDA: Because no one would find me here. And because I read Mr. Fink's letter.

FINK: [*Quite recovering himself*] But of course! My letter. I knew you'd notice it among the thousands. Pretty good, wasn't it?

FANNY: I helped him with it.

FINK: [*Laughing*] What a glorious coincidence! I had no idea when I wrote it, that . . . But how wonderfully things work out!

KAY GONDA: [*Looking at him*] I am wanted for murder.

FINK: Oh, don't worry about that. We don't mind. We're broadminded.

FANNY: [*Hastily pulling down the window shade*] You'll be perfectly safe here. You'll excuse the . . . informal appearance of things, won't you? We were considering moving out of here.

FINK: Please sit down, Miss Gonda.

KAY GONDA: [*Sitting down, removing her hat*] Thank you.

FINK: I've dreamed of a chance to talk to you like this. There are so many things I've always wanted to ask you.

KAY GONDA: There are many things I've always wanted to be asked.

FINK: Is it true, what they say about Granton Sayers? You ought to know. They say he was a regular pervert and what he didn't do to women . . .

FANNY: Chuck! That's entirely irrelevant and . . .

KAY GONDA: [*With a faint smile at her*] No. It isn't true.

FINK: Of course, I'm not one to censure anything. I despise morality. Then there's another thing I wanted to ask you: I've always been interested, as a sociologist, in the influence of the economic factor on the individual. How much does a movie star actually get?

KAY GONDA: Fifteen or twenty thousand a week on my new contract—I don't remember.

[FANNY *and* FINK *exchange startled glances*]

FINK: What an opportunity for social good! I've always believed that you were a great humanitarian.

KAY GONDA: Am I? Well, perhaps I am. I hate humanity.

FINK: You don't mean that, Miss Gonda!

KAY GONDA: There are some men with a purpose in life. Not many, but there are. And there are also some with a purpose—and with integrity. These are very rare. I like them.

FINK: But one must be tolerant! One must consider the pressure of the economic factor. Now, for instance, take the question of a star's salary . . .

KAY GONDA: [*Sharply*] I do not want to talk about it. [*With a note that sounds almost like pleading in her voice*] Have you nothing to ask me about my work?

FINK: Oh, God, so much! . . . [*Suddenly earnest*] No. Nothing. [KAY GONDA *looks at him closely, with a faint smile. He adds, suddenly simple, sincere for the first time:*] Your work . . . one shouldn't talk about it. I can't. [*Adds*] I've never looked upon you as a movie star. No one does. It's not like looking at Joan Tudor or Sally Sweeney, or the rest of them. And it's not the trashy stories you make—you'll excuse me, but they are trash. It's something else.

KAY GONDA: [*Looking at him*] What?

FINK: The way you move, and the sound of your voice, and your eyes. Your eyes.

FANNY: [*Suddenly eager*] It's as if you were not a human being at all, not the kind we see around us.

FINK: We all dream of the perfect being that man could be. But no one has ever seen it. You have. And you're showing it to us. As if you knew a great secret, lost by the world, a great secret and a great hope. Man washed clean. Man at his highest possibility.

FANNY: When I look at you on the screen, it makes me feel guilty, but it also makes me feel young, new and proud. Somehow, I want to raise my arms like this. . . . [*Raises her arms over her head in a triumphant, ecstatic ges-*

ture; then, embarrassed:] You must forgive us. We're being perfectly childish.

FINK: Perhaps we are. But in our drab lives, we have to grasp at any ray of light, anywhere, even in the movies. Why not in the movies, the great narcotic of mankind? You've done more for the damned than any philanthropist ever could. How do you do it?

KAY GONDA: [*Without looking at him*] One can do it just so long. One can keep going on one's own power, and wring dry every drop of hope—but then one has to find help. One has to find an answering voice, an answering hymn, an echo. I am very grateful to you. [*There is a knock at the door. They look at one another.* FINK *walks to the door resolutely*]

FINK: Who's there?

WOMAN'S VOICE: [*Offstage*] Say, Chuck, could I borrow a bit of cream?

FINK: [*Angrily*] Go to hell! We haven't any cream. You got your nerve disturbing people at this hour! [*A muffled oath and retreating steps are heard offstage. He returns to the others*] God, I thought it was the police!

FANNY: We mustn't let anyone in tonight. Any of those starving bums around here would be only too glad to turn you in for a—[*Her voice changes suddenly, strangely, as if the last word had dropped out accidentally*]—a reward.

KAY GONDA: Do you realize what chance you are taking if they find me here?

FINK: They'll get you out of here over my dead body.

KAY GONDA: You don't know what danger . . .

FINK: We don't have to know. We know what your work means to us. Don't we, Fanny?

FANNY: [*She has been standing aside, lost in thought*] What?

FINK: We know what Miss Gonda's work means to us, don't we?

FANNY: [*In a flat voice*] Oh, yes . . . yes . . .

KAY GONDA: [*Looking at* FINK *intently*] And that which it means to you . . . you will not betray it?

FINK: One doesn't betray the best in one's soul.

KAY GONDA: No. One doesn't.

FINK: [*Noticing* FANNY's *abstraction*] Fanny!

FANNY: [*With a jerk*] Yes? What?

FINK: Will you tell Miss Gonda how we've always . . .

FANNY: Miss Gonda must be tired. We should really allow her to go to bed.

KAY GONDA: Yes. I am very tired.

FANNY: [*With brisk energy*] You can have our bedroom. . . . Oh, yes, please don't protest. We'll be very comfortable here, on the couch. We'll stay here on guard, so that no one will try to enter.

KAY GONDA: [*Rising*] It is very kind of you.

FANNY: [*Taking the lamp*] Please excuse this inconvenience. We're having a little trouble with our electricity. [*Leading the way to the bedroom*] This way, please. You'll be comfortable and safe.

FINK: Good night, Miss Gonda. Don't worry. We'll stand by you.

KAY GONDA: Thank you. Good night. [*She exits with* FANNY *into the bedroom.* FINK *lifts the window shade. A broad band of moonlight falls across the room. He starts clearing the couch of its load of junk.* FANNY *returns into the room, closing the door behind her*]

FANNY: [*In a low voice*] Well, what do you think of that? [*He stretches his arms wide, shrugging*] And they say miracles don't happen!

FINK: We'd better keep quiet. She may hear us. . . . [*The band of light goes out in the crack of the bedroom door*] How about the packing?

FANNY: Never mind the packing now. [*He fishes for sheets and blankets in the cartons, throwing their contents out again.* FANNY *stands aside, by the window, watching him silently. Then, in a low voice:*] Chuck . . .

FINK: Yes?

FANNY: In a few days, I'm going on trial. Me and eleven of the kids.

FINK: [*Looking at her, surprised*] Yeah.

FANNY: It's no use fooling ourselves. They'll send us all up.

FINK: I know they will.

FANNY: Unless we can get money to fight it.

FINK: Yeah. But we can't. No use thinking about it. [*A short silence. He continues with his work*]

FANNY: [*In a whisper*] Chuck . . . do you think she can hear us?

FINK: [*Looking at the bedroom door*] No.

FANNY: It's a murder that she's committed.

FINK: Yeah.

FANNY: It's a millionaire that she's killed.

FINK: Right.

FANNY: I suppose his family would like to know where she is.

FINK: [*Raising his head, looking at her*] What are you talking about?

FANNY: I was thinking that if his family were told where she's hiding, they'd be glad to pay a reward.

FINK: [*Stepping menacingly toward her*] You lousy . . . what are you trying to . . .

FANNY: [*Without moving*] Five thousand dollars, probably.

FINK: [*Stopping*] Huh?

FANNY: Five thousand dollars, probably.

FINK: You lousy bitch! Shut up before I kill you! [*Silence. He starts to undress. Then:*] Fanny . . .

FANNY: Yes?

FINK: Think they'd—hand over five thousand?

FANNY: Sure they would. People pay more than that for ordinary kidnappers.

FINK: Oh, shut up! [*Silence. He continues to undress*]

FANNY: It's jail for me, Chuck. Months, maybe years in jail.

FINK: Yeah . . .

FANNY: And for the others, too. Bud, and Pinky, and Mary, and the rest. Your friends. Your comrades. [*He stops his undressing*] You need them. The cause needs them. Twelve of our vanguard.

FINK: Yes . . .

FANNY: With five thousand, we'd get the best lawyer from New York. He'd beat the case. . . . And we wouldn't have to move out of here. We wouldn't have to worry. You could continue your great work ... [*He does not answer*] Think of all the poor and helpless who need you. ... [*He does not answer*] Think of twelve human beings you're sending to jail ... twelve to one, Chuck. ... [*He does not answer*] Think of your duty to millions of your brothers. Millions to one. [*Silence*]

FINK: Fanny ...

FANNY: Yes?

FINK: How would we go about it?

FANNY: Easy. We get out while she's asleep. We run to the police station. Come back with the cops. Easy.

FINK: What if she hears?

FANNY: She won't hear. But we got to hurry. [*She moves to the door. He stops her*]

FINK: [*In a whisper*] She'll hear the door opening. [*Points to the open window*] This way. ...

[*They slip out through the window. The room is empty for a brief moment. Then the bedroom door opens.* KAY GONDA *stands on the threshold. She stands still for a moment, then walks across the room to the entrance door and goes out, leaving the door open*]

CURTAIN

SCENE 3

The screen unrolls a letter written in a bold, aggressive handwriting:

Dear Miss Gonda,

I am an unknown artist. But I know to what heights I shall rise, for I carry a sacred banner which cannot fail—and which is you. I have painted nothing that was not you. You stand as a goddess on every canvas I've done. I have never seen you in person. I do not need to. I can draw your face with my eyes closed. For my spirit is but a mirror of yours.

Someday you shall hear men speak of me. Until then, this is only a first tribute from your devoted priest—

Dwight Langley
. . . Normandie Avenue
Los Angeles, California

Lights go out, screen disappears, and stage reveals studio of DWIGHT LANGLEY. *It is a large room, flashy, dramatic, and disreputable. Center back, large window showing the dark sky and the shadows of treetops; entrance door center Left; door into next room upstage Right. A profusion of paintings and sketches on the walls, on the easels, on the floor; all are of* KAY GONDA; *heads, full figures, in modern clothes, in flowering drapes, naked.*

A mongrel assortment of strange types fills the room: men and women in all kinds of outfits, from tails and evening gowns to beach pajamas and slacks, none too prosperous-looking, all having one attribute in common—a glass in hand—and all showing signs of its effect.

DWIGHT LANGLEY *lies stretched in the middle of a couch; he is young, with a tense, handsome, sunburnt face, dark, disheveled hair, and a haughty, irresistible smile.* EUNICE HAMMOND *keeps apart from the guests, her eyes returning constantly, anxiously, to* LANGLEY; *she is a beautiful young girl, quiet, reticent, dressed in a smart, simple dark dress obviously more expensive than any garment in the room.*

As the curtain rises, the guests are lifting their glasses in a grand toast to LANGLEY, *their voices piercing the raucous music coming over the radio.*

MAN IN DRESS SUIT: Here's to Lanny!
MAN IN SWEATER: To Dwight Langley of California!
WOMAN IN EVENING GOWN: To the winner and the best of us—from the cheerful losers!
TRAGIC GENTLEMAN: To the greatest artist ever lived!

LANGLEY: [*Rising, waving his hand curtly*] Thanks.

[ALL *drink. Someone drops a glass, breaking it reso-
nantly. As* LANGLEY *steps aside from the others,* EUNICE
approaches him]

EUNICE: [*Extending her glass to his, whispers softly*] To
the day we've dreamed of for such a long time, dear.

LANGLEY: [*Turning to her indifferently*] Oh . . . oh, yes . . .
[*Clinks glass to hers automatically, without looking
at her*]

WOMAN IN SLACKS: [*Calling to her*] No monopoly on him,
Eunice. Not anymore. From now on—Dwight Langley
belongs to the world!

WOMAN IN EVENING GOWN: Well, not that I mean to mini-
mize Lanny's triumph, but I must say that for the greatest exhibition of the decade, it was rather a fizz, wasn't
it? Two or three canvases with some idea of something,
but the rest of the trash people have the nerve to exhibit
these days . . .

EFFEMINATE YOUNG MAN: Dear me! It is positively
preposterous!

MAN IN DRESS SUIT: But Lanny beat them all! First prize of
the decade!

LANGLEY: [*With no trace of modesty*] Did it surprise you?

TRAGIC GENTLEMAN: Because Lanny's a geniush!

EFFEMINATE YOUNG MAN: Oh, my yes! Positively a genius!

[LANGLEY *walks over to a sideboard to refill his glass.*
EUNICE, *standing beside him, slips her hand over his*]

EUNICE: [*In a low voice, tenderly*] Dwight, I haven't had a
moment with you to congratulate you. And I do want to
say it tonight. I'm too happy, too proud of you to know
how to say it, but I want you to understand . . . my dearest . . . how much it means to me.

LANGLEY: [*Jerking his hand away, indifferently*] Thanks.

EUNICE: I can't help thinking of the years past. Remember,
how discouraged you were at times, and I talked to you
about your future, and . . .

LANGLEY: You don't have to bring that up now, do you?

EUNICE: [*Trying to laugh*] I shouldn't. I know. Utterly bad form. [*Breaking down involuntarily*] But I can't help it. I love you.

LANGLEY: I know it. [*Walks away from her*]

BLOND GIRL: [*Sitting on the couch, next to the woman in slacks*] Come here, Lanny! Hasn't anyone got a chance with a real genius?

LANGLEY: [*Flopping down on the couch, between the two girls*] Hello.

WOMAN IN SLACKS: [*Throwing her arms around his shoulders*] Langley, I can't get over that canvas of yours. I still see it as it hung there tonight. The damn thing haunts me.

LANGLEY: [*Patronizingly*] Like it?

WOMAN IN SLACKS: Love it. You do get the damnedest titles, though. What was it called? Hope, faith, or charity? No. Wait a moment. Liberty, equality, or . . .

LANGLEY: *Integrity*.

WOMAN IN SLACKS: That's it. "Integrity." Just what did you really mean by it, darling?

LANGLEY: Don't try to understand.

MAN IN DRESS SUIT: But the woman! The woman in your painting, Langley! Ah, that, my friend, is a masterpiece!

WOMAN IN SLACKS: That white face. And those eyes. Those eyes that look straight through you!

WOMAN IN EVENING GOWN: You know, of course, who she is?

MAN IN DRESS SUIT: Kay Gonda, as usual.

MAN IN SWEATSHIRT: Say, Lanny, will you ever paint any other female? Why do you always have to stick to that one?

LANGLEY: An artist *tells*. He does not *explain*.

WOMAN IN SLACKS: You know, there's something damn funny about Gonda and that Sayers affair.

MAN IN DRESS SUIT: I bet she did it all right. Wouldn't put it past her.

EFFEMINATE YOUNG MAN: Imagine Kay Gonda being hanged! The blond hair and the black hood and the noose. My, it would be *perfectly* thrilling!

WOMAN IN EVENING GOWN: There's a new theme for you, Lanny. "Kay Gonda on the Gallows."

LANGLEY: [*Furiously*] Shut up, all of you! She didn't do it! I won't have you discussing her in my house!

[*The guests subside for a brief moment*]

MAN IN DRESS SUIT: Wonder how much Sayers actually left.

WOMAN IN SLACKS: The papers said he was just coming into a swell setup. A deal with United California Oil or some such big-time stuff. But I guess it's off now.

MAN IN SWEATER: No, the evening papers said his sister is rushing the deal through.

WOMAN IN EVENING GOWN: But what're the police doing? Have they issued any warrants?

MAN IN DRESS SUIT: Nobody knows.

WOMAN IN EVENING GOWN: Damn funny. . . .

MAN IN SWEATER: Say, Eunice, any more drinks left in this house? No use asking Lanny. He never knows where anything is.

MAN IN DRESS SUIT: [*Throwing his arm around Eunice*] The greatest little mother-sister-and-all-the-rest combination an artist ever had!

[EUNICE *disengages herself, not too brusquely, but obviously displeased*]

EFFEMINATE YOUNG MAN: Do you know that Eunice darns his socks? Oh, my, yes! I've seen a pair. Positively the cutest things!

MAN IN SWEATER: The woman behind the throne! The woman who guided his footsteps, washed his shirts, and kept up his courage in his dark years of struggle.

WOMAN IN EVENING GOWN: [*To the* WOMAN IN SLACKS, *in a low voice*] Kept up his courage—and his bank account.

WOMAN IN SLACKS: No. Really?

WOMAN IN EVENING GOWN: My dear, it's no secret. Where do you suppose the money came from for the "dark years of struggle"? The Hammond millions. Not that

old man Hammond didn't kick her out of the house. He
did. But she had some money of her own.

EFFEMINATE YOUNG MAN: Oh, my yes. The Social Regis-
ter dropped her, too. But she didn't care one bit, not
one bit.

MAN IN SWEATER: [*To* EUNICE] How about it, Eunice?
Where are the drinks?

EUNICE: [*Hesitating*] I'm afraid . . .

LANGLEY: [*Rising*] She's afraid she doesn't approve. But
we're going to drink whether she approves of it or not.
[*Searches through the cupboards frantically*]

WOMAN IN SLACKS: Really, folks, it's getting late and . . .

MAN IN DRESS SUIT: Oh, just one more drink, and we'll all
toddle home.

LANGLEY: Hey, Eunice, where's the gin?

EUNICE: [*Opening a cabinet and producing two bottles,
quietly*] Here.

MAN IN SWEATER: Hurrah! Wait for baby!

[*There is a general rush to the bottles*]

MAN IN DRESS SUIT: Just one last drink and we'll scram.
Hey everybody! Another toast. To Dwight Langley and
Eunice Hammond!

EUNICE: To Dwight Langley and his future!

[*All roar approval and drink*]

EVERYONE: [*Roaring at once*] Speech, Lanny! . . . Yes! . . .
Come on, Lanny! . . . Speech! . . . Come on!

LANGLEY: [*Climbs up on a chair, stands a little unsteadily,
speaks with a kind of tortured sincerity*] The bitterest
moment of an artist's life is the moment of his triumph.
The artist is but a bugle calling to a battle no one wants
to fight. The world does not see and does not want to
see. The artist begs men to throw the doors of their lives
open to grandeur and beauty, but those doors will remain closed forever . . . forever . . . [*Is about to add
something, but drops his hand in a gesture of hopelessness and ends in a tone of quiet sadness*] . . . forever . . . .

[*Applause. The general noise is cut short by a knock at the door.* LANGLEY *jumps off his chair*] Come in!

[*The door opens, disclosing an irate* LANDLADY *in a soiled Chinese kimono*]

LANDLADY: [*In a shrill whine*] Mr. Langley, this noise will have to stop! Don't you know what time it is?

LANGLEY: Get out of here!

LANDLADY: The lady in 315 says she'll call the police! The gentleman in . . .

LANGLEY: You heard me! Get out! Think I have to stay in a lousy dump like this?

EUNICE: Dwight! [*To* LANDLADY] We'll keep quiet, Mrs. Johnson.

LANDLADY: Well, you'd better! [*She exits angrily*]

EUNICE: Really, Dwight, we shouldn't . . .

LANGLEY: Oh, leave me alone! No one's going to tell *me* what to do from now on!

EUNICE: But I only . . .

LANGLEY: You're turning into a damnable, nagging, middle-class female!

[EUNICE *stares at him, frozen*]

WOMAN IN SLACKS: Going a bit too far, Langley!

LANGLEY: I'm sick and tired of people who can't outgrow their possessiveness! You know the hypocritical trick— the chains of *gratitude*!

EUNICE: Dwight! You don't think that I . . .

LANGLEY: I know damn well what *you* think! Think you've bought me, don't you? Think you own me for the rest of my life in exchange for some grocery bills?

EUNICE: What did you say? [*Screaming suddenly*] I didn't hear you right!

MAN IN SWEATER: Look here, Langley, take it easy, you don't know what you're saying, you're . . .

LANGLEY: [*Pushing him aside*] Go to hell! You can all go to hell if you don't like it! [*To* EUNICE] And as for you . . .

EUNICE: Dwight . . . please . . . not now . . .

LANGLEY: Yes! Right here and now! I want them all to hear! [*To the guests*] So you think I can't get along without her? I'll show you! I'm through! [*To* EUNICE] Do you hear that? I'm through! [EUNICE *stands motionless*] I'm free! I'm going to rise in the world! I'm going places none of you ever dreamed of! I'm ready to meet the only woman I've ever wanted—Kay Gonda! I've waited all these years for the day when I would meet her! That's all I've lived for! And no one's going to stand in my way!

EUNICE: [*She walks to door Left, picks up her hat and coat from a pile of clothing in a corner, turns to him again, quietly*] Goodbye, Dwight . . . [*Exits*]

[*There is a second of strained silence in the room: the* WOMAN IN SLACKS *is the first one to move; she goes to pick up her coat, then turns to Langley*]

WOMAN IN SLACKS: I thought you had just done a painting called "Integrity."

LANGLEY: If that was intended for a dirty crack . . . [*The* WOMAN IN SLACKS *exits, slamming the door*] Well, go to hell! [*To the others*] Get out of here! All of you! Get out!

[*There is a general shuffle for hats and coats*]

WOMAN IN EVENING GOWN: Well, if we're being kicked out . . .

MAN IN DRESS SUIT: That's all right. Lanny's a bit upset.

LANGLEY: [*Somewhat gentler*] I'm sorry. I thank you all. But I want to be alone. [*The guests are leaving, waving halfhearted goodbyes*]

BLOND GIRL: [*She is one of the last to leave. She hesitates, whispering tentatively:*] Lanny . . .

LANGLEY: Out! All of you! [*She exits. The stage is empty but for* LANGLEY *surveying dazedly the havoc of his studio. There is a knock at the door*] Out, I said! Don't want any of you! [*The knock is repeated. He walks to the door, throws it open.* KAY GONDA *enters. She stands looking at him without a word. He asks impatiently:*] Well? [*She does not answer*] What do you want?

KAY GONDA: Are you Dwight Langley?

LANGLEY: Yes.

KAY GONDA: I need your help.

LANGLEY: What's the matter?

KAY GONDA: Don't you know?

LANGLEY: How should I know? Just who are you?

KAY GONDA: [*After a pause*] Kay Gonda.

LANGLEY: [*Looks at her and bursts out laughing*] So? Not Helen of Troy? Nor Madame Du Barry? [*She looks at him silently*] Come on, out with it. What's the gag?

KAY GONDA: Don't you know me?

LANGLEY: [*Looks her over contemptuously, his hands in his pockets, grinning*] Well, you do look like Kay Gonda. So does her stand-in. So do dozens of extra girls in Hollywood. What is it you're after? I can't get you into pictures, my girl. I'm not even the kind to promise you a screen test. Drop the racket. Who are you?

KAY GONDA: Don't you understand? I am in danger. I have to hide. Please let me stay here for the night.

LANGLEY: What do you think this is? A flop house?

KAY GONDA: I have no place to go.

LANGLEY: That's an old one in Hollywood.

KAY GONDA: They will not look for me here.

LANGLEY: Who?

KAY GONDA: The police.

LANGLEY: Really? And why would Kay Gonda pick my house to hide in of all places? [*She starts to open her handbag, but closes it again and says nothing*] How do I know you're Kay Gonda? Have you any proof?

KAY GONDA: None, but the honesty of your vision.

LANGLEY: Oh, cut the tripe! What are you after? Taking me for a . . . [*There is a loud knock at the door*] What's this? A frame-up? [*Walks to door and throws it open. A uniformed* POLICEMAN *enters.* KAY GONDA *turns away quickly, her back to the others*]

POLICEMAN: [*Good-naturedly*] 'Evening. [*Looking about*

him, helplessly] Where's the drunken party we got a complaint about?

LANGLEY: Of all the nerve! There's no party, officer. I had a few friends here, but they left long ago.

POLICEMAN: [*Looking at* KAY GONDA *with some curiosity*] Between you and me, it's a lotta cranks that call up complaining about noise. As I see it, there's no harm in young people having a little fun.

LANGLEY: [*Watching curiously the* POLICEMAN's *reaction to* KAY GONDA] We really weren't disturbing anyone. I'm sure there's nothing you want here, *is there,* officer?

POLICEMAN: No, sir. Sorry to have bothered you.

LANGLEY: We are really alone here—[*Points to* KAY GONDA]—*this lady* and I. But you're welcome to *look around.*

POLICEMAN: Why, no, sir. No need to. Good night. [*Exits*]

LANGLEY: [*Waits to hear his steps descending the stairs. Then turns to* KAY GONDA *and bursts out laughing*] That gave the show away, didn't it, my girl?

KAY GONDA: What?

LANGLEY: The cop. If you were Kay Gonda and if the police were looking for you, wouldn't he have grabbed you?

KAY GONDA: He did not see my face.

LANGLEY: He would have looked. Come on, what kind of racket are you really working?

KAY GONDA: [*Stepping up to him, in full light*] Dwight Langley! Look at me! Look at all these pictures of me that you've painted! Don't you know me? You've lived with me in your hours of work, your best hours. Were you lying in those hours?

LANGLEY: Kindly leave my art out of it. My art has nothing to do with your life or mine.

KAY GONDA: Of what account is an art that preaches things it does not want to exist?

LANGLEY: [*Solemnly*] Listen. Kay Gonda is the symbol of all the beauty I bring to the world, a beauty we can never reach. We can only sing of her, who is the unattainable. That is the mission of the artist. We can only strive, but never succeed. Attempt, but never achieve.

That is our tragedy, but our hopelessness is our glory.
Get out of here!

KAY GONDA: I need your help.

LANGLEY: Get out!!

[*Her arms fall limply. She turns and walks out.* DWIGHT
LANGLEY *slams the door*]

CURTAIN

ACT II

The letter projected on the screen is written in an ornate, old-fashioned handwriting:

Dear Miss Gonda,

Some may call this letter a sacrilege. But as I write it, I do not feel like a sinner. For when I look at you on the screen, it seems to me that we are working for the same cause, you and I. This may surprise you, for I am only a humble Evangelist. But when I speak to men about the sacred meaning of life, I feel that you hold the same Truth which my words struggle in vain to disclose. We are traveling different roads, Miss Gonda, but we are bound to the same destination.

Respectfully yours,

Claude Ignatius Hix
. . . Slosson Blvd.
Los Angeles, California

Lights go out, screen disappears. When the curtain rises on the temple of CLAUDE IGNATIUS HIX, *the stage is almost completely black. Nothing can be seen of the room save the dim outline of a door, downstage Right, open upon a dark street. A small cross of electric lights burns high on wall Center. It throws just enough light to*

155

show the face and shoulders of CLAUDE IGNATIUS HIX *high above the ground (he is standing in the pulpit, but this cannot be distinguished in the darkness). He is tall, gaunt, clothed in black; his hair is receding off a high forehead. His hands rise eloquently as he speaks into the darkness.*

HIX: . . . but even in the blackest one of us, there is a spark of the sublime, a single drop in the desert of every barren soul. And all the suffering of men, all the twisted agonies of their lives, come from their treason to that hidden flame. All commit the treason, and none can escape the payment. None can . . . [*Someone sneezes loudly in the darkness, by the door Right.* HIX *stops short, calls in a startled voice:*] Who's there?

[*He presses a switch that lights two tall electric tapers by the sides of his pulpit. We can now see the temple. It is a long, narrow barn with bare rafters and unpainted walls. There are no windows and only a single door. Rows of old wooden benches fill the room, facing the pulpit*]

[SISTER ESSIE TWOMEY *stands downstage Right, by the door. She is a short, plump woman nearing forty, with bleached blond hair falling in curls on her shoulders, from under the brim of a large pink picture hat trimmed with lilies-of-the-valley. Her stocky little figure is draped in the long folds of a sky blue cape*]

ESSIE TWOMEY: [*She raises her right arm solemnly*] Praise the Lord! Good evening, Brother Hix. Keep going. Don't let me interrupt you.
HIX: [*Startled and angry*] You? What are *you* doing here?
ESSIE TWOMEY: I heard you way from the street—it's a blessed voice you have, though you don't control your belly tones properly—and I didn't want to intrude. I just slipped in.
HIX: [*Icily*] And of what service may I be to *you*?
ESSIE TWOMEY: Go ahead with the rehearsal. It's an inspir-

ing sermon you have there, a peach of a sermon. Though a bit on the old-fashioned side. Not modern enough, Brother Hix. That's not the way I do it.

HIX: I do not recall having solicited advice, Sister Twomey, and I should like to inquire for the reason of this sudden visitation.

ESSIE TWOMEY: Praise the Lord! I'm a harbinger of good news. Yes, indeed. I got a corker for you.

HIX: I shall point out that we have never had any matters of common interest.

ESSIE TWOMEY: Verily, Brother Hix. You smacked the nail right on the head. That's why you'll be overjoyed at the proposition. [*Settling herself comfortably down on a bench*] It's like this, brother: there's no room in this neighborhood for you and me both.

HIX: Sister Twomey, these are the first words of truth I have ever heard emerging from your mouth.

ESSIE TWOMEY: The poor dear souls in these parts are heavily laden, indeed. They cannot support two temples. Why, the mangy bums haven't got enough to feed the fleas on a dog!

HIX: Dare I believe, sister, that your conscience has spoken at last, and you are prepared to leave this neighborhood?

ESSIE TWOMEY: Who? *Me* leave this neighborhood? [*Solemnly*] Why, Brother Hix, you have no idea of the blessed work my temple is doing. The lost souls milling at its portals—praise the Lord! . . . [*Sharply*] No, brother, keep your shirt on. I'm going to buy you out.

HIX: What?!

ESSIE TWOMEY: Not that I really have to. You're no competition. But I thought I might as well clear it up once and for all. I want this territory.

HIX: [*Beside himself*] You had the infernal presumption to suppose that the Temple of Eternal Truth was for sale?

ESSIE TWOMEY: Now, now, Brother Hix, let's be modern. That's no way to talk business. Just look at the facts. You're washed up here, brother.

HIX: I will have you understand . . .

ESSIE TWOMEY: What kind of a draw do you get? Thirty or fifty heads on a big night. Look at me. Two thousand souls every evening, seeking the glory of God! *Two thousand* noses, actual count! I'm putting on a Midnight Service tonight—"The Night Life of the Angels"—and I'm expecting three thousand.

HIX: [*Drawing himself up*] There come moments in a man's life when he is sorely pressed to remember the lesson of charity to all. I have no wish to insult you. But I have always considered you a tool of the Devil. My temple has stood in this neighborhood for . . .

ESSIE TWOMEY: I know. For twenty years. But times change, brother. You haven't got what it takes any more. You're still in the horse-and-buggy age—praise the Lord!

HIX: The faith of my fathers is good enough for me.

ESSIE TWOMEY: Maybe so, brother, maybe so. But not for the customers. Now, for instance, take the name of your place: "Temple of Eternal Truth." Folks don't go for that nowadays. What have I got? "The Little Church of the Cheery Corner." That draws 'em, brother. Like flies.

HIX: I do not wish to discuss it.

ESSIE TWOMEY: Look at what you were just rehearsing here. That'll put 'em to sleep. Verily. You can't hand out that line anymore. Now take my last sermon—"The Service Station of the Spirit." There's a lesson for you, brother! I had a whole service station built—[*Rises, walks to pulpit*]—right there, behind my pulpit. Tall pumps, glass and gold, labeled "Purity," "Prayer," "Prayer with Faith Super-Mixture." And young boys in white uniforms—good-lookers, every one of 'em!— with gold wings, and caps inscribed "Creed Oil, Inc." Clever, eh?

HIX: It's a sacrilege!

ESSIE TWOMEY: [*Stepping up on the pulpit*] And the pulpit here was—[*Looks at her fingers*]—hm, dust, Brother Hix. Bad business! . . . And the pulpit was made up like a gold automobile. [*Greatly inspired*] Then I preached to my flock that when you travel the hard road of life, you must be sure that your tank is filled with the best gas of Faith, that your tires are inflated with the air of Charity, that your radiator is cooled with the sweet water of Temperance, that your battery is charged with the power of Righteousness, and that you beware of treacherous Detours which lead to perdition! [*In her normal voice*] Boy, did that wow 'em! Praise the Lord! It brought the house down! And we had no trouble at all when we passed the collection box made up in the shape of a gasoline can!

HIX: [*With controlled fury*] Sister Twomey, you will please step down from my pulpit!

ESSIE TWOMEY: [*Coming down*] Well, brother, to make a long story short, I'll give you five hundred bucks and you can move your junk out.

HIX: *Five hundred dollars for the Temple of Eternal Truth?*

ESSIE TWOMEY: Well, what's the matter with five hundred dollars? It's a lot of money. You can buy a good second-hand car for five hundred dollars.

HIX: Never, in twenty years, have I shown the door to anyone in this temple. But I am doing it now. [*He points to the door*]

ESSIE TWOMEY: [*Shrugging*] Well, have it your own way, brother. They have eyes, but they see not! . . . I should worry, by Jesus! [*Raising her arm*] Praise the Lord! [*Exits*]

[*The minute she is out,* EZRY'S *head comes peering cautiously from behind the door.* EZRY *is a lanky, gangling youth, far from bright*]

EZRY: [*Calls in a whisper*] Oh, Brother Hix!

HIX: [*Startled*] Ezry! What are you doing there? Come in.

EZRY: [*Enters, awed*] Gee, it was better'n a movie show!

HIX: Have you been listening?

EZRY: Gee! Was that Sister Essie Twomey?

HIX: Yes, Ezry, it was Sister Essie Twomey. Now you mustn't tell anyone about what you heard here.

EZRY: No, sir. Cross my heart, Brother Hix. [*Looking at the door with admiration*] My, but Sister Twomey talks pretty!

HIX: You mustn't say that. Sister Twomey is an evil woman.

EZRY: Yes, sir. . . . Gee, but she's got such pretty curls!

HIX: Ezry, do you believe in me? Do you like to come here for the services?

EZRY: Yes, sir. . . . The Crump twins, they said Sister Twomey had a airyplane in her temple, honest to goodness!

HIX: [*Desperately*] My boy, listen to me, for the sake of your immortal soul . . . [*He stops short.* KAY GONDA *enters*]

KAY GONDA: Mr. Hix?

HIX: [*Without taking his eyes from her, in a choked voice*] Ezry. Run along.

EZRY: [*Frightened*] Yes, sir. [*Exits hurriedly*]

HIX: You're not . . .

KAY GONDA: Yes. I am.

HIX: To what do I owe the great honor of . . .

KAY GONDA: To a murder.

HIX: Do you mean that those rumors are true?

KAY GONDA: You can throw me out, if you wish. You can call the police, if you prefer. Only do so *now*.

HIX: You are seeking shelter?

KAY GONDA: For one night.

HIX: [*Walks to the open door, closes it, and locks it*] This door has not been closed for twenty years. It shall be closed tonight. [*He returns to her and silently hands her the key*]

KAY GONDA: [*Astonished*] Why are you giving it to me?

HIX: The door will not be opened, until you wish to open it.

KAY GONDA: [*She smiles, takes the key and slips it into her bag. Then:*] Thank you.

HIX: [*Sternly*] No. Do not thank me. I do not want you to stay here.

KAY GONDA: [*Without understanding*] You—don't?

HIX: But you are safe—if this is the safety you want. I have turned the place over to you. You may stay here as long as you like. The decision will be yours.

KAY GONDA: You do not want me to hide here?

HIX: I do not want you to hide.

KAY GONDA: [*She looks at him thoughtfully, then walks to

a bench and sits down, watching him. She asks slowly:].
What would you have me do?

HIX: [*He stands before her, austerely erect and solemn*]
You have taken a heavy burden upon your shoulders.

KAY GONDA: Yes. A heavy burden. And I wonder how
much longer I will be able to carry it.

HIX: You may hide from the men who threaten you. But of
what importance is that?

KAY GONDA: Then you do not want to save me?

HIX: Oh, yes. I want to save you. But not from the police.

KAY GONDA: From whom?

HIX: From yourself. [*She looks at him for a long moment,
a fixed, steady glance, and does not answer*] You have
committed a mortal sin. You have killed a human being.
[*Points to the room*] Can this place—or any place—
give you protection from that?

KAY GONDA: No.

HIX: You cannot escape from your crime. Then do not try
to run from it. Give up. Surrender. Confess.

KAY GONDA: [*Slowly*] If I confess, they will take my life.

HIX: If you don't, you will lose your life—the eternal life
of your soul.

KAY GONDA: Is it a choice, then? Must it be one or the
other?

HIX: It has always been a choice. For all of us.

KAY GONDA: Why?

HIX: Because the joys of this earth are paid for by damna-
tion in the Kingdom of Heaven. But if we choose to suffer, we are rewarded with eternal happiness.

KAY GONDA: Then we are on earth only in order to suffer?

HIX: And the greater the suffering, the greater our virtue.
[*Her head drops slowly*] You have a sublime chance before you. Accept, of your own will, the worst that can be
done to you. The infamy, the degradation, the prison
cell, the scaffold. Then your punishment will become
your glory.

KAY GONDA: How?

HIX: It will let you enter the Kingdom of Heaven.

KAY GONDA: Why should I want to enter it?

HIX: If you know that a life of supreme beauty is possible—how can you help but want to enter it?

KAY GONDA: How can I help but want it *here,* on earth?

HIX: Ours is a dark, imperfect world.

KAY GONDA: Why is it not perfect? Because it cannot be? Or because we do not want it to be?

HIX: This world is of no consequence. Whatever beauty it offers us is here only that we may sacrifice it—for the greater beauty beyond. [*She is not looking at him. He stands watching her for a moment; then, his voice low with emotion:*] You don't know how lovely you are at this moment. [*She raises her head*] You don't know the hours I've spent watching you across the infinite distance of a screen. I would give my life to keep you here in safety. I would let myself be torn to shreds, rather than see you hurt. Yet I am asking you to open this door and walk out to martyrdom. *That* is *my* chance of sacrifice. I am giving up the greatest thing that ever came to me.

KAY GONDA: [*Her voice soft and low*] And after you and I have made our sacrifice, what will be left on this earth?

HIX: Our example. It will light the way for all the miserable souls who flounder in helpless depravity. They, too, will learn to renounce. Your fame is great. The story of your conversion will be heard the world over. You will redeem the scrubby wretches who come to this temple and all the wretches in all the slums.

KAY GONDA: Such as that boy who was here?

HIX: Such as that boy. Let *him* be the symbol, not a nobler figure. That, too, is part of the sacrifice.

KAY GONDA: [*Slowly*] What do you want me to do?

HIX: Confess your crime. Confess it publicly, to a crowd, to the hearing of all!

KAY GONDA: Tonight?

HIX: Tonight!

KAY GONDA: But there is no crowd anywhere at this hour.

HIX: At this hour . . . [*With sudden inspiration*] Listen. At this hour, a large crowd is gathered in a temple of error, six blocks away. It is a dreadful place, run by the most contemptible woman I've ever known. I'll take you there. I'll let you offer that woman the greatest gift—the kind of sensation she's never dared to imagine for her audience. You will confess to her crowd. Let her take the credit and the praise for your conversion. Let her take the fame. She is the one least worthy of it.

KAY GONDA: That, too, is part of the sacrifice?

HIX: Yes.

[KAY GONDA *rises. She walks to the door, unlocks it, and flings it open. Then she turns to* HIX *and throws the key in his face. It strikes him as she goes out. He stands motionless, only his head dropping and his shoulders sagging*]

CURTAIN

SCENE 2

The letter projected on the screen is written in a sharp, precise, cultured handwriting:

Dear Miss Gonda,

I have had everything men ask of life. I have seen it all, and I feel as if I were leaving a third-rate show on a disreputable side street. If I do not bother to die, it is only because my life has all the emptiness of the grave and my death would have no change to offer me. It may happen, any day now, and nobody—not even the one writing these lines—will know the difference.

But before it happens, I want to raise what is left of my soul in a last salute to you, you who are that which the world should have been. Morituri te salutamus.

> Dietrich von Esterhazy
> Beverly-Sunset Hotel
> Beverly Hills, California

Lights go out, screen disappears, and stage reveals drawing room in the hotel suite of DIETRICH VON ESTER-HAZY. *It is a large, luxurious room, modern, exquisitely*

*simple. Wide entrance door in center wall Left. Smaller
door to bedroom in wall Right, upstage. Large window
in wall Left, showing the dark view of a park far below.
Downstage Right a fireplace. One single lamp burning.*

As the curtain rises the entrance door opens to admit
DIETRICH VON ESTERHAZY *and* LALO JANS. DIETRICH
VON ESTERHAZY *is a tall, slender man in his early forties, whose air of patrician distinction seems created
for the trim elegance of his full dress suit.* LALO JANS *is
an exquisite female, hidden in the soft folds of an er-
mine wrap over a magnificent evening gown. She walks
in first and falls, exhausted, on a sofa downstage,
stretching out her legs with a gesture of charming lassi-
tude.* DIETRICH VON ESTERHAZY *follows her silently.
She makes a little gesture, expecting him to take her
wrap. But he does not approach her or look at her, and
she shrugs, throwing her wrap back, letting it slide
halfway down her bare arms.*

LALO: [*Looking at a clock on the table beside her, lazily*]
Only two o'clock. . . . Really, we didn't have to leave so
early, darling. . . . [ESTERHAZY *does not answer. He
does not seem to hear. There is no hostility in his attitude, but a profound indifference and a strange tension.
He walks to the window and stands looking out thoughtfully, unconscious of* LALO'S *presence. She yawns, lighting a cigarette*] I think I'll go home. . . . [*No answer*] I
said, I think I'll go home. . . . [*Coquettishly*] Unless, of
course, you insist. . . . [*No answer. She shrugs and set-
tles down more comfortably. She speaks lazily, watching the smoke of her cigarette*] You know, Rikki, we'll
just have to go to Agua Caliente. And this time I'll put
it all on Black Rajah. It's a cinch. . . . [*No answer*] By
the way, Rikki, my chauffeur's wages were due yesterday. . . . [*Turns to him. Slightly impatient:*] Rikki?

ESTERHAZY: [*Startled, turning to her abruptly, polite and
completely indifferent*] What were you saying, my dear?

LALO: [*Impatiently*] I said my chauffeur's wages were due
yesterday.

ESTERHAZY: [*His thoughts miles away*] Yes, of course. I shall take care of it.

LALO: What's the matter, Rikki? Just because I lost that money?

ESTERHAZY: Not at all, my dear. Glad you enjoyed the evening.

LALO: But then you know I've always had the damnedest luck at roulette. And if we hadn't left so early, I'm sure I'd have won it back.

ESTERHAZY: I'm sorry. I was a little tired.

LALO: And anyway, what's one thousand and seventy something?

ESTERHAZY: [*Stands looking at her silently. Then, with a faint smile of something like sudden decision, he reaches into his pocket and calmly hands her a checkbook*] I think you might as well see it.

LALO: [*Taking the book indifferently*] What's that? Some bank book?

ESTERHAZY: See what's left . . . at some bank.

LALO: [*Reading*] Three hundred and sixteen dollars. . . . [*Looks quickly through the check stubs*] Rikki! You wrote that thousand-dollar check on *this* bank! [*He nods silently, with the same smile*] You'll have to transfer the money from another bank, first thing in the morning.

ESTERHAZY: [*Slowly*] I have no other bank.

LALO: Huh?

ESTERHAZY: I have no other money. You're holding there all that's left.

LALO: [*Her lazy nonchalance gone*] Rikki! You're kidding me!

ESTERHAZY: Far be it from me, my dear.

LALO: But . . . but you're crazy! Things like that don't happen like . . . like that! One sees . . . in advance . . . one knows.

ESTERHAZY: [*Calmly*] I've known it. For the last two years. But a fortune does not vanish without a few last convulsions. There has always been something to sell, to pawn, to borrow on. Always someone to borrow from. But not this time. This time, it's done.

LALO: [*Aghast*] But . . . but where did it go?

ESTERHAZY: [*Shrugging*] How do I know? Where did all the rest of it go, those other things, inside, that you start life with? Fifteen years is a long time. When they threw me out of Austria, I had millions in my pocket, but the rest—the rest, I think, was gone already.

LALO: That's all very beautiful, but what are you going to do?

ESTERHAZY: Nothing.

LALO: But tomorrow . . .

ESTERHAZY: Tomorrow, Count Dietrich von Esterhazy will be called upon to explain the matter of a bad check. *May* be called upon.

LALO: Stop grinning like that! Do you think it's funny?

ESTERHAZY: I think it's curious. . . . The first Count Dietrich von Esterhazy died fighting under the walls of Jerusalem. The second died on the ramparts of his castle, defying a nation. The last one wrote a bad check in a gambling casino with chromium and poor ventilation. . . . It's curious.

LALO: What are you talking about?

ESTERHAZY: About what a peculiar thing it is—a leaking soul. You go through your days and it slips away from you, drop by drop. With each step. Like a hole in your pocket and coins dropping out, bright little coins, bright and shining, never to be found again.

LALO: To hell with that! What's to become of *me*?

ESTERHAZY: I've done all I could, Lalo. I've warned you before the others.

LALO: You're not going to stand there like a damn fool and let things . . .

ESTERHAZY: [*Softly*] You know, I think I'm glad it happened like this. A few hours ago I had problems, a thick web of problems I was much too weary to untangle. Now I'm free. Free at one useless stroke I did not intend striking.

LALO: Don't you care at all?

ESTERHAZY: I would not be frightened if I still cared.

LALO: Then you *are* frightened?

ESTERHAZY: I should like to be.

LALO: Why don't you do something? Call your friends!

ESTERHAZY: Their reaction, my dear, would be precisely the same as yours.

LALO: You're blaming *me,* now!

ESTERHAZY: Not at all. I appreciate you. You make my prospect so simple—and so *easy.*

LALO: But good God! What about the payments on my new Cadillac? And those pearls I charged to you? And . . .

ESTERHAZY: And my hotel bill. And my florist's bill. And that last party I gave. And the mink coat for Colette Dorsay.

LALO: [*Jumping up*] What?!

ESTERHAZY: My dear, you really didn't think you were . . . the only one?

LALO: [*Looks at him, her eyes blazing. Is on the point of screaming something. Laughs suddenly instead, a dry insulting laughter*] Do you think I care—*now*? Do you think I'm going to cry over a worthless . . .

ESTERHAZY: [*Quietly*] Don't you think you'd better go home now?

LALO: [*Tightens her wrap furiously, rushes to the door, turns abruptly*] Call me up when you come to your senses. I'll answer—if I feel like it tomorrow.

ESTERHAZY: And if I'm here to call—*tomorrow.*

LALO: Huh?

ESTERHAZY: I said, if I'm here to call—tomorrow.

LALO: Just what do you mean? Do you intend to run away or . . .

ESTERHAZY: [*With quiet affirmation*] Or.

LALO: Oh, don't be a melodramatic fool! [*Exits, slamming the door*]

[ESTERHAZY *stands motionless, lost in thought. Then he shudders slightly, as if recovering himself. Shrugs. Walks into bedroom Right, leaving the door open. The telephone rings. He returns, his evening coat replaced by a trim lounging jacket*]

ESTERHAZY: [*Picking up receiver*] Hello? . . . [*Astonished*] At this hour? What's her name? . . . She won't? . . . All right, have her come up. [*Hangs up. Lights a cigarette. There is a knock at the door. He smiles*] Come in!

[KAY GONDA *enters. His smile vanishes. He does not move. He stands looking at her for a moment, two motionless fingers holding the cigarette at his mouth. Then he flings the cigarette aside with a violent jerk of his wrist—his only reaction—and bows calmly, formally*]

Good evening, *Miss Gonda.*

KAY GONDA: Good evening.

ESTERHAZY: A veil or black glasses?

KAY GONDA: What?

ESTERHAZY: I hope you didn't let the clerk downstairs recognize you.

KAY GONDA: [*Smiles suddenly, pulling her glasses out of her pocket*] Black glasses.

ESTERHAZY: It was a brilliant idea.

KAY GONDA: What?

ESTERHAZY: Your coming here to hide.

KAY GONDA: How did you know that?

ESTERHAZY: Because it could have occurred only to you. Because you're the only one capable of the exquisite sensitiveness to recognize the only sincere letter I've ever written in my life.

KAY GONDA: [*Looking at him*] Was it?

ESTERHAZY: [*Studying her openly, speaking casually, matter-of-factly*] You look taller than you do on the screen—and less real. Your hair is blonder than I thought. Your voice about a tone higher. It is a pity that the camera does not photograph the shade of your lipstick. [*In a different voice, warm and natural*] And now that I've done my duty as a fan reacting, sit down and let's forget the unusual circumstances.

KAY GONDA: Do you really want me to stay here?

ESTERHAZY: [*Looking at the room*] The place is not too uncomfortable. There's a slight draft from the window at times, and the people upstairs become noisy occasionally, but not often. [*Looking at her*] No, I won't tell you how glad I am to see you here. I never speak of the things that mean much to me. The occasions have been too rare. I've lost the habit.

KAY GONDA: [*Sitting down*] Thank you.

ESTERHAZY: For what?

KAY GONDA: For what you didn't say.

ESTERHAZY: Do you know that it is really I who must thank you? Not only for coming, but for coming tonight of all nights.

KAY GONDA: Why?

ESTERHAZY: Perhaps you have taken a life in order to save another. [*Pause*] A long time ago—no, isn't that strange?—it was only a few minutes ago—I was ready to kill myself. Don't look at me like that. It isn't frightening. But what did become frightening was that feeling of utter indifference, even to death, even to my own indifference. And then you came. . . . I think I could hate you for coming.

KAY GONDA: I think you will.

ESTERHAZY: [*With sudden fire, the first, unexpected emotion*] I don't want to be proud of myself again. I had given it up. Yet now I am. Just because I see you here. Just because a thing has happened which is like nothing I thought possible on earth.

KAY GONDA: You said you would not tell me how glad you were to see me. Don't tell me. I do not want to hear it. I have heard it too often. I have never believed it. And I do not think I shall come to believe it *tonight*.

ESTERHAZY: Which means that you have always believed it. It's an incurable disease, you know—to have faith in the better spirit of man. I'd like to tell you to renounce it. To destroy in yourself all hunger for anything above the dry rot that others live by. But I can't. Because you will never be able to do it. It's your curse. And mine.

KAY GONDA: [*Angry and imploring at once*] I do not want to hear it!

ESTERHAZY: [*Sitting down on the arm of a chair, speaking softly, lightly*] You know, when I was a boy—a very young boy—I thought my life would be a thing immense and shining. I wanted to kneel to my own future. . . . [*Shrugs*] One gets over that.

KAY GONDA: Does one?

ESTERHAZY: Always. But never completely.

KAY GONDA: [*Breaking down, suddenly eager and trusting*] I saw a man once, when I was very young. He stood on a rock, high in the mountains. His arms were spread out and his body bent backward, and I could see him as an arc against the sky. He stood still and tense, like a string trembling to a note of ecstasy no man had ever heard. . . . I have never known who he was. I knew only that this was what life should be. . . . [*Her voice trails off*]

ESTERHAZY: [*Eagerly*] And?

KAY GONDA: [*In a changed voice*] And I came home, and my mother was serving supper, and she was happy because the roast had a thick gravy. And she gave a prayer of thanks to God for it. . . . [*Jumps up, whirls to him suddenly, angrily*] Don't listen to me! Don't look at me like that! . . . I've tried to renounce it. I thought I must close my eyes and bear anything and learn to live like the others. To make me as they were. To make me forget. I bore it. All of it. But I can't forget the man on the rock. I can't!

ESTERHAZY: We never can.

KAY GONDA: [*Eagerly*] You understand? I'm not alone? . . . Oh, God! I can't be alone! [*Suddenly quiet*] Why did you give it up?

ESTERHAZY: [*Shrugging*] Why does anyone give it up? Because it never comes. What did I get instead? Racing boats, and horses, and cards, and women—all those blind alleys—the pleasures of the moment. All the things I never wanted.

KAY GONDA: [*Softly*] Are you certain?

ESTERHAZY: There was nothing else to take. But if it came, if one had a chance, a last chance . . .

KAY GONDA: Are you certain?

ESTERHAZY: [*Looks at her, then walks resolutely to the telephone and picks up the receiver*] Gladstone 2-1018. . . . Hello, Carl? . . . Those two staterooms on the *Empress of Panama* that you told me about—do you still want to get rid of them? Yes . . . yes, I do . . . At seven thirty a.m.? . . .

I'll meet you there.... I understand.... Thank you. [*Hangs up.* KAY GONDA *looks at him questioningly. He turns to her, his manner calm, matter-of-fact*] The *Empress of Panama* leaves San Pedro at seven thirty in the morning. For Brazil. No extradition laws there.

KAY GONDA: What are you attempting?

ESTERHAZY: We're escaping together. We're outside the law—both of us. I have something worth fighting for now. My ancestors would envy me if they could see me. For my Holy Grail is of this earth, it is real, alive, possible. Only they would not understand. It is our secret. Yours and mine.

KAY GONDA: You have not asked me whether I want to go.

ESTERHAZY: I don't have to. If I did—I would have no right to go with you.

KAY GONDA: [*Smiles softly; then:*] I want to tell you.

ESTERHAZY: [*Stops, faces her, earnestly*] Tell me.

KAY GONDA: [*Looking straight at him, her eyes trusting, her voice a whisper*] Yes, I want to go.

ESTERHAZY: [*Holds her glance for an instant; then, as if deliberately refusing to underscore the earnestness of the moment, glances at his wristwatch and speaks casually again*] We have just a few hours to wait. I'll make a fire. We'll be more comfortable. [*He speaks gaily as he proceeds to light the fire*] I'll pack a few things.... You can get what you need aboard ship.... I haven't much money, but I'll raise a few thousands before morning.... I don't know where, as yet, but I'll raise it.... [*She sits down in an armchair by the fire. He sits down on the floor at her feet, facing her*] The sun is terrible down in Brazil. I hope your face doesn't get sunburnt.

KAY GONDA: [*Happily, almost girlishly*] It always does.

ESTERHAZY: We'll build a house somewhere in the jungle. It will be curious to start chopping trees down—that's another experience I've missed. I'll learn it. And you'll have to learn to cook.

KAY GONDA: I will. I'll learn everything we'll need. We'll start from scratch, from the beginning of the world—*our* world.

ESTERHAZY: You're not afraid?

KAY GONDA: [*Smiling softly*] I'm terribly afraid. I have never been happy before.

ESTERHAZY: The work will ruin your hands . . . your lovely hands. . . . [*He takes her hand, then drops it hurriedly. Speaks with a little effort, suddenly serious:*] I'll be only your architect, your valet, and your watchdog. And nothing else—until I deserve it.

KAY GONDA: [*Looking at him*] What were you thinking?

ESTERHAZY: [*Absently*] I was thinking about tomorrow and all the days thereafter. . . . They seem such a long way off. . . .

KAY GONDA: [*Gaily*] I'll want a house by the seashore. Or by a great river.

ESTERHAZY: With a balcony off your room, over the water, facing the sunrise. . . . [*Involuntarily*] And the moonlight streaming in at night. . . .

KAY GONDA: We'll have no neighbors . . . nowhere . . . not for miles around. . . . No one will look at me . . . no one will pay to look at me. . . .

ESTERHAZY: [*His voice low*] I shall allow no one to look at you. . . . In the morning, you will swim in the sea . . . alone . . . in the green water . . . with the first sun rays on your body. . . . [*He rises, bends over her, whispers*] And then I'll carry you up to the house . . . up the rocks . . . in my arms . . . [*He seizes her and kisses her violently. She responds. He raises his head and chuckles with a sound of cynical intimacy*] That's all we're really after, you and I, aren't we? Why pretend?

KAY GONDA: [*Not understanding*] What?

ESTERHAZY: Why pretend that we're important? We're no better than the others. [*Tries to kiss her again*]

KAY GONDA: Let me go! [*She tears herself away*]

ESTERHAZY: [*Laughing harshly*] Where? You have no place to go! [*She stares at him, wide-eyed, incredulous*] After all, what difference does it make, whether it's now or later? Why should we take it so seriously? [*She whirls toward the door. He seizes her. She screams, a muffled scream, stopped by his hand on her mouth*] Keep still! You can't call for help! . . . It's a death sentence—or this. . . . [*She starts laughing hysterically*]

Keep still! . . . Why should I care what you'll think of me afterwards? . . . Why should I care about tomorrow?

[*She tears herself away, runs to the door, and escapes. He stands still. He hears her laughter, loud, reckless, moving away*]

CURTAIN

SCENE 3

The letter projected on the screen is written in a sharp, uneven handwriting:

Dear Miss Gonda,
This letter is addressed to you, but I am writing it to myself.

I am writing and thinking that I am speaking to a woman who is the only justification for the existence of this earth, and who has the courage to want to be. A woman who does not assume a glory of greatness for a few hours, then return to the children-dinner-friends-football-and-God reality. A woman who seeks that glory in her every minute and her every step. A woman in whom life is not a curse, nor a bargain, but a hymn.

I want nothing except to know that such a woman exists. So I have written this, even though you may not bother to read it, or reading it, may not understand. I do not know what you are. I am writing to what you could have been.

Johnnie Dawes
. . . Main Street
Los Angeles, California

Lights go out, screen disappears, and stage reveals garret of JOHNNIE DAWES. *It is a squalid, miserable room with a low, slanting ceiling, with dark walls showing beams under cracked plaster. The room is so*

*bare that it gives the impression of being uninhabited, a
strange, intangible impression of unreality. A narrow
iron cot, at wall Right; a broken table, a few boxes for
chairs. A narrow door opens diagonally in the Left upstage corner. The entire wall Center is a long window
checkered into small panes. It opens high over the sky-
line of Los Angeles. Behind the black shadows of skyscrapers, there is a first hint of pink in the dark sky.
When the curtain rises, the stage is empty, dark. One
barely distinguishes the room and sees only the faintly
luminous panorama of the window. It dominates the
stage, so that one forgets the room, and it seems as if
the setting is only the city and the sky. (Throughout the
scene, the sky lightens slowly, the pink band of dawn
grows, rising.)*

*Steps are heard coming up the stairs. A quivering
light shows in the cracks of the door. The door opens to
admit* KAY GONDA. *Behind her,* MRS. MONAGHAN, *an old
landlady, shuffles in, with a lighted candle in hand. She
puts the candle down on the table, and stands panting
as after a long climb, studying* KAY GONDA *with a suspicious curiosity.*

MRS. MONAGHAN: Here ye are. This is it.

KAY GONDA: [*Looking slowly over the room*] Thank you.

MRS. MONAGHAN: And ye're a relative of him, ye are?

KAY GONDA: No.

MRS. MONAGHAN: [*Maliciously*] Sure, and I was thinking that.

KAY GONDA: I have never seen him before.

MRS. MONAGHAN: Well, I'm after tellin' ye he's no good,
that's what he is, no good. It's a born bum he is. No rent
never. He can't keep a job more'n two weeks.

KAY GONDA: When will he be back?

MRS. MONAGHAN: Any minute at all—or never, for all I
know. He runs around all night, the good Lord only
knows where. Just walks the streets like the bum he is,
just walks. Comes back drunk like, only he's not drunk,
'cause I know he don't drink.

KAY GONDA: I will wait for him.

MRS. MONAGHAN: Suit yerself. [*Looks at her shrewdly*] Maybe ye got a job for him?

KAY GONDA: No. I have no job for him.

MRS. MONAGHAN: He's got himself kicked out again, three days ago it was. He had a swell job bellhoppin'. Did it last? It did not. Same as the soda counter. Same as the waitin' at Hamburger Looey's. He's no good, I'm tellin' ye. I know him. Better'n ye do.

KAY GONDA: I do not know him at all.

MRS. MONAGHAN: And I can't say I blame his bosses, either. He's a strange one. Never a laugh, never a joke out of him. [*Confidentially*] Ye know what Hamburger Looey said to me? He said, "Stuck up little snot," said Hamburger Looey, "makes a regular guy feel creepy."

KAY GONDA: So Hamburger Looey said that?

MRS. MONAGHAN: Faith and he did. [*Confidentially*] And d'ye know? He's been to college, that boy. Ye'd never believe it from the kind of jobs he can't keep, but he has. What he learned there the good Lord only knows. It's no good it done him. And . . . [*Stops, listening. Steps are heard rising up the stairs*] That's him now! Nobody else'd be shameless enough to come home at this hour of the night. [*At the door*] Ye think it over. Maybe ye could do somethin' for him. [*Exits*]

[JOHNNIE DAWES *enters. He is a tall, slender boy in his late twenties; a gaunt face, prominent cheekbones, a hard mouth, clear, steady eyes. He sees* KAY GONDA *and stands still. They look at each other for a long moment*]

JOHNNIE: [*Slowly, calmly, no astonishment and no question in his voice*] Good evening, Miss Gonda.

KAY GONDA: [*She cannot take her eyes from him, and it is her voice that sounds astonished*] Good evening.

JOHNNIE: Please sit down.

KAY GONDA: You do not want me to stay here.

JOHNNIE: You're staying.

KAY GONDA: You have not asked me why I came.

JOHNNIE: You're here. [*He sits down*]

KAY GONDA: [*She approaches him suddenly, takes his face in her hands and raises it*] What's the matter, Johnnie?

JOHNNIE: Nothing—now.

KAY GONDA: You must not be so glad to see me.

JOHNNIE: I knew you'd come.

KAY GONDA: [*She walks away from him, falls wearily down on the cot. She looks at him and smiles; a smile that is not gay, not friendly*] People say I am a great star, Johnnie.

JOHNNIE: Yes.

KAY GONDA: They say I have everything one can wish for.

JOHNNIE: Have you?

KAY GONDA: No. But how do you know it?

JOHNNIE: How do you know that I know it?

KAY GONDA: You are never afraid when you speak to people, are you, Johnnie?

JOHNNIE: Yes. I am very much afraid. Always. I don't know what to say to them. But I'm not afraid—now.

KAY GONDA: I am a very bad woman, Johnnie. Everything you've heard about me is true. Everything—and more. I came to tell you that you must not think of me what you said in your letter.

JOHNNIE: You came to tell me that everything I said in my letter was true. Everything—and more.

KAY GONDA: [*With a harsh little laugh*] You're a fool! I'm not afraid of you. . . . Do you know that I get twenty thousand dollars a week?

JOHNNIE: Yes.

KAY GONDA: Do you know that I have fifty pairs of shoes and three butlers?

JOHNNIE: I suppose so.

KAY GONDA: Do you know that my pictures are shown in every town on earth?

JOHNNIE: Yes.

KAY GONDA: [*Furiously*] Stop looking at me like that! . . . Do you know that people pay millions to see me? I don't need your approval! I have plenty of worshipers! I mean a great deal to them!

JOHNNIE: You mean nothing at all to them. You know it.

KAY GONDA: [*Looking at him almost with hatred*] I

thought I knew it—an hour ago. [*Whirling upon him*] Oh, why don't you ask me for something?

JOHNNIE: What do you want me to ask you?

KAY GONDA: Why don't you ask me to get you a job in the movies, for instance?

JOHNNIE: The only thing I could ask you, you have given to me already.

KAY GONDA: [*She looks at him, laughs harshly, speaks in a new voice, strange to her, an unnaturally common voice*] Look, Johnnie, let's stop kidding each other. I'll tell you something. I've killed a man. It's dangerous, hiding a murderess. Why don't you throw me out? [*He sits looking at her silently*] No? That one won't work? Well, then, look at me. I'm the most beautiful woman you've ever seen. Don't you want to sleep with me? Why don't you? Right now. I won't struggle. [*He does not move*] Not that? But listen: do you know that there's a reward on my head? Why don't you call the police and turn me over to them? You'd be set for life.

JOHNNIE: [*Softly*] Are you as unhappy as that?

KAY GONDA: [*Walks to him, then falls on her knees at his feet*] Help me, Johnnie!

JOHNNIE: [*Bends down to her, his hands on her shoulders, asks softly:*] Why did you come here?

KAY GONDA: [*Raising her head*] Johnnie. If all of you who look at me on the screen hear the things I say and worship me for them—where do I hear them? Where can I hear them, so that I might go on? I want to see, real, living, and in the hours of my own days, that glory I create as an illusion! I want it real! I want to know that there is someone, somewhere, who wants it, too! Or else what is the use of seeing it, and working, and burning oneself for an impossible vision? A spirit, too, needs fuel. It can run dry.

JOHNNIE: [*He rises, leads her to the cot, makes her sit down, stands before her*] I want to tell you only this: there are a few on earth who see you and understand. These few give life its meaning. The rest—well, the rest are what you see they are. You have a duty. To live. Just to remain on earth. To let them know you do and can exist. To fight, even a fight without hope. We can't give up the earth to all those others.

KAY GONDA: [*Looking at him, softly*] Who are you, Johnnie?

JOHNNIE: [*Astonished*] I? . . . I'm—nothing.

KAY GONDA: Where do you come from?

JOHNNIE: I've had a home and parents somewhere. I don't remember much about them . . . I don't remember much about anything that's ever happened to me. There's not a day worth remembering.

KAY GONDA: You have no friends?

JOHNNIE: No.

KAY GONDA: You have no work?

JOHNNIE: Yes . . . no, I was fired three days ago. I forgot.

KAY GONDA: Where have you lived before?

JOHNNIE: Many places. I've lost count.

KAY GONDA: Do you hate people, Johnnie?

JOHNNIE: No. I never notice them.

KAY GONDA: What do you dream of?

JOHNNIE: Nothing. Of what account are dreams?

KAY GONDA: Of what account is life?

JOHNNIE: None. But who made it so?

KAY GONDA: Those who cannot dream.

JOHNNIE: No. Those who can *only* dream.

KAY GONDA: Are you very unhappy?

JOHNNIE: No. . . . I don't think you should ask me these questions. You won't get a decent answer from me to anything.

KAY GONDA: There was a great man once who said: "I love those that know not how to live today."

JOHNNIE: [*Quietly*] I think I am a person who should never have been born. This is not a complaint. I am not afraid and I am not sorry. But I have often wanted to die. I have no desire to change the world—nor to take any part in it, as it is. I've never had the weapons which you have. I've never even found the desire to find weapons. I'd like to go, calmly and willingly.

KAY GONDA: I don't want to hear you say that.

JOHNNIE: There has always been something holding me here. Something that had to come to me before I went. I want to know one living moment of that which is *mine,* not theirs. Not their dismal little pleasures. One moment of ecstasy, utter and absolute, a moment that must not be survived. . . . They've never given me a life. I've always hoped I would choose my death.

KAY GONDA: Don't say that. I need you. I'm here. I'll never let you go.

JOHNNIE: [*After a pause, looking at her in a strange new way, his voice dry, flat*] You? You're a murderess who'll get caught someday and die on the gallows.

[*She looks at him, astonished. He walks to the window, stands looking out. Beyond the window it is now full daylight. The sun is about to rise. Rays of light spread like halos from behind the dark silhouettes of skyscrapers. He asks suddenly, without turning to her:*]

You killed him?

KAY GONDA: We don't have to talk about that, do we?

JOHNNIE: [*Without turning*] I knew Granton Sayers. I worked for him once, as a caddy, at a golf club in Santa Barbara. A hard kind of man.

KAY GONDA: He was a very unhappy man, Johnnie.

JOHNNIE: [*Turning to her*] Was anyone present?

KAY GONDA: Where?

JOHNNIE: When you killed him?

KAY GONDA: Do we have to discuss that?

JOHNNIE: It's something I must know. Did anyone see you kill him?

KAY GONDA: No.

JOHNNIE: Have the police got anything on you?

KAY GONDA: No. Except what I could tell them. But I will not tell it to them. Nor to you. Not now. Don't question me.

JOHNNIE: How much is the reward on your head?

KAY GONDA: [*After a pause, in a strange kind of voice*] What did you say, Johnnie?

JOHNNIE: [*Evenly*] I said, how much is the reward on your head? [*She stares at him*] Never mind. [*He walks to the door, throws it open, calls:*] Mrs. Monaghan! Come here!

KAY GONDA: What are you doing? [*He does not answer or look at her.* MRS. MONAGHAN *shuffles up the stairs and appears at the door*]

MRS. MONAGHAN: [*Angrily*] What d'ye want?

JOHNNIE: Mrs. Monaghan, listen carefully. Go downstairs to your phone. Call the police. Tell them to come here at once. Tell them that Kay Gonda is here. You understand? *Kay Gonda.* Now hurry.

MRS. MONAGHAN: [*Aghast*] Yes, sir. . . . [*Exits hurriedly*]

[JOHNNIE *closes the door, turns to* KAY GONDA. *She tries to dash for the door. The table is between them. He opens a drawer, pulls out a gun, points it at her*]

JOHNNIE: Stand still. [*She does not move. He backs to the door and locks it. She sags suddenly, still standing up*]

KAY GONDA: [*Without looking at him, in a flat, lifeless voice*] Put it away. I will not try to escape. [*He slips the gun into his pocket and stands leaning against the door. She sits down, her back turned to him*]

JOHNNIE: [*Quietly*] We have about three minutes left. I am thinking now that nothing has happened to us and nothing will happen. The world stopped a minute ago and in three minutes it will go on again. But this—this pause is ours. You're here. I look at you. I've seen your eyes—and all the truth that man has ever sought. [*Her head falls down on her arms*] There are no other men on earth right now. Just you and I. There's nothing but a world in which you live. To breathe for once that air, to move in it, to hear my own voice on waves that touch no ugliness, no pain . . . I've never known gratitude. But now, of all the words I'd like to say to you, I'll say just three: I thank you. When you leave, remember I have thanked you. Remember—no matter what may happen in this room. . . . [*She buries her head in her arms. He stands silently, his head thrown back, his eyes closed*]

[*Hurried steps are heard rising up the stairs.* JOHNNIE *and* KAY GONDA *do not move. There is a violent knock at*

the door. JOHNNIE *turns, unlocks the door, and opens it.*
A police CAPTAIN *enters, followed by two* POLICEMEN.
KAY GONDA *rises, facing them*]

CAPTAIN: Jesus Christ! [*They stare at her, aghast*]

POLICEMAN: And I thought it was another crank calling!

CAPTAIN: Miss Gonda, I'm sure glad to see you. We've been driven crazy with . . .

KAY GONDA: Take me away from here. Anywhere you wish.

CAPTAIN: [*Making a step toward her*] Well, we have no . . .

JOHNNIE: [*In a quiet voice which is such an implacable command that all turn to him*] Stay away from her. [*The* CAPTAIN *stops.* JOHNNIE *motions to a* POLICEMAN *and points to the table*] Sit down. Take a pencil and paper. [*The* POLICEMAN *looks at the* CAPTAIN, *who nods, baffled. The* POLICEMAN *obeys*] Now write this: [*Dictates slowly, his voice precise, emotionless*] I, John Dawes, confess that on the night of May fifth, willfully and with premeditation, I killed Granton Sayers of Santa Barbara, California. [KAY GONDA *takes a deep breath, which is almost a gasp*] I have been absent from my home for the last three nights, as my landlady, Mrs. Sheila Monaghan, can testify. She can further testify that I was dismissed from my job at the Alhambra Hotel on May third. [KAY GONDA *starts laughing suddenly. It is the lightest, happiest laughter in the world*] I had worked for Granton Sayers a year ago, at the Greendale Golf Club of Santa Barbara. Being jobless and broke, I went to Granton Sayers on the evening of May fifth, determined to extort money from him through blackmail, under threat of divulging certain information I possessed. He refused my demands even at the point of a gun. I shot him. I disposed of the gun by throwing it into the ocean on my way back from Santa Barbara. I was alone in committing this crime. No other person was or is to be implicated. [*Adds*] Have you got it all? Give it to me. [*The* POLICEMAN *hands the confession to him.* JOHNNIE *signs it*]

CAPTAIN: [*He cannot quite collect his wits*] Miss Gonda, what have you got to say about this?

KAY GONDA: [*Hysterically*] Don't ask me! Not now! Don't speak to me!

JOHNNIE: [*Hands the confession to the* CAPTAIN] You will please let Miss Gonda depart now.

CAPTAIN: Wait a minute, my boy. Not so fast. There's a lot of explaining you have to do yet. How did you get into the Sayers house? How did you leave it?

JOHNNIE: I have told you all I'm going to tell.

CAPTAIN: What time was it when you did the shooting? And what is Miss Gonda doing here?

JOHNNIE: You know all you have to know. You know enough not to implicate Miss Gonda. You have my confession.

CAPTAIN: Sure. But you'll have to prove it.

JOHNNIE: It will stand—even if I do not choose to prove it. Particularly if I am not here to prove it.

CAPTAIN: Gonna be tough, eh? Well, you'll talk at headquarters all right. Come on, boys.

KAY GONDA: [*Stepping forward*] Wait! You must listen to me now. I have a statement to make. I . . .

JOHNNIE: [*Steps back, pulls the gun out of his pocket, covering the group*] Stand still, all of you. [*To* KAY GONDA] Don't move. Don't say a word.

KAY GONDA: Johnnie! You don't know what you're doing! Wait, my dearest! Put that gun down.

JOHNNIE: [*Without lowering the gun, smiles at her*] I heard it. Thank you.

KAY GONDA: I'll tell you everything! You don't know! I'm safe!

JOHNNIE: I know you're safe. You will be. Step back. Don't be afraid. I won't hurt anyone. [*She obeys*] I want you all to look at me. Years from now you can tell your grandchildren about it. You are looking at something you will never see again and they will never see—*a man who is perfectly happy!* [*Points the gun at himself, fires, falls*]

CURTAIN

SCENE 4

> *Entrance hall in the residence of* KAY GONDA. *It is high, bare, modern in its austere simplicity. There is no furniture, no ornaments of any kind. The upper part of the hall is a long raised platform, dividing the room horizontally, and three broad continuous steps lead down from it to the foreground. Tall, square columns rise at the upper edge of the steps. Door into the rest of the house downstage in wall Left. The entire back wall is of wide glass panes, with an entrance door in the center. Beyond the house, there is a narrow path among jagged rocks, a thin strip of the high coast with a broad view of the ocean beyond and of a flaming sunset sky. The hall is dim. There is no light, save the glow of the sunset.*
>
> *At curtain rise,* MICK WATTS *is sitting on the top step, leaning down toward a dignified* BUTLER *who sits on the floor below, stiff, upright, and uncomfortable holding a tray with a full highball glass on it.* MICK WATTS' *shirt collar is torn open, his tie hanging loose, his hair disheveled. He is clutching a newspaper ferociously. He is sober.*

MICK WATTS: [*Continuing a discourse that has obviously been going on for some time, speaking in an even, expressionless monotone, his manner earnest, confidential*] . . . and so the king called them all before his throne and he said: "I'm weary and sick of it. I am tired of my kingdom where not a single man is worth ruling. I am tired of my lusterless crown, for it does not reflect a single flame of glory anywhere in my land." . . . You see, he was a very foolish king. Some scream it, like he did, and squash their damn brains out against a wall. Others stagger on, like a dog chasing a shadow, knowing damn well that there is no shadow to chase, but still going on, their hearts empty and their paws bleeding. . . . So the king said to them on his deathbed—oh, this was another time, he was on his deathbed this time— he said: "It is the end, but I am still hoping. There is no end. Ever shall I go on hoping . . . ever . . . ever." [*Looks suddenly at the* BUTLER, *as if noticing him for the first time, and asks in an entirely different voice, pointing at him:*] What the hell are you doing here?

BUTLER: [*Rising*] May I observe, sir, that you have been speaking for an hour and a quarter?

MICK WATTS: Have I?

BUTLER: You have, sir. So, if I may be forgiven, I took the liberty of sitting down.

MICK WATTS: [*Surprised*] Fancy, you were here all the time!

BUTLER: Yes, sir.

MICK WATTS: Well, what did you want here in the first place?

BUTLER: [*Extending the tray*] Your whiskey, sir.

MICK WATTS: Oh! [*Reaches for the glass, but stops, jerks the crumpled newspaper at the* BUTLER, *asks:*] Have you read this?

BUTLER: Yes, sir.

MICK WATTS: [*Knocking the tray aside; it falls, breaking the glass*] Go to hell! I don't want any whiskey!

BUTLER: But you ordered it, sir.

MICK WATTS: Go to hell just the same! [*As the* BUTLER *bends to pick up the tray*] Get out of here! Never mind! Get out! I don't want to see any human snoot tonight!

BUTLER: Yes, sir. [*Exits Left*]

[MICK WATTS *straightens the paper out, looks at it, crumples it viciously again. Hears steps approaching outside and whirls about.* FREDERICA SAYERS *is seen outside, walking hurriedly toward the door; she has a newspaper in her hand.* MICK WATTS *walks to door and opens it, before she has time to ring*]

MISS SAYERS: Good evening.

[*He does not answer, lets her enter, closes the door and stands silently, looking at her. She looks around, then at him, somewhat disconcerted*]

MICK WATTS: [*Without moving*] Well?

MISS SAYERS: Is this the residence of Miss Kay Gonda?

MICK WATTS: It is.

MISS SAYERS: May I see Miss Gonda?

MICK WATTS: No.

MISS SAYERS: I am Miss Sayers. Miss Frederica Sayers.

MICK WATTS: I don't care.

MISS SAYERS: Will you please tell Miss Gonda that I am here? If she is at home.

MICK WATTS: She is not.

MISS SAYERS: When do you expect her back?

MICK WATTS: I don't expect her.

MISS SAYERS: My good man, this is getting to be pre-posterous!

MICK WATTS: It is. You'd better get out of here.

MISS SAYERS: Sir?!

MICK WATTS: She'll be back any minute. I know she will. And there's nothing to talk about now.

MISS SAYERS: My good man, do you realize . . .

MICK WATTS: I realize everything that you realize, and then some. And I'm telling you there's nothing to be done. Don't bother her now.

MISS SAYERS: May I ask who you are and what you're talk-ing about?

MICK WATTS: Who I am doesn't matter. I'm talking about—[*Extends the newspaper*]—this.

MISS SAYERS: Yes, I've read it, and I must say it is utterly bewildering and . . .

MICK WATTS: Bewildering? Hell, it's monstrous! You don't know the half of it! . . . [*Catching himself, adds flatly*] I don't, either.

MISS SAYERS: Look here, I must get to the bottom of this thing. It will go too far and . . .

MICK WATTS: It *has gone* too far.

MISS SAYERS: Then I must . . .

[KAY GONDA *enters from the outside. She is dressed as in all the preceding scenes. She is calm, but very tired*]

MICK WATTS: So here you are! I knew you'd be back *now*!

KAY GONDA: [*In a quiet, even voice*] Good evening, Miss Sayers.

MISS SAYERS: Miss Gonda, this is the first sigh of relief I've breathed in two days! I never thought the time should come when I'd be so glad to see you! But you must understand . . .

KAY GONDA: [*Indifferently*] I know.

MISS SAYERS: You must understand that I could not foresee the astounding turn of events. It was most kind of you to go into hiding, but, really, you did not have to hide from me.

KAY GONDA: I was not hiding from anyone.

MISS SAYERS: But where were you?

KAY GONDA: Away. It had nothing to do with Mr. Sayers' death.

MISS SAYERS: But when you heard those preposterous rumors accusing you of his murder, you should have come to me at once! When I asked you, at the house that night, not to disclose to anyone the manner of my brother's death, I had no way of knowing what suspicions would arise. I tried my best to get in touch with you. Please believe me that I did not start those rumors.

KAY GONDA: I never thought you did.

MISS SAYERS: I wonder who started them.

KAY GONDA: I wonder.

MISS SAYERS: I do owe you an apology. I'm sure you felt it was my duty to disclose the truth at once, but you know why I had to keep silent. However, the deal is closed, and I thought it best to come to you first and tell you that I'm free to speak now.

KAY GONDA: [*Indifferently*] It was very kind of you.

MISS SAYERS: [*Turning to* MICK WATTS] Young man, you can tell that ridiculous studio of yours that Miss Gonda did not murder my brother. Tell them they can read his suicide letter in tomorrow's papers. He wrote that he had no desire to struggle any longer, since his business was ruined and since the only woman he'd ever loved had, that night, refused to marry him.

KAY GONDA: I'm sorry, Miss Sayers.

MISS SAYERS: This is not a reproach, Miss Gonda. [*To* MICK WATTS] The Santa Barbara police knew everything, but promised me silence. I had to keep my brother's suicide

secret for a while, because I was negotiating a merger
with . . .

MICK WATTS: . . . with United California Oil, and you
didn't want them to know the desperate state of the Sayers Company. Very smart. Now you've closed the deal
and gypped United California. My congratulations.

MISS SAYERS: [*Aghast, to* KAY GONDA] This peculiar
gentleman knew it all?

MICK WATTS: So it seems, doesn't it?

MISS SAYERS: Then, in heaven's name, why did you allow
everybody to suspect Miss Gonda?

KAY GONDA: Don't you think it best, Miss Sayers, not to
discuss this any further? It's done. It's past. Let's leave
it at that.

MISS SAYERS: As you wish. There is just one question I
would like to ask you. It baffles me completely. I
thought perhaps you may know something about it.
[*Points at the newspaper*] This. That incredible story . . .
that boy I've never heard of, killing himself . . . that in-
sane confession. . . . What does it mean?

KAY GONDA: [*Evenly*] I don't know.

MICK WATTS: Huh?

KAY GONDA: I have never heard of him before.

MISS SAYERS: Then I can explain it only as the act of a
crank, an abnormal mind . . .

KAY GONDA: Yes, Miss Sayers. A mind that was not
normal.

MISS SAYERS: [*After a pause*] Well if you'll excuse me,
Miss Gonda, I shall wish you good night. I shall give
my statement to the papers immediately and clear your
name completely.

KAY GONDA: Thank you, Miss Sayers. Good night.

MISS SAYERS: [*Turning at the door*] I wish you luck with
whatever it is you're doing. You have been most courte-
ous in this unfortunate matter. Allow me to thank you.

[KAY GONDA *bows.* MISS SAYERS *exits*]

MICK WATTS: [*Ferociously*] Well?

KAY GONDA: Would you mind going home, Mick? I am
very tired.

MICK WATTS: I hope you've . . .

KAY GONDA: Telephone the studio on your way. Tell them that I will sign the contract tomorrow.

MICK WATTS: I hope you've had a good time! I hope you've enjoyed it! But I'm through!

KAY GONDA: I'll see you at the studio tomorrow at nine.

MICK WATTS: I'm through! God, I wish I could quit!

KAY GONDA: You know that you will never quit, Mick.

MICK WATTS: That's the hell of it! That you know it, too! Why do I serve you like a dog and will go on serving you like a dog for the rest of my days? Why can't I resist any crazy whim of yours? Why did I have to go and spread rumors about a murder you never committed? Just because you wanted to find out something? Well, have you found it out?

KAY GONDA: Yes.

MICK WATTS: What have you found out?

KAY GONDA: How many people saw my last picture? Do you remember those figures?

MICK WATTS: Seventy-five million, six hundred thousand, three hundred and twelve.

KAY GONDA: Well, Mick, seventy-five million, six hundred thousand people hate me. They hate me in their hearts for the things they see in me, the things they have betrayed. I mean nothing to them, except a reproach. . . . But there are three hundred and twelve others—perhaps only the twelve. There are a few who want the highest possible and will take nothing less and will not live on any other terms. . . . It is with them that I am signing a contract tomorrow. We can't give up the earth to all those others.

MICK WATTS: [*Holding out the newspaper*] And what about *this*?

KAY GONDA: I've answered you.

MICK WATTS: But you *are* a murderess, Kay Gonda! You killed that boy!

KAY GONDA: No, Mick, not I alone.

MICK WATTS: But the poor fool thought that he had to save your life!

KAY GONDA: He has.

MICK WATTS: What?!

KAY GONDA: He wanted to die that I may live. He did just that.

MICK WATTS: But don't you realize what you've done?

KAY GONDA: [*Slowly, looking past him*] That, Mick, was the kindest thing I have ever done.

CURTAIN

Think Twice

PREFACE

The Depression years in New York City (to which she moved in 1934) were a difficult financial struggle for Ayn Rand: she lived on the earnings from *Night of January 16th* and from a series of jobs she held as reader for various movie companies. She wrote when she could find the time. Nevertheless, the work moved ahead. In 1935, she began making notes for *The Fountainhead* and planning the architectural research that it would require. Realizing that the novel would be a long-term project, she interrupted it several times to do shorter pieces. In 1937, she wrote the novelette *Anthem* (published separately by New American Library). In 1939, she wrote a stage adaptation of *We the Living,* produced on Broadway under the title of *The Unconquered* (it was not successful). In the same year, she wrote her third and last original stage play, the philosophical murder mystery *Think Twice.* It has never been produced.

Think Twice, written five years later than *Ideal,* is finished, mature work, in all major respects characteristic of the author of *The Fountainhead.* The theme is the distinctive Ayn Rand approach to ethics: the evil of altruism, and the need of man to live an independent, egoistic existence. The hero, who now has primacy over the heroine, is a completely recognizable Ayn Rand type. The plot, fast-moving and logical, has an ingenious twist; the story presents an altruist who, acting on his ideas, specializes in seeking power over others, thereby giving them compelling reasons to want to kill him. (The Russian character was originally a German Nazi; in the 1950s, Miss Rand updated the play, turning him into a Communist.) The style is smoothly assured; the mechanics of alibis, motives, and clues are deftly handled; and the writing displays Ayn Rand's clarity, her sense of drama, her intellectual wit. There is even the first sign of the science-fiction element which, years later, would become John Galt's motor in *Atlas Shrugged*.

One of Ayn Rand's most impressive literary skills, brilliantly demonstrated in her novels, is her ability to integrate theme and plot. That ability is evidenced in *Think Twice*—in the union of philosophy and murder mystery. This is not a routine murder story, with some abstract talk thrown in for effect. Nor is it a drawing-room discussion interrupted now and again by some unrelated events. The play is a union of thought and action: the philosophic ideas of the characters actually motivate and explain their actions, which in turn concretize and demonstrate the philosophic point, and acquire significance because of it. The result is a seamless blend of depth and excitement, at once art and entertainment.

A decade later, in her journal of August 28, 1949, Ayn Rand wrote the following:

> The idea that "art" and "entertainment" are opposites, that art is serious and dull, while entertainment is empty and stupid, but enjoyable—is the result of the nonhuman, altruistic morality. That which is *good* [in this view] must be unpleasant. That which is enjoyable is sinful. Pleasure is an indulgence of a low order, to be apologized for. The serious is the performance of a duty, unpleasant and, therefore, uplifting. If a work of art examines life seriously, it must necessarily be unpleasant and unexciting, because such is the nature of life for man. An entertaining, enjoyable play cannot possibly be true to the deeper essence of life, it *must* be superficial, since life is not to be enjoyed.

It is unlikely that Miss Rand had her early work in mind when she wrote these words, but the present piece does illustrate her point. *Think Twice* is an entertaining, enjoyable play that is true to the deeper essence of life.

I first read the play in the 1950s, with Miss Rand present, asking me now and then who I thought the murderer was. I guessed just about every possibility, except the right one. Each time, Miss Rand beamed and said: "Think twice." When I finished, she told me that anyone who knew her and her philosophy should have been able to guess right away. She could not, she went on, ever write a series of mysteries, because everyone would know who the murderers were. "How?" I asked.

Now see if you can guess the murderer. After the play, I will quote her answer.

—Leonard Peikoff

CHARACTERS

WALTER BRECKENRIDGE
CURTISS
SERGE SOOKIN
HARVEY FLEMING
TONY GODDARD
STEVE INGALLS
BILLY BRECKENRIDGE
FLASH KOZINSKY
ADRIENNE KNOWLAND
HELEN BRECKENRIDGE
GREGORY HASTINGS
DIXON

Place   Living room of a home in Connecticut

Time   Act I, Scene 1—Afternoon of July 3rd
           Act I, Scene 2—That evening
           Act II, Scene 1—Half an hour later
           Act II, Scene 2—Next morning

Think Twice

ACT I

SCENE 1

Afternoon of July 3rd. The living room of a home in Connecticut. A large room, not offensively wealthy, but evidencing both money and an unsuccessful attempt at good taste. The room is stately and Colonial—too deliberately so. Everything is brand-new, resplendently unused; one expects to see price tags on the furniture.

Large French windows, Center, opening upon a lovely view of the grounds with a lake in the distance, a view marred only by a dismal, gray sky. Stairway, Stage Right, leading to a door, and another door downstage, leading to the rest of the ground floor. Entrance door upstage Left. Downstage Left an unused fireplace, with logs stacked neatly, and above the fireplace—a large portrait of WALTER BRECKENRIDGE.

At curtain rise, WALTER BRECKENRIDGE *stands alone in front of the fireplace. He is a stately, gray-haired man of fifty, who looks like a saint; a very "human" saint, however: benevolent, dignified, humorous, and a little portly. He stands, looking up at the portrait, deeply absorbed, a gun in his hand.*

After a while, CURTISS, *the butler, enters from door Right, carrying two empty flower vases.* CURTISS *is elderly, and severely well-mannered. He deposits the vases on a table and a cabinet.* BRECKENRIDGE *does not turn and* CURTISS *does not see the gun.*

CURTISS: Anything else, sir? [BRECKENRIDGE *does not move*] Mr. Breckenridge . . . [*No answer*] Is anything the matter, sir?

BRECKENRIDGE: [*Absently*] Oh . . . no . . . no . . . I was just wondering . . . [*Points at the portrait*] Do you think that in the centuries to come people will say he was a great man? [*Turns to face* CURTISS] Is it a good likeness of me, Curtiss? [CURTISS *sees the gun and steps back with a little gasp*] What's the matter?

CURTISS: Mr. Breckenridge!

BRECKENRIDGE: What's the matter with you?

CURTISS: Don't do it, sir! Whatever it is, don't do it!

BRECKENRIDGE: [*Looks at him in amazement, then notices the gun in his own hand and bursts out laughing*] Oh, that? . . . I'm sorry, Curtiss. I'd quite forgotten I held it.

CURTISS: But, sir . . .

BRECKENRIDGE: Oh, I just sent the car down to meet Mrs. Breckenridge at the station, and I didn't want her to find this in the car, so I brought it in. We mustn't tell her about . . . you know, about why I have to carry this. It would only worry her.

CURTISS: Yes, of course, sir. I'm so sorry. It just gave me a jolt.

BRECKENRIDGE: I don't blame you. You know, I hate the damn thing myself. [*Walks to a cabinet and slips the gun into a drawer*] Funny, isn't it? I'm actually afraid of it. And when I think of all the deadly stuff I've handled in the laboratory. Radioactive elements. Cosmic rays. Things that could wipe out the whole population of the state of Connecticut. Never been afraid of them. In fact, never felt anything at all. But this . . . [*Points to the drawer*] Do you suppose it's my old age and I'm being sensitive about any . . . reminder?

CURTISS: [*Reproachfully*] Your old age, sir!

BRECKENRIDGE: Well, time passes, Curtiss, time passes. Why do they celebrate birthdays? It's just one year closer to the grave. And there's so much to be done. [*Looks at the portrait*] That's what I was thinking when you came in. Have I done enough in my life? Have I done enough?

[SERGE SOOKIN *enters through the French doors.* SERGE *is about thirty-two, pale, blond, with the face and the manner of a fervent idealist. His clothes are neat, but very poor. His arms are loaded with an enormous bunch of freshly cut flowers*]

Ah, Serge . . . thank you. . . . So kind of you to help us.

SERGE: I hope this flowers Mrs. Breckenridge will like.

BRECKENRIDGE: She loves flowers. We must have lots of flowers. . . . Over here, Serge. . . . [*Indicating the vases as* SERGE *arranges the flowers*] We'll put them here—and over there, on the cabinet—and on the fireplace, just one or two sprays on the fireplace.

SERGE: [*Wistfully*] By us in Moscow, we had the more beautiful flowers.

BRECKENRIDGE: Try not to think of all that, Serge. There are things it's best to forget. [*To* CURTISS] Have you taken care of the cigarettes, Curtiss?

[CURTISS *busies himself filling cigarette boxes*]

SERGE: [*Grimly*] There are the things never one can forget. But I am so sorry. That we should not discuss about. Not today, no? This is a great day.

BRECKENRIDGE: Yes, Serge. This is a great day for me. [*Indicating an armchair*] I don't think that chair is right, over there. Curtiss, would you move it please this way, to the table? [*As* CURTISS *obeys*] That's better, thank you. We must have everything right, Curtiss. For our guests. They are very important guests.

CURTISS: Yes, sir.

[*From offstage, there comes the sound of Tchaikovsky's "Autumn Song" expertly played on the piano.* BRECKENRIDGE *looks in the direction of the sound, a little annoyed, then shrugs and turns to* SERGE]

BRECKENRIDGE: You will meet some very interesting people today, Serge. I want you to meet them. Perhaps it
will give you a better idea of me. You know, one can
judge a man best by his friends.

SERGE: [*Looking up the stairs, a little grimly*] Not always,
I hope.

BRECKENRIDGE: [*Looking up*] Oh, Steve? You mustn't
mind Steve. You mustn't let him upset you.

SERGE: [*Coldly*] Mr. Ingalls he is not kind.

BRECKENRIDGE: No. Steve's never been kind. But then,
you know, strictly speaking, Steve is not a friend. He's
my business partner—just a junior partner, as we call
it, but darn useful. One of the best physicists in the
country.

SERGE: You are so modest, Mr. Breckenridge. *You* are
in the country the greatest physicist. That everybody
knows.

BRECKENRIDGE: Perhaps everybody but me.

SERGE: You are to mankind the benefactor. But Mr. Ingalls
he is not a friend to the world. In his heart for the world
there is no place. Today the world needs friends.

BRECKENRIDGE: That's true. But—

•

[*Doorbell rings.* CURTISS *opens the door.* HARVEY
FLEMING *stands on the threshold. He is a man in his late
forties, tall, gaunt, disreputably unkempt. He looks like
anything but an "important" guest: he needs a shave,
his clothes need pressing; he is not drunk, but not quite
sober. He carries a small, battered overnight bag. He
stands for a moment, studying the room glumly*]

CURTISS: [*Bowing*] Good afternoon, sir. Come right in, sir.

FLEMING: [*Enters, without removing his hat. Snaps
glumly:*] Billy arrived yet?

CURTISS: Yes, sir.

BRECKENRIDGE: [*Advancing toward* FLEMING *with a
broad smile*] Well, Harvey! Greetings and welcome.
Harvey, I want you to meet—

FLEMING: [*Nods curtly in the general direction of* BRECK-

ENRIDGE *and* SERGE] Hello. [*To* CURTISS] Where's Billy's room?

CURTISS: This way, sir.

[FLEMING *exits with him through door Right, without a glance at the others*]

SERGE: [*A little indignant*] But what is the matter?

BRECKENRIDGE: You mustn't mind him, Serge. He is a very unhappy man. [*Looks impatiently in the direction of the music*] I do wish Tony would stop playing.

SERGE: It is so sad, this piece. It is not appropriate today.

BRECKENRIDGE: Ask him to stop, will you?

[SERGE *exits Right while* BRECKENRIDGE *continues rearranging the room. The music stops.* SERGE *returns, followed by* TONY GODDARD. TONY *is young, tall, slender, modestly dressed, and a little high-strung, which he does his best to conceal.* BRECKENRIDGE *speaks gaily:*]

Did you notice that there's a phonograph right by the piano, Tony? Why didn't you put on a record by Egon Richter? He plays that piece ever so much better.

TONY: It *was* the record.

BRECKENRIDGE: Well, well! That's one on me.

TONY: I know you don't like to hear me playing.

BRECKENRIDGE: I? Why shouldn't I, Tony?

TONY: I'm sorry. . . . [*Indifferently, but not at all offensively*] Have I wished you a happy birthday, Mr. Breckenridge?

BRECKENRIDGE: Yes, of course you have. When you arrived. Why, Tony! How unflattering!

TONY: Guess I shouldn't have asked. Makes it worse. I always do things like that.

BRECKENRIDGE: Anything wrong, Tony?

TONY: No. No. [*Listlessly*] Where are our host and hostess?

BRECKENRIDGE: [*With a broad smile*] They haven't arrived.

TONY: Not yet?

BRECKENRIDGE: No.

TONY: Isn't that rather peculiar?

BRECKENRIDGE: Why, no. Mrs. Dawson asked me to take care of everything—it was very kind of her, she wanted so much to please me.

SERGE: It is unusual, no?—your preparing the party for your own birthday in the house of somebody else?

BRECKENRIDGE: Oh, the Dawsons are old friends of mine—and they insisted that they wanted to give the party and give it here.

TONY: Well, the house isn't old. It doesn't look as if they'd ever lived in it.

BRECKENRIDGE: It was built very recently.

STEVE INGALLS: [*From the top of the stairway*] And in very bad taste.

[INGALLS *is a man of about forty, tall and lean, with a hard, inscrutable face. He looks like a man who should have great energy—and his appearance is a contrast to his manner and movements: slow, lazy, casual, indifferent. He wears simple sports clothes. He comes lazily down the stairs, while* BRECKENRIDGE *speaks sharply, looking up at him:*]

BRECKENRIDGE: Was that necessary, Steve?

INGALLS: Not at all. They could have chosen a better architect.

BRECKENRIDGE: That's not what I meant.

INGALLS: Don't be obvious, Walter. Was there ever a time when I didn't know what you meant? [*To* TONY] Hello, Tony. You here, too? As was to be expected. Sacrificial offerings—needed at one's birthday party.

SERGE: [*Stiffly*] It is *Mr. Breckenridge's* birthday party.

INGALLS: So it is.

SERGE: If you think you—

BRECKENRIDGE: Please, Serge. Really, Steve, do let's drop the personal remarks just for today, shall we? Particularly about the house and particularly when the Dawsons arrive.

INGALLS: When or if?

BRECKENRIDGE: What do you mean?

INGALLS: And another thing, Walter, is that you always know what I mean.

BRECKENRIDGE: [*Does not answer. Then looks impatiently at door Right*] I wish they'd bring Billy out. What is he doing there with Harvey? [*Goes to ring bell*]

TONY: Who else is coming?

BRECKENRIDGE: We're almost all here, except Adrienne. I've sent the car to meet Helen.

SERGE: Adrienne? It is not perhaps Miss Adrienne Knowland?

BRECKENRIDGE: Yes.

[CURTISS *enters Right*]

CURTISS: Yes, sir?

BRECKENRIDGE: Please tell Mr. Kozinsky to bring Billy out here.

CURTISS: Yes, sir. [*Exits Right*]

SERGE: It is not the great Adrienne Knowland?

INGALLS: There's only one Adrienne Knowland, Serge. But the adjective is optional.

SERGE: Oh, I am so happy that I should meet her in the person! I have seen her in that so beautiful play—*Little Women*. I have wondered so often what she is like in the real life. I have thought she must be sweet and lovely—like Mademoiselle Shirley Temple in the cinema, when I was a little boy in Moscow.

INGALLS: Yeah?

BRECKENRIDGE: Please, Steve. We know you don't like Adrienne, but couldn't you control it for just a few hours?

[HARVEY FLEMING *enters Right and holds the door open for* FLASH KOZINSKY, *who comes in pushing* BILLY BRECKENRIDGE *in a wheelchair.* BILLY *is a boy of fifteen, pale, thin, strangely quiet and a little too well-mannered.* FLASH *does not carry a college pennant, but "football hero" is written all over him as plainly as if he did. He is young, husky, pleasant-looking, and not too bright. As he wheels the chair in, he bumps it against the doorjamb*]

FLEMING: Careful, you clumsy fool!

BILLY: It's all right . . . Mr. Fleming.

BRECKENRIDGE: Well, Billy! Feel rested after the trip?

BILLY: Yes, Father.

INGALLS: Hello, Bill.

BILLY: Hello, Steve.

FLASH: [*Turns to* FLEMING. *It has taken all this time to penetrate*] Say, you can't talk to me like that!

FLEMING: Huh?

FLASH: Who are you to talk to me like that?

FLEMING: Skip it.

BRECKENRIDGE: [*Indicating* SERGE] Billy, you remember Mr. Sookin?

BILLY: How do you do, Mr. Sookin.

SERGE: Good afternoon, Billy. Feeling better, no? You look wonderful.

FLEMING: He looks like hell.

BILLY: I'm all right.

SERGE: You are not comfortable maybe? This pillow it is not right. [*Adjusts the pillow behind* BILLY'*s head*] So! It is better?

BILLY: Thank you.

SERGE: I think the footrest it should be higher. [*Adjusts the footrest*] So?

BILLY: Thank you.

SERGE: I think perhaps it is a little chilly. You want I should bring the warm shawl?

BILLY: [*Very quietly*] Leave me alone, will you please?

BRECKENRIDGE: There, there! Billy's just a little nervous. The trip was too much for him—in his condition.

[FLEMING *walks brusquely to the sideboard and starts pouring himself a glass of whiskey*]

BILLY: [*His eyes following* FLEMING *anxiously, his voice low and almost pleading*] Don't do that, Mr. Fleming.

FLEMING: [*Looks at him, then puts the bottle down. Quietly:*] Okay, kid.

SERGE: [*To* BRECKENRIDGE, *in what he intends to be a whisper*] Your poor son, how long he has this paralysis?

BRECKENRIDGE: Sh-sh.

BILLY: Six years and four months, Mr. Sookin.

[*There is a moment of embarrassed silence.* FLASH *looks from one face to another, then bursts out suddenly and loudly:*]

FLASH: Well, I don't know what the rest of you think, but *I* think Mr. Sookin shouldn't've asked that.

FLEMING: Keep still.

FLASH: Well, *I* think—

[*There is a frightening screech of brakes offstage and the sound of a car being stopped violently. A car door is slammed with a bang and a lovely, husky feminine voice yells: "Goddamn it!"*]

INGALLS: [*With a courtly gesture of introduction in the direction of the sound*] There's Mademoiselle Shirley Temple . . . !

[*The entrance door flies open as* ADRIENNE KNOWLAND *enters without ringing. She is as great a contrast to the conception of a Shirley Temple or of* Little Women *as can be imagined. She is a woman of about twenty-eight, beautiful and completely unconcerned about her beauty, with sharp, angular movements and a tense, restless energy. Her clothes are simple and tailored, such as a woman would wear for a walk in the country, not the kind one would expect from a glamorous actress. She carries a small suitcase. She enters like a gust of wind and whirls upon* BRECKENRIDGE]

ADRIENNE: Walter! Why in hell do they have a horse running loose out there?

BRECKENRIDGE: Adrienne, my dear! How do you—

TONY: [*At the same time*] A *horse*?

ADRIENNE: A horse. Hello, Tony. Why do they have a horse cavorting in the middle of the driveway? I almost killed the damn beast and I think I should have.

BRECKENRIDGE: I'm so sorry, my dear. Somebody's carelessness. I shall give orders to—

ADRIENNE: [*Forgetting him entirely, to* FLEMING] Hello, Harvey. Where have you been hiding yourself lately? Hello, Bill, old pal. I really came here just to see you again. Hello, Flash.

BRECKENRIDGE: Adrienne, my dear, may I present Serge Sookin, a new and very dear friend of mine?

ADRIENNE: How do you do, Mr. Sookin.

SERGE: [*Clicking his heels and bowing*] I am honored, Miss Knowland.

ADRIENNE: [*Looking at the room*] Well, I think this place is—[*Her glance stops on* INGALLS, *who is standing aside. She throws at him curtly, as an afterthought:*] Hello, Steve. [*She turns away from him before he has had time to complete his bow*] I think this place is—what one would expect it to be.

BRECKENRIDGE: Would you like to see your room, my dear?

ADRIENNE: No hurry. [*Tears her hat off and tosses it halfway across the room. To* FLASH, *indicating her suitcase:*] Flash, be an angel and take my stuff out of the way, will you? [FLASH *exits up the stairs with the suitcase.* ADRIENNE *walks to sideboard and pours herself a drink*] Incidentally, where's the host?

BRECKENRIDGE: Mr. and Mrs. Dawson are not here yet.

ADRIENNE: Not here? That's a new one in etiquette. Oh, and yes, of course, happy birthday.

BRECKENRIDGE: Thank you, my dear.

ADRIENNE: How's the infernal machine?

BRECKENRIDGE: The what?

ADRIENNE: The gadget with cosmic rays that the papers have been yelping about.

BRECKENRIDGE: The papers might do some real yelping about it soon. Very soon.

TONY: I heard it's really a colossal invention, Adrienne.

ADRIENNE: Another one? I think it's outrageous—the amount of space that the Breckenridge Laboratories have always managed to hog in the newspapers. But then, Walter has a genius for not remaining unnoticed. Like a stripteaser.

INGALLS: Or an actress.

ADRIENNE: [*Whirls to him, then away, and repeats calmly, her voice a little hard*] Or an actress.

SERGE: [*Breaks the uncomfortable little silence, speaking hotly and with a defiant sort of respect*] The stage—it is a great art. It helps such as suffer and are poor, all the misery and the sadness it makes forget for the few hours. The theater—it is the noble work of the humanitarianism.

ADRIENNE: [*Looks at him very coldly, then turns to* BRECKENRIDGE *and says dryly:*] Congratulations, Walter.

BRECKENRIDGE: What?

ADRIENNE: Your very dear friend is a real find, isn't he? Out of what gutter did you pick him up?

SERGE: [*Stiffly*] Miss Knowland . . . !

ADRIENNE: But, sweetheart, there's no need to look so Russian about it. I meant it in the nicest way. Besides, it goes for me, too, and for all of us here. We were all picked up by Walter out of one gutter or another. That's why he's a great man.

SERGE: I do not understand.

ADRIENNE: You didn't know? But it's no secret. I was singing in a dive, just one step better than a cat house—not a very long step—when Walter discovered me, and he built the Breckenridge Theater. Tony here is studying medicine—on a Breckenridge scholarship. Harvey has nothing but Breckenridge cash between him and the Bowery Mission—only nobody would let him into the Mission, just as nobody will give him a job, because he drinks. That's all right, Harvey—I do, too, at times. Billy here—

TONY: For God's sake, Adrienne!

ADRIENNE: But we're among friends. We're all in the same boat, aren't we? Except Steve, of course. Steve is a special case and the less you know about him, the better.

BRECKENRIDGE: Adrienne, my dear, we know you have a wonderful sense of humor, but why overdo it?

ADRIENNE: Oh, I just thought I'd initiate your Volga Boatman here. He's joining the brotherhood, isn't he? He's got all the earmarks.

SERGE: It is very strange, all this, Miss Knowland, but I think it is beautiful.

ADRIENNE: [*Dryly*] It is very beautiful.

[FLASH *comes back down the stairs*]

SERGE: And it is the noble thing—the Breckenridge Theater in the so very vile Fourteenth Street, for the poor people to see the drama. The art brought to the masses, as it should. I have often wondered how Mr. Breckenridge can do it, with the such low prices of the tickets.

INGALLS: He can't. The noble thing costs him a hundred thousand dollars a season, out of his own pocket.

SERGE: Miss Knowland?

INGALLS: No, Serge. Not Miss Knowland. The theater. That would have been much more sensible. But Walter never asks anything in return. He discovered her, he built the theater for her, he made her the star of Fourteenth Street, he made her famous—in fact, he made her in every sense but the proper one. Which is outrageous, when you look at Adrienne.

BRECKENRIDGE: Really, Steve!

SERGE: [*To* INGALLS] You are not able to understand the unselfish action?

INGALLS: No.

SERGE: You do not have the feeling that it is beautiful?

INGALLS: I've never had any beautiful feelings, Serge.

SERGE: [*To* ADRIENNE] I shall beg your forgiveness, Miss Knowland, since the person who should do so will not.

BRECKENRIDGE: Don't take Steve too seriously, Serge. He's not really as rotten as he sounds at times.

SERGE: By us in Moscow, a gentleman does not insult an artist.

BRECKENRIDGE: Oh, no matter what Steve says, he's always attended her every opening night.

ADRIENNE: [*It is almost a scream*] He . . . *what*?

BRECKENRIDGE: Didn't you know it? Steve's always been there, at every opening of yours—though I never caught him applauding, but the others made up for it; you've never lacked applause, have you, my dear?

ADRIENNE: [*She has been looking at* INGALLS *all through* BRECKENRIDGE's *speech. She asks, still looking at* INGALLS:] Walter . . . with whom?

BRECKENRIDGE: I beg your pardon?

ADRIENNE: With whom did he come to my openings?

BRECKENRIDGE: How can one ever ask "with whom" about Steve? Alone, of course.

ADRIENNE: [*To* INGALLS, *her voice trembling with anger*] You didn't see me in *Little Women,* did you?

INGALLS: Oh, yes, my dear, I did. You were very sweet and very coy. Particularly the way you let your hands flutter about. Like butterflies.

ADRIENNE: Steve, you didn't—

INGALLS: Yes, I did. I saw you in *Peter Pan.* You have beautiful legs. I saw you in *Daughter of the Slums*— very touching when you died of unemployment. I saw you in *The Yellow Ticket.*

ADRIENNE: Goddamn you, you didn't see *that*!

INGALLS: I did.

TONY: But, Adrienne, why are you so upset about it? Your greatest hits.

ADRIENNE: [*She has not even heard* TONY] Why did you go to my openings?

INGALLS: Well, my dear, there could be two explanations: either I'm a masochist or I wanted material for a conversation such as this.

[*He turns away from her, the conversation ended, as far as he's concerned. There is a silence. Then* FLASH *says loudly:*]

FLASH: Well, I don't know about you all, but *I* don't think it was a nice conversation.

TONY: [*As* FLEMING *is about to snap at* FLASH] Never mind, Harvey. I'll kill him for you one of these days.

FLEMING: Why in hell should Billy have a moron for a tutor?

BRECKENRIDGE: And why, may I ask, should you exhibit public concern about Billy's tutors, Harvey?

[FLEMING *looks at him, then steps back, somehow defeated*]

FLASH: [*Belligerently*] Whom you calling a moron, huh? Whom?
FLEMING: You.
FLASH: [*Taken aback*] Oh. . . .
BILLY: Father, could I please be taken back to my room?
BRECKENRIDGE: Why, I didn't think you'd want to miss the party, Billy. However, if you prefer—
BILLY: [*Indifferently*] No. It's all right. I'll stay here.

[*Doorbell rings*]

TONY: The Dawsons?
BRECKENRIDGE: [*Mysteriously*] Yes, I think it's time for the Dawsons.

[CURTISS *enters Right and crosses to open the door.* HELEN BRECKENRIDGE *enters. She is a woman of about thirty-six, tall, blond, exquisitely groomed. She is the perfect lady in the best sense of the word and she looks like the picture of a perfect wife who has always been perfectly cared for. She carries a small gift package*]

HELEN: [*Astonished*] Why, Curtiss! What are *you* doing here?
CURTISS: [*Bowing*] Good afternoon, madam.
BRECKENRIDGE: Helen, my dear! [*Kisses her on the cheek*] What a pleasant surprise to see you enter! As a matter of fact, it's always a surprise to me. I can't get used to it—not after sixteen years of married life.
HELEN: [*Smiling*] Too nice, Walter, much too nice. [*To the others*] Shall I say "hello" collectively? I'm afraid I'm late and last, as usual.

[*The others answer ad-lib greetings.* CURTISS *whispers something to* BRECKENRIDGE, *who nods.* CURTISS *exits Right*]

HELEN: [*To* BILLY] How do you feel, dear? Was the trip too hard?

BILLY: It was all right.

HELEN: I really don't quite see why I wasn't allowed to come down with you.

BRECKENRIDGE: [*Smiling*] There was a reason, my dear.

HELEN: I had a perfectly beastly time getting away from the city. I envy you, Steve—living right here in Connecticut. You have no idea of the traffic on a holiday eve. Besides, I had to stop at a bookstore—and why is it that they never seem to have any clerks in bookstores? [*To* BRECKENRIDGE, *indicating her package*] I bought *How Deep the Shadows* for Mrs. Dawson. Mrs. Dawson has such a regrettable taste in books. But it was so nice of her—giving this party.

INGALLS: Too nice, Helen, much too nice.

HELEN: Not if it got you out of that laboratory of yours. How long since you last attended a party, Steve?

INGALLS: I'm not sure. Maybe a year.

HELEN: Maybe two?

INGALLS: Possible.

HELEN: But I'm being terribly rude. Shouldn't I say hello to our hostess? Where is our hostess?

[*Nobody answers. Then* BRECKENRIDGE *steps forward*]

BRECKENRIDGE: [*His voice gay and solemn at once*] Helen, my dear, *that* is my surprise. *You* are the hostess. [*She looks at him without understanding*] You have always wanted a house in the country. This is it. It's yours. I had it built for you. [*She stares at him, frozen*] Why, my dear, what's the matter?

HELEN: [*A smile coming very slowly—and not too naturally—to her face*] I . . . I'm just . . . speechless . . . Walter. [*The smile improving*] You can't expect me not to be a little—overwhelmed, can you? . . . And I haven't even thanked you yet. I'm late again. I'm always too late. . . . [*She looks about, a little helplessly, notices the package in her hand*] Well . . . well, I guess I'll have to read *How Deep the Shadows* myself. It serves me right.

BRECKENRIDGE: I am fifty years old today, Helen. Fifty. It's a long time. Half a century. And I was just . . . just vain and human enough to want to mark the occasion. Not for myself—but for others. How can we ever leave a mark—except upon others? This is my gift—to you.

HELEN: Walter . . . when did you start building it . . . this house?

BRECKENRIDGE: Oh, almost a year ago. Think of what I've spared you: all the bother and trouble and arguments with architects and contractors, and shopping for furniture and kitchen ranges and bathroom fixtures. Let me tell you, it's a headache and a heartache.

HELEN: Yes, Walter. You have never let me be exposed to a headache or a heartache. You have been very kind. . . . Well . . . well, I hardly know where to begin . . . if I'm to be hostess—

BRECKENRIDGE: Everything's taken care of, my dear. Curtiss is here, and Mrs. Pudget is in the kitchen, the dinner is ordered, the drinks are ready, even the soap is in the bathrooms. I wanted you to come and find the party complete—from guests to ashtrays. I planned it that way. I don't want you to exert yourself at all.

HELEN: Well, I suppose that's that. . . .

BRECKENRIDGE: [*Turning to* BILLY] And, Billy, I wouldn't forget *you* today. Did you see—from the window of your room—that horse out on the lawn?

BILLY: Yes, Father.

BRECKENRIDGE: Well, it's yours. That's *your* present.

[*There's a little gasp—from* ADRIENNE]

HELEN: [*With shocked reproach*] *Really,* Walter!

BRECKENRIDGE: But why are you all looking at me like that? Don't you understand? If Billy concentrates on how much he would like to be able to ride that horse— it will help him to get well. It will give him a concrete objective for a healthy mental attitude.

BILLY: Yes, Father. Thank you very much, Father.

FLEMING: [*Screams suddenly, to* BRECKENRIDGE] Goddamn you! You dirty bastard! You lousy, rotten sadist! You—

INGALLS: [*Seizing him as he swings out at* BRECKENRIDGE]
Easy, Harvey. Take it easy.

BRECKENRIDGE: [*After a pause, very gently*] Harvey . . .
[*The kindness of his tone makes* FLEMING *cringe, almost
visibly*] I'm sorry, Harvey, that I should be the cause of
your feeling as ashamed as you will feel later.

FLEMING: [*After a pause, dully*] I apologize, Walter. . . .
[*He turns abruptly, walks to sideboard, pours himself a
drink, swallows it, refills the glass. No one is looking at
him, except* BILLY]

BRECKENRIDGE: It's all right. I understand. I'm your
friend, Harvey. I've always been your friend.

[*Silence*]

FLASH: Well, *I* think Mr. Fleming is drunk.

[CURTISS *enters with a tray bearing filled cocktail
glasses*]

BRECKENRIDGE: [*Brightly*] I think Mr. Fleming has the
right idea—for the moment. It's time we all had a drink.

[CURTISS *passes the cocktails to the guests. When he
comes to* ADRIENNE *he stands waiting politely. She is
lost in thought and does not notice him*]

Adrienne, my dear . . .

ADRIENNE: [*With a little jerk of returning to reality*] What?
[*Sees* CURTISS] Oh . . . [*Takes a glass absently*]

BRECKENRIDGE: [*Taking the last glass, stands solemnly
facing the others*] My friends! Not I, but *you* are to be
honored today. Not what I have been, but those whom I
have served. You—all of you—are the justification of
my existence—for help to one's fellow men is the only
justification of anyone's existence. That is why I chose
you as my guests today. That is why we shall drink a
toast—not to me, but—[*Raising his glass*]—to you, my
friends! [*Drinks. The others stand silently*]

SERGE: I would so very much like to give the toast also, please?

BRECKENRIDGE: If you wish, Serge.

SERGE: [*Fervently*] To the man who has his life devoted so that the other men's lives should be better. To the man the genius of whom to the world gave the machine for the Vitamin X separating, which little babies makes so healthier. To the man who the new violet-ray diffuser gave us, so cheaper that the poor people in the slums the sunlight could have. To the man who the electric saw for the surgery invented, which so many lives has saved. To the friend of the mankind—Walter Breckenridge!

INGALLS: Sure. Walter's invented everything but a bust developer for social workers.

FLASH: *I* think that's in bad taste.

ADRIENNE: [*Rising*] And now that we've done our duty, may I go up to my room, Walter?

BRECKENRIDGE: Wait, Adrienne, do you mind? There's something I want you all to hear. [*To the others*] My friends, I have an announcement to make. It is important. I want you to be the first to hear it.

INGALLS: More gifts?

BRECKENRIDGE: Yes, Steve. One more gift. My greatest— and my last. [*To the others*] My friends! You have heard of the invention on which I have worked for the last ten years—the one Adrienne referred to so charmingly as a "gadget." There has been quite a great deal of mystery about it—unavoidably, as you shall see. It is a device to capture the energy of cosmic rays. You may have heard that cosmic rays possess a tremendous potential of energy, which scientists have struggled to harness for years and years. I was fortunate enough to find the secret of it—with Steve's able assistance, of course. I have been asked so often whether the device is completed. I have refused to answer. But I can say it now: it is completed. It is tried, tested, and proved beyond doubt. Its possibilities are tremendous. [*Pauses. Continues, very simply, almost wearily:*] Tremendous. And its financial promises are unlimited. [*Stops*]

INGALLS: Well?

BRECKENRIDGE: Well . . . My friends, a man controlling such an invention and keeping its secret could be rich. *Rich.* But I am not going to keep it. [*Pauses, looks at them, then says slowly:*] Tomorrow, at twelve o'clock noon, I shall give this invention to mankind. *Give,* not sell it. For all and any to use. Without charge. To all mankind. [TONY *emits a long whistle.* FLASH *stands with his mouth hanging open, and utters only one awed:* "*Gee!*"] Think what that will do. Free power—drawn out of space. It will light the poorest slum and the shack of the sharecropper. It will throw the greedy utility companies out of business. It will be mankind's greatest blessing. And no one will hold private control over it.

ADRIENNE: Beautiful showmanship, Walter. You've always been a master of the theater.

TONY: But I suppose it *is* sort of grand—

ADRIENNE:—opera.

HELEN: What exactly is to happen tomorrow at noon, Walter?

BRECKENRIDGE: I have invited the press to be at the laboratory tomorrow at noon. I shall give them the blueprints—the formulas—everything—to spread in every tabloid.

ADRIENNE: Don't forget the Sunday magazine sections.

BRECKENRIDGE: Adrienne, my dear, surely you don't disapprove?

ADRIENNE: What's it to me?

SERGE: Ah, but it is so beautiful! It is an example for the whole world to follow. To me Mr. Breckenridge has spoken about this gift many weeks ago and I said: "Mr. Breckenridge, if you do this, I will be proud a human being to be!"

BRECKENRIDGE: [*Turning to* INGALLS] Steve?

INGALLS: What?

BRECKENRIDGE: What do you say?

INGALLS: I? Nothing.

BRECKENRIDGE: Of course, Steve doesn't quite approve. Steve is rather . . . old-fashioned. He would have preferred to keep the whole thing secret in our own hands, and to make a tremendous fortune. Wouldn't you, Steve?

INGALLS: [*Lazily*] Oh, yes. I like to make money. I think money is a wonderful thing. I don't see what's wrong with making a fortune—if you deserve it and people are willing to pay for what you offer them. Besides, I've never liked things that are given away. When you get something for nothing—you always find a string attached somewhere. Like the fish when it swallows the worm. But then, I've never had any noble feelings.

SERGE: Mr. Ingalls, that is contemptible!

INGALLS: Cut it, Serge. You bore me.

BRECKENRIDGE: But, Steve, I want you to understand why—

INGALLS: Don't waste your time, Walter. I've never understood the noble, the selfless, or any of those things. Besides, it's not my fortune you're giving away. It's yours. I'm only a junior partner. All I lose is two bits to your dollar. So I'm not going to argue about it.

BRECKENRIDGE: I'm glad, Steve. I made this decision after a great deal of time and meditation.

INGALLS: You did? [*Rises*] You know, Walter, I think decisions are made quickly. And the more important the step—the quicker. [*Walks to stairs*]

SERGE: [*With a little touch of triumph*] I begged Mr. Breckenridge to do this.

INGALLS: [*Stops on the stairs on his way up, looks at him. Then:*] I know you did. [*Exits up the stairs*]

HELEN: [*Rising*] It seems so foolish to ask this—when I'm hostess—but what time is dinner ordered for, Walter?

BRECKENRIDGE: Seven o'clock.

HELEN: Would you mind if I took a look at what my house is like?

BRECKENRIDGE: But of course! How thoughtless of me! Holding you here—when you must be dying of curiosity.

HELEN: [*To the others*] Shall we make an inspection tour together? The hostess needs someone to guide her.

TONY: I'll show you. I've been all through the house. The laundry in the basement is wonderful.

HELEN: Shall we start with Billy's room?

BILLY: Yes, please, Mother. I want to go back to my room.

[*As* FLEMING *and* FLASH *are wheeling* BILLY *out, Right,*
BRECKENRIDGE *is about to follow*]

ADRIENNE: Walter. I'd like to speak to you. [BRECKEN-
RIDGE *stops, frowning*] For just a few minutes.

BRECKENRIDGE: Yes, of course, my dear.

[HELEN *and* TONY *exit after* BILLY, FLEMING, *and* FLASH.
SERGE *remains*]

ADRIENNE: Serge, when you hear someone say to someone else: "I'd like to speak to you"—it usually means
"alone."

SERGE: Ah, but of course! I am so sorry, Miss Knowland!
[*Bows and exits Right*]

BRECKENRIDGE: [*Sitting down and indicating a chair*] Yes,
my dear?

ADRIENNE: [*She remains standing, looking at him. After a
moment, she says in a flat, hard, expressionless voice:*]
Walter, I want you to release me from my contract.

BRECKENRIDGE: [*Leans back. Then:*] You're not serious,
my dear.

ADRIENNE: Walter, please. Please don't make me say too
much. I can't tell you how serious I am.

BRECKENRIDGE: But I thought it was understood, a year
ago, that we would not discuss that subject again.

ADRIENNE: And I've stuck it out, haven't I? For another
whole year. I've tried. Walter. I can't go on.

BRECKENRIDGE: You are not happy?

ADRIENNE: Don't make me say anything else.

BRECKENRIDGE: But I don't understand. I—

ADRIENNE: Walter. I'm trying so hard not to have another
scene like last year. Don't ask me any questions. Just
say that you will release me.

BRECKENRIDGE: [*After a pause*] If I released you, what
would you do?

ADRIENNE: That play I showed you last year.

BRECKENRIDGE: For a commercial producer?

ADRIENNE: Yes.

BRECKENRIDGE: For a cheap, vulgar, commercial Broadway producer?

ADRIENNE: For the cheapest and most vulgar one I could find.

BRECKENRIDGE: Let's see. If I remember correctly, your part would be that of a very objectionable young woman who wants to get rich, who drinks and swears and—

ADRIENNE: [*Coming to life*] And how she swears! And she sleeps with men! And she's ambitious! And she's selfish! And she laughs! And she's not sweet— Oh, Walter! She's not sweet at all!

BRECKENRIDGE: You're overestimating yourself, my dear. You can't play a part like that.

ADRIENNE: Maybe not. I'll try.

BRECKENRIDGE: You want a disastrous flop?

ADRIENNE: Perhaps. I'll take the chance.

BRECKENRIDGE: You want to be panned?

ADRIENNE: Perhaps. If I have to be.

BRECKENRIDGE: And your audience? What about your audience? [*She doesn't answer*] What about the people who love you and respect you for what you represent to them?

ADRIENNE: [*Her voice flat and dead again*] Walter, skip that. *Skip that.*

BRECKENRIDGE: But you seem to have forgotten. The Breckenridge Theater is not a mere place of amusement. It was not created just to satisfy your exhibitionism or my vanity. It has a social mission. It brings cheer to those who need it most. It gives them what they like. They need you. They get a great deal from you. You have a duty and a standing above those of a mere actress. Isn't that precious to you?

ADRIENNE: Oh, Goddamn you! [*He stares at her*] All right! You asked for it! I hate it! Do you hear me? I hate it! All of it! Your noble theater and your noble plays and all the cheap, trite, trashy, simpering bromides that are so sweet! So sweet! God, so sweet I can hear them grating on my teeth every evening! I'm going to scream in the middle of one of those noble speeches, some night, and bring the curtain down! I can't go on with it, Goddamn you and your audience! I can't! Do you understand me? I can't!

BRECKENRIDGE: Adrienne, my child, I cannot let you ruin yourself.

ADRIENNE: Listen, Walter, please listen. . . . I'll try to explain it. I'm not ungrateful. I want the audience to like me. But that's not enough. Just to do what they want me to do, just because they like it—it's not enough. I've got to like it, too. I've got to believe in what I'm doing. I've got to be proud of it. You can't do any kind of work without that. That comes first. Then you take a chance—and hope that others will like it.

BRECKENRIDGE: Isn't that rather selfish?

ADRIENNE: [*Simply*] I guess it is. I guess I'm selfish. It's selfish to breathe, also—isn't it? You don't breathe for anyone but yourself. . . . All I want is a chance—for myself—to do something strong, living, intelligent, difficult—just once.

BRECKENRIDGE: [*Sadly*] I believed in you, Adrienne. I did my best for you.

ADRIENNE: I know. And I hate to hurt you. That's why I've stood it for such a long time. But, Walter, the contract—it's for five more years. I couldn't take five years. I couldn't even take it for five days this coming season. I've reached my last minute—it's very terrible, when a person is driven to his last minute, and very ugly. You must let me go.

BRECKENRIDGE: Who's been talking to you? Steve's influence?

ADRIENNE: Steve? You know what I think of Steve. When would I talk to him? When do I ever see him?

BRECKENRIDGE: [*Shrugging*] It just sounds like him.

ADRIENNE: Do you know what made me speak to you today? That stupendous thing you announced. I thought . . . you're doing so much for humanity, and yet . . . why is it that the people who worry most about mankind have the least concern for any actual human being?

BRECKENRIDGE: My dear, try to understand. I'm acting for your own good. I can't let you ruin your career.

ADRIENNE: Let me go, Walter. Give me my freedom.

BRECKENRIDGE: Freedom—for what? Freedom to hurt yourself.

ADRIENNE: Yes!—if necessary. To make mistakes. To fail. To be alone. To be rotten. To be selfish. But to be free.

BRECKENRIDGE: [*Rising*] No, Adrienne.

ADRIENNE: [*In a dead, flat voice*] Walter . . . do you remember . . . last summer . . . when I ran my car into a tree? . . . Walter, it was not an accident. . . .

BRECKENRIDGE: [*Severely*] I refuse to understand what you mean. You're being indecent.

ADRIENNE: [*Screams*] Goddamn you! Goddamn you, you rotten, holy, saintly bastard!

INGALLS: [*Appearing at the top of the stairs*] You'll ruin your voice, Adrienne—and you won't be able to do *Little Women* again.

[ADRIENNE *whirls around and stops short*]

BRECKENRIDGE: [*As* INGALLS *comes down the stairs*] I believe this is the kind of performance you'll enjoy, Steve. So I'll leave Adrienne to you. You'll find you have a great deal in common. [*Exits Right*]

INGALLS: The acoustics in this room are great, Adrienne. Does wonders for your diaphragm—and your vocabulary.

ADRIENNE: [*Stands looking at him with hatred*] Listen, you. I have something to tell you. Now. I don't care. If you want to make wisecracks, I'll give you something real to wisecrack about.

INGALLS: Go ahead.

ADRIENNE: I know what you think of me—and you're right. I'm just a lousy ham who's done nothing but trash all her life. I'm no better than a slut—not because I haven't any talent, but worse: because I have and sold it. Not even for money, but for someone's stupid, drooling kindness—and I'm more contemptible than an honest whore!

INGALLS: That's a pretty accurate description.

ADRIENNE: Well, that's what I am. I know also what you are. You're a hard, cold, ruthless egoist. You're just a laboratory machine—all chromium and stainless steel. You're as efficient and bright and vicious as a car going ninety miles an hour. Only the car would bump if it ran over someone's body. You wouldn't. You wouldn't even know it. You're going ninety miles every one of the twenty-four hours—through a desert island, as far as you're concerned. A desert island full of charts, blueprints, coils, tubes, and batteries. You've never known a human emotion. You're worse than any of us. I think you're the rottenest person I've ever met. I'm inexcusably, contemptibly, completely in love with you and have been for years. [*She stops. He stands motionless, looking at her silently. She snaps:*] Well? [*He does not move*] You're not going to pass up a chance like this for one of your brilliant wisecracks? [*He does not move*] Shouldn't you answer—something?

INGALLS: [*His voice is very soft and very earnest. It is the first sound of simple sincerity to be heard from him:*] Adrienne . . . [*She looks at him, astonished*] I am thinking that I haven't heard it. I can't answer. Had you said it to me yesterday—or the day after tomorrow—I'd answer. Today, I can't.

ADRIENNE: Why?

INGALLS: You know, sound vibrations never die in space. Let's think that what you said hasn't reached me yet. It will reach me day after tomorrow. Then—if I'm still able to hear it and if you still want me to hear it—I'll give you my answer.

ADRIENNE: Steve . . . what's the matter?

INGALLS: Day after tomorrow, Adrienne. Perhaps sooner. But if not then—then never.

ADRIENNE: Steve, I don't understa—

INGALLS: [*Picking up a magazine from the table, in his normal, conversational tone*] Have you seen this week's *World*? There's a very interesting article on the progressive income tax. It demonstrates how the tax works for the protection of mediocrity. . . . The problem of taxation, of course, is extremely complex.

ADRIENNE: [*She is turned away from him, her shoulders sagging a little, but she does her best to follow his lead*

*and speaks obediently, in as good an imitation of a con-
versational tone as she can manage—but her voice
sounds very tired*] Yes. I've never been able to figure out
an income tax blank or an insurance policy.

[HELEN, BRECKENRIDGE, SERGE, *and* TONY *enter, coming down the stairs*]

INGALLS: Well? What do you think of the house, Helen?

HELEN: [*Without enthusiasm*] It's lovely.

BRECKENRIDGE: [*Proudly*] She couldn't think of one thing
that I hadn't thought of already.

INGALLS: As usual.

BRECKENRIDGE: Oh say, I mustn't forget. I'll tell you all
while Billy isn't here; it's a little surprise for him.
Tonight, at ten o'clock, when it gets dark, I shall give you
a demonstration of my invention. Its first public demonstration. We'll start celebrating the Fourth of July tonight,
a little in advance. We'll have fireworks—I've had them
lined up—[*Points*]—over there, on the other side of the
lake. I'll set them off—from the garden—without touching them, without wires, by remote control—by mere
electrical impulses through the air.

TONY: Could I see the machine?

BRECKENRIDGE: No, Tony. Nobody can see the machine
till tomorrow. Don't try to find it. You won't. But you
will all be the first witnesses of its action. [*Shrugs gaily*]
Think of it! If someday they make a movie of my life,
you will all be impersonated in that scene.

SERGE: They always make the lives of the great men in the
cinema.

INGALLS: All that Walter needs now to be a great man is to
get assassinated.

HELEN: Steve!

INGALLS: Well, he came pretty close to it once—so I guess
that'll have to do.

HELEN: He . . . did what?

INGALLS: Didn't you know that Walter almost got bumped
off—about a month ago?

HELEN: [*Aghast*] No! . . .

INGALLS: Oh, yes. Someone's tried to get him. Under very mysterious circumstances, too.

BRECKENRIDGE: Just an accident, probably. Why talk about it?

HELEN: Please tell me, Steve.

INGALLS: There isn't really much to tell. Walter and Serge drove down to Stamford, one evening, and stopped at the laboratory, and dragged me down here to see the house—the "Dawsons'" house—it was just being finished then. Well, the three of us got separated, looking around, and then I heard a shot—and I saw Walter picking up his hat, with a hole through it. It was a new hat, too.

HELEN: Oh! . . .

INGALLS: Well, we called the police, and all the building workers were searched, but we never found the man who did it or the gun.

HELEN: But it's fantastic! Walter doesn't have an enemy in the world!

INGALLS: I guess you never can tell.

[FLEMING *enters, Right, goes to sideboard, pours himself a drink, and stands drinking, ignoring the others*]

HELEN: And then?

INGALLS: That's all. . . . Oh, yes, there was another funny thing. I had a bag in the car—just a small bag with some old junk in it. When we got back to the car, we found the lock of that bag broken open. There was nothing inside that anyone would want, and whoever did it hadn't even looked inside, because the things were just as I'd left them, but the lock was broken. We never figured that out, either.

HELEN: Walter! . . . Why didn't you tell me about this?

BRECKENRIDGE: That is precisely why, dear—so that you wouldn't be upset, as you are now. Besides, it was nothing. An accident or a crank. I told Curtiss about it—told him not to admit any strangers to the house—but nobody came and nothing happened.

INGALLS: I told Walter that he should carry a gun—just in case—but he wouldn't do it.

HELEN: But you should, Walter!

BRECKENRIDGE: I do. I got one.

INGALLS: I don't believe it. You know, Walter is afraid of guns.

BRECKENRIDGE: Nonsense.

INGALLS: You said so yourself.

BRECKENRIDGE: [*Indicating cabinet*] Look in that drawer.

[INGALLS *opens the drawer and takes out the gun*]

INGALLS: You're right—for once. [*Examining the gun*] Nice little job. That will take care of any—emergency.

HELEN: Oh, put it away! I don't like them myself.

[INGALLS *replaces the gun in the drawer and closes it*]

TONY: It doesn't make sense. A man like Mr. Breckenridge— why would anyone—

BRECKENRIDGE: Of course it doesn't make sense. And I don't see why Steve had to bring that up—today of all days. . . . Well, shall we go on to look at the grounds? Wait till you see the grounds, Helen!

HELEN: [*Rising*] Yes, of course.

[FLEMING *swallows another drink and exits Right*]

BRECKENRIDGE: Adrienne, my dear—coming?

ADRIENNE: [*In a flat voice*] Yes.

BRECKENRIDGE: No hard feelings, of course?

ADRIENNE: No.

BRECKENRIDGE: I knew you'd be all right. I wasn't angry. An actress' temper is like a summer storm.

ADRIENNE: Yes.

[*She walks out through the French doors, followed by* BRECKENRIDGE, SERGE, *and* TONY]

HELEN: [*Stops at the French doors, turns*] Coming, Steve?

[*He does not answer and stands looking at her. Then:*]

INGALLS: Helen . . .

HELEN: Yes?

INGALLS: You are not happy, are you?

HELEN: [*With amused reproach*] Steve! That's one of those questions that should never be answered—one way or the other.

INGALLS: I'm asking it only . . . in self-defense.

HELEN: In . . . your *own* defense?

INGALLS: Yes.

HELEN: [*Decisively*] Don't you think we'd better join the others?

INGALLS: No. [*She does not move. She stands looking at him. After a moment, he adds:*] You know what I'm going to say.

HELEN: No. I don't know . . . I don't know. . . . [*Involuntarily*] I don't want to know . . . !

INGALLS: I love you, Helen.

HELEN: [*Trying to be amused*] Really, Steve, we're about ten years too late, aren't we? I'm sure I am. I thought things like that weren't being said anymore. At least . . . not to me. . . .

BRECKENRIDGE'S VOICE: [*Calling from garden*] Helen! . . .

INGALLS: I have wanted to say it for more than ten years.

HELEN: It's too . . . foolish . . . and conventional, isn't it? My husband's partner . . . and . . . and I'm the perfect wife who's always had everything . . .

INGALLS: Have you?

HELEN: . . . and you've never seemed to notice that I existed. . . .

INGALLS: Even if I know it's hopeless—

HELEN: Of course it's hopeless. . . . It . . . it *should* be hopeless. . . . [*There is the sound of voices approaching from the garden.* INGALLS *moves suddenly to take her in his arms*] Steve! . . . Steve, they're coming back! They're—

[*The voices are closer. He stops her words with a violent kiss. Her first movement is to struggle against him, then her body relaxes in surrender, her arms rise to embrace him—very eagerly—just as* ADRIENNE, BRECKENRIDGE, SERGE, *and* TONY *enter from the garden.* HELEN *and* INGALLS *step apart, she shocked, he perfectly calm.* IN- GALLS *is first to break the silence*]

INGALLS: I've always wanted to know what one really did at such a moment.

SERGE: [*Choking with indignation*] This . . . this . . . it is monstrous! . . . It is unspeakable! . . . It is—

BRECKENRIDGE: [*With great poise*] Now, Serge. No hysterics please. From anyone. Let us act grown-up. [*To* HELEN, *gently*] I'm sorry, Helen. I know this is harder for you than for any of us. I shall try to make it easier, if I can. [*Notices* ADRIENNE, *who looks more stunned and crushed than all the others*] What's the matter, Adrienne?

ADRIENNE: [*Barely able to answer*] Nothing . . . nothing. . . .

BRECKENRIDGE: Steve, I should like to speak to you alone.

INGALLS: I have wanted to speak to you alone, Walter, for a long time.

CURTAIN

SCENE 2

That evening. The room is in semidarkness, with just one lamp burning on a table.

At curtain rise, BRECKENRIDGE *is sitting in an armchair, a little slumped, looking tired and dejected.* SERGE *sits on a low hassock—at a little distance, but almost as if he were sitting at* BRECKENRIDGE'S *feet.*

SERGE: It is terrible. It is too terrible and I am sick. I cannot help that it should make me sick.

BRECKENRIDGE: You're young, Serge. . . .

SERGE: Is it only the young who have the feeling of decency?

BRECKENRIDGE: It is only the young who condemn. . . .

SERGE: At the dinner . . . you were . . . as if nothing had happened. . . . You were magnificent.

BRECKENRIDGE: There's Billy to think about.

SERGE: And now? What is to happen now?

BRECKENRIDGE: Nothing.

SERGE: Nothing?

BRECKENRIDGE: Serge, my position does not allow me to make this public. People believe in me. I cannot have scandal attached to my name. Besides, think what it would do to Helen. Do you suppose I'd do that to her?

SERGE: Mrs. Breckenridge she did not think of *you*.

BRECKENRIDGE: [*Slowly*] There's something about it that I can't understand. It's unlike Helen. But it's much more unlike Steve.

SERGE: Mr. Ingalls? Of him I expect anything.

BRECKENRIDGE: That's not what I mean, Serge. It wouldn't surprise me that Steve should be unscrupulous. But that he should be stupid!

SERGE: Stupid?

BRECKENRIDGE: If Steve had wanted to carry on a secret love affair with Helen, he could have done so for years and years, and none of us would ever guess—if he didn't want us to guess. He's clever. He's too terribly clever. But to start . . . to start an embrace in broad daylight—when he knew we'd be back for her any moment—a fool wouldn't do that. *That's* what I can't understand.

SERGE: What did he say when you spoke to him?

BRECKENRIDGE: [*Evasively*] We spoke of . . . many things.

SERGE: I cannot understand that this to *you* should happen! The gratitude it does not exist in the world.

BRECKENRIDGE: Ah, Serge. We must never think of gratitude. We must do what we think is good for our fellow men—and let kindness be its own reward. [FLASH *enters Right, wheeling* BILLY *in, followed by* FLEMING *and* HELEN. BRECKENRIDGE *rises*]

BILLY: You wanted me here, Father?

BRECKENRIDGE: Yes, Billy. Not too tired?

BILLY: No.

BRECKENRIDGE: [*To* HELEN, *indicating his chair*] Sit down, my dear. This is the most comfortable chair in the room. [HELEN *obeys silently.* INGALLS *enters from the garden and remains standing at the French doors*] But why are we sitting in the dark like this? [*Turns more lights on*] Your dress is so light, Helen. It's rather chilly tonight for this time of the year. Are you sure you're not too cold?

HELEN: No.

BRECKENRIDGE: [*Offering her a cigarette box*] Cigarette, my dear?

HELEN: No, thank you.

INGALLS: [*Without moving*] You're exceptionally rotten tonight, Walter. Worse than usual.

BRECKENRIDGE: I beg your pardon? [ADRIENNE *enters, coming down the stairs, but stops and stands watching those below*]

INGALLS: You know what I'd do if I were you? I'd yell at Helen at the slightest provocation or without any. I'd swear at her. I think I'd slap her.

BRECKENRIDGE: *You* would.

INGALLS: And do you know what the result would be? It would make things easier for her.

HELEN: Please, Steve.

INGALLS: I'm sorry, Helen . . . I'm terribly sorry.

[*Silence.* ADRIENNE *comes down the stairs. At the bottom, she stops: she sees* INGALLS *looking at her. For a moment they stand face to face, holding the glance. Then she turns sharply and goes to sit down alone in a corner of the room*]

FLASH: [*Looking helplessly at everybody*] What the hell is going on in this house?

BRECKENRIDGE: Flash. You are not to swear in Billy's presence.

FLASH: Gee, I beg your pardon. But I feel something. You may not know it, but I'm sensitive.

SERGE: By us in Moscow, things like this would not happen.

INGALLS: [*Casually*] Say, Serge, I heard something interesting today about some compatriots of yours. About the Soviet Culture and Friendship Society.

SERGE: [*Looks at him for a distinct moment, then:*] So? What did you hear?

INGALLS: That the FBI has caught up with them. Seems they're just a front for Soviet espionage in this country. One of the biggest fronts. Heard the FBI has cracked down on them and seized their files.

SERGE: When? That is not true!

INGALLS: Today.

SERGE: I do not believe it!

INGALLS: It ought to be in the papers—by now. I got a tip from my old friend Joe Cheeseman of the New York *Courier*—the *Courier* was first to get the story—he said it would be on their front page this afternoon.

BRECKENRIDGE: Never knew you had friends among the press.

SERGE: Do you have the today's *Courier*?

INGALLS: No.

SERGE: [*To the others*] Has anybody the—

INGALLS: Why are you so interested, Serge? What do you know about the Soviet Culture and Friendship Society?

SERGE: What do I know! A great deal I know! I know for long time they are the Soviet spies. I knew Makarov, their president, in Moscow. He was one of the worst. When I escaped during the World War Number Two . . . That is why I escaped—because the men like him they betrayed the people. They had the noble ideals, but the so cruel methods! They did not believe in God. They lost the spirit of our Holy Mother Russia. They lost our beautiful dream of the brotherhood and the equal sharing and the—

BRECKENRIDGE: Don't talk about it, Serge.

SERGE: All the time I am in this country, I wanted to tell the police what I know about Makarov and the Soviet Culture and Friendship Society. But I could not speak. If I open my mouth . . . [*Shudders*] You see, my family—they are still in Russia. My mother . . . and my sister.

FLASH: Gee, Mr. Sookin! That's awful.

SERGE: But if the Soviet Culture and Friendship it got caught now—I'm glad. I'm so glad! . . . Has anyone the today's *Courier* here? [*All the others answer "No" or shake their heads*] But I must see it! Where can I get the New York newspapers?

BRECKENRIDGE: Nowhere around here—at this hour.

INGALLS: In Stamford, Serge.

SERGE: Ah, yes? Then I will go to Stamford.

BRECKENRIDGE: Oh, but Serge! It's a long drive—three quarters of an hour at the least, there and back.

SERGE: But I so much want to read it tonight.

BRECKENRIDGE: You will miss the . . . the surprise.

SERGE: But you will excuse me, Mr. Breckenridge, no? I will try most quick as I can to be back. Would you permit that I take the car?

BRECKENRIDGE: Certainly, if you insist.

SERGE: [*To* INGALLS] Where do I find the nearest place with the newspapers?

INGALLS: Just follow the road straight to Stamford. The first drugstore you come to—a little place called Lawton's, on the corner, near the Breckenridge Laboratories. They have all the papers. Let's see . . . [*Looks at his watch*] They get the last city editions at ten o'clock. In fifteen minutes. They'll have them by the time you get there. Joe Cheeseman said it would be in today's last edition.

SERGE: Thank you so much. [*To* BRECKENRIDGE] You will please excuse me?

BRECKENRIDGE: Sure. [SERGE *exits Left*]

FLASH: [*As no one seems inclined to talk*] And another thing that bothers me is why nobody ate any dinner tonight. The lobster was wonderful. [*There is the distant sound of a small explosion, and far away, beyond the lake, a rocket rises, bursts in the air and vanishes*]

BRECKENRIDGE: Our neighbors across the lake are celebrating early.

BILLY: I want to see it.

BRECKENRIDGE: You'll see something much bigger than this—in a little while.

[FLASH *turns the wheelchair toward the French doors. Another rocket goes off in the distance.* TONY *enters, Left*]

TONY: Say, where's Serge going in such a hurry? Just saw him driving off.

BRECKENRIDGE: To Stamford. To get a newspaper.

INGALLS: You haven't got today's *Courier* by any chance, have you, Tony?

TONY: The *Courier*? No. [*Hesitates, then:*] Mr. Breckenridge, could I speak to you? For just a moment. I've tried all day—

BRECKENRIDGE: Well, what is it, Tony? What is it?

TONY: It's . . . about Billy. I didn't want to—[*Looks at* BILLY]

FLEMING: About Billy? What?

BRECKENRIDGE: Surely it can't be a secret. Go ahead.

TONY: If you wish. I saw Professor Doyle this morning.

BRECKENRIDGE: Oh, *that*? You're not going to begin again to—

FLEMING: Doyle? That's the doctor who's taking care of Billy?

TONY: Yes. He's my teacher at college.

FLEMING: What did he say?

BRECKENRIDGE: Really, Tony, I thought we had settled—

FLEMING: What did he say?

TONY: [*To* BRECKENRIDGE] He said that I must speak to you and beg you on my knees if I have to. He said that if you don't send Billy to Montreal this summer and let Dr. Harlan perform that operation—Billy will never walk again. [FLEMING *makes a step forward slowly, ominously*]

BRECKENRIDGE: Just a minute, Harvey.

FLEMING: [*In a strange, hoarse voice*] Why didn't you tell me about this?

BRECKENRIDGE: Because I didn't have to.

TONY: Mr. Fleming, it's Billy's last chance. He's almost fifteen now. If we wait longer, the muscles will become atrophied and it will be too late. Professor Doyle said—

BRECKENRIDGE: Did Professor Doyle say also that we'd risk Billy's life in that operation?

TONY: Yes.

BRECKENRIDGE: That's my answer.

HELEN: Walter, please. Please let's reconsider. Professor Doyle said the risk wasn't too great. It's a small chance against . . . against the certainty of being a cripple for life!

BRECKENRIDGE: A small chance is too much—where Billy is concerned. I would rather have Billy as he is than take the risk of losing him.

FLEMING: [*Screams ferociously*] That's going too far, you lousy bastard! You won't get away with this! Goddamn you, not with this! I demand, do you hear me?—I *demand* that you let them do the operation!

BRECKENRIDGE: You demand? By what right? [FLEMING *stands looking at him, helplessness coming almost visibly to his gaunt, slumping figure*]

INGALLS: [*His voice hard*] Do you mind if I don't witness this? [*Turns and exits through the French doors*]

BRECKENRIDGE: I must warn you, Harvey. If we have any more . . . incidents such as this, I shall be forced to forbid you to visit Billy.

HELEN: Oh, no, Walter!

FLEMING: You . . . wouldn't do that, Walter? You . . . you *can't.*

BRECKENRIDGE: You know very well that I can.

BILLY: [*It is the first time that his voice is alive—and desperate*] Father! You won't do *that*! [*As* BRECKENRIDGE *turns to him*] Please, Father. I don't mind anything else. I don't have to have the operation. Only you won't . . . Mr. Fleming, it's all right about the operation. I don't mind.

BRECKENRIDGE: Of course, Billy. And I'm sorry that Harvey upsets you so much. You understand. Anything I do is only for your own good. I wouldn't take a chance on your life with some unproved new method. [*As* HELEN *is about to speak*] And so, Helen, we shall consider the matter closed.

[FLEMING *turns abruptly. On his way to the stairs, he seizes a bottle from the sideboard and exits up the stairs*]

FLASH: Well, *I* think this is one hell of a birthday party!

BRECKENRIDGE: We mustn't mind poor Harvey. He is an unfortunate case. [*Looks at his watch*] And now we'll turn to a much more cheerful subject. [*Rises*] Billy, my dear, just watch the lake. You'll see something interesting in a few minutes. [*To the others*] Now, please, I don't want anyone to follow me. I don't want anyone to see how it's done. Not till tomorrow. You'll get the best view from here. [*Turns at the French doors*] Who knows? Perhaps what you are about to see will be of great importance to all mankind. [*Exits through French doors and walks off Right into the garden*]

HELEN: [*Rises suddenly as if with a decision taken, starts toward the stairs, then stops and says to the others, vaguely, as an afterthought:*] You will excuse me, please? . . . [*Exits up the stairs*]

TONY: I'm sorry, Bill. I've tried.

BILLY: It's all right. . . . When you'll be a doctor on your own, Tony, I'll still be . . . like this. And then I'd like you to be my doctor.

TONY: [*With an oddly stressed bitterness*] When I'll be . . . a doctor. . . .

BILLY: Everybody says you'll be a good one. Father says very nice things about you. About your hands, too. He says you have the hands of a great surgeon.

TONY: [*Looks at his hands*] Yes . . . he does . . . doesn't he? [*Turns abruptly to go*]

FLASH: Say, don't you want to see the fireworks?

TONY: Oh, take your fireworks and shove— [*Exits Right*]

FLASH: [*Looking after him with open mouth*] Well, *I* think he meant . . .

ADRIENNE: Yes, Flash. He meant exactly what you think.

[*From offstage Right there comes the sound of Rachmaninoff's Prelude in G Minor played on the piano*]

BILLY: Don't go, Miss Knowland. Everybody's going.

ADRIENNE: I'll stay, Bill. Let's open the doors and turn out the light, we'll see better. [*She turns the light off, while* FLASH *throws the French doors open*]

BILLY: Why does Tony always play such sad things?

ADRIENNE: Because he's very unhappy, Bill.

FLASH: You know, I can't figure it out. Nobody's happy in this house.

BILLY: Father is happy. [*A magnificent rocket rises over the lake, much closer than the ones we've seen, and bursts into showers of stars*]

FLASH: There it goes!

BILLY: Oh! . . . . [*The rockets continue at slow intervals*]

FLASH: [*Excitedly, between the sounds of the explosions*] You see, Billy . . . you see . . . that's your father's new invention! . . . It works! . . . Those rockets are set off without any wires . . . without touching them . . . just like that, through space. . . . Imagine? Just some sort of tiny little rays blasting those things to pieces!

ADRIENNE: Lovely precision . . . right on target. . . . What if one chose a larger . . . [*Then, suddenly, she gasps; it is almost a stifled scream*]

FLASH: What's the matter?

ADRIENNE: [*In a strange voice*] I . . . just thought of something. . . . [*She is suddenly panicky, as she makes a movement to rush out, stops helplessly before the vast darkness of the garden, whirls around to ask:*] Where's Walter? Where did he go?

FLASH: I don't know. We're not supposed to follow him.

ADRIENNE: Where's Steve?

FLASH: Don't know. I think he went out.

ADRIENNE: [*Screaming into the garden*] Steve! . . . Steve! . . .

FLASH: He won't hear you. This place is so big, there's miles and miles to the grounds, you can't find anybody out there at night.

ADRIENNE: I've got to—
BILLY: Look, Miss Knowland! *Look!*

[*The fireworks are now forming letters, high over the lake, taking shape gradually, one tiny dot of light after another. The letters spell out:* "GOD BLESS . . ."]

ADRIENNE: I've got to find Walter!
FLASH: Miss Knowland! Don't! Mr. Breckenridge will be angry!

[ADRIENNE *rushes out and disappears Left into the garden. The fireworks continue to spell:* "GOD BLESS AMER . . ." *Then, suddenly, the last dot of light flashes on with a jerk, spreads out, the letters tremble, smear, and vanish altogether. There is nothing but darkness and silence*]

Well! . . . what's the matter? . . . What happened? . . . [*They wait. Nothing happens*] Well, I guess maybe the invention's not right yet. Something's gone screwy there. Maybe the great discovery's not so perfect. . . .
BILLY: It will start again in a minute.
FLASH: Maybe the old-fashioned way is best. [*They wait. Nothing happens*] Say, Bill. What's the matter with everybody in this house?
BILLY: Nothing.
FLASH: I can't figure it out. You're the nicest people I ever lived with. But there's something wrong. Very wrong.
BILLY: Skip it, Flash.
FLASH: Now take you, for instance. That operation. You wanted it pretty badly?
BILLY: I guess maybe I did. . . . I don't know . . . I don't know how it really feels to want things. I've been trying to learn not to.
FLASH: Bill, what do you want most in the world?
BILLY: I? . . . [*Thinks for a moment, then:*] I guess . . . I guess to get a glass of water.
FLASH: *What?* Want me to get you a drink?
BILLY: No. You don't understand. To get a glass of water—

myself. [FLASH *stares at him*] You see what I mean? To
get thirsty and not to have to tell anybody about it, but to
walk down to the kitchen, and turn the faucet, and fill a
glass, and drink it. Not to need anybody, not to thank
anybody, not to ask for it. To *get* it. Flash. You don't
know how important it is—not to need anybody.

FLASH: But people *want* to help you.

BILLY: Flash, when it's—everything, all the time, everything I do . . . I can't be thirsty—alone, without telling
somebody. I can't be hungry—alone. I'm not a person.
I'm only something being helped. . . . If I could stand
up just once—stand up on my own feet and tell them all
to go to hell! Oh, Flash, I wouldn't tell them to! But just
to know that I could! Just once!

FLASH: Well, what for, if you wouldn't? You don't make
sense. People are very kind to you and—[*There is the
sound of a distant explosion in the garden*] There! There
it goes again! [*Looks out. There is nothing but darkness*]
No. Guess it was a dud.

BILLY: They're kind to me. It's such a horrible thing—that
sort of kindness. Sometimes I want to be nasty just to
have somebody snap at me. But they won't. They don't
respect me enough to get angry. I'm not important
enough to resent. I'm only something to be kind to.

FLASH: *Listen,* how about that glass of water? Do you want
me to get it or don't you?

BILLY: [*His head dropping, his voice dull*] Yes. Get me a
glass of water.

FLASH: Look, water's not good for you. How about my fixing you some nice hot chocolate and a little toast?

BILLY: Yes.

FLASH: That's what I said: nobody ate anything tonight.
All that grand dinner going to waste. It's a crazy house.
[*Turns at the door*] Want the light on?

BILLY: No. [FLASH *exits Right.* BILLY *sits alone for a moment, without moving, his head down.* INGALLS *enters
from the garden*]

INGALLS: Hello, Bill. What are you doing here alone in the
dark? [*Switches the light on*] The fireworks over?

BILLY: Something went wrong. They stopped.

INGALLS: Oh? Where's Walter?

BILLY: Fixing it, I guess. He hasn't come back. [*As IN-GALLS turns to the stairs*] Steve.

INGALLS: Yes?

BILLY: Steve, do you know why I like you? . . . Because you've never been kind to me.

INGALLS: But I want to be kind to you, kid.

BILLY: That's not what I mean. You couldn't be what . . . what I'm talking about. I mean, people who use kindness like some sort of weapon. . . . Steve! It's a horrible weapon. I think it's worse than poison gas. It gets in deeper, it hurts more, and there's no gas mask to wear against it. Because people would say you're wicked to want such a mask.

INGALLS: Bill. Listen to me. It doesn't matter. Even your legs and the wheelchair—it doesn't matter, so long as you don't let anyone into your mind. Keep your mind, Bill—keep it free and keep it your own. Don't let anyone help you—inside. Don't let anyone tell you what you must think. Don't let anyone tell you what you must feel. Don't ever let them put your soul in a wheelchair. Then you'll be all right, no matter what they do.

BILLY: You understand. Steve, you're the only one who understands. [*FLASH enters Right*]

FLASH: Come on, Bill. The grub's ready. Do you want it here?

BILLY: I'm not hungry. Take me to my room, please. I'm tired.

FLASH: Aw, hell! After I went to all the bother—

BILLY: Please, Flash. [*FLASH starts wheeling the chair out*] Good night, Steve.

INGALLS: Good night, kid. [*FLASH and BILLY exit, and we hear TONY's voice in the next room*]

TONY'S VOICE: Going, Billy? Good night.

BILLY'S VOICE: Good night. [*TONY enters Right*]

TONY: What about the great fireworks? All over?

INGALLS: I guess so. Billy said something went wrong.

TONY: You didn't watch them?

INGALLS: No.

TONY: I didn't either.

[HELEN *appears at the top of the stairs. She has her hat and coat on, and carries a small suitcase. She stops short, seeing the two men below, then comes resolutely down the stairs*]

INGALLS: Helen? Where are you going?

HELEN: Back to town.

TONY: *Now?*

HELEN: Yes.

INGALLS: But, Helen—

HELEN: Please don't ask me any questions. I didn't know that someone would still be here. I wanted to . . . I wanted not to have to talk to anyone.

INGALLS: But what's happened?

HELEN: Later, Steve. Later. I'll talk to you afterward. To-morrow, in town, if you wish. I'll explain. Please don't—

[*From a distance in the garden there comes* ADRIENNE'S *scream—a horrified scream. They whirl to the French doors*]

INGALLS: Where's Adrienne?

HELEN: I don't know. She—

[INGALLS *rushes out into the garden.* TONY *follows him.* FLASH *comes running in, Right*]

FLASH: What was that?

HELEN: I . . . don't . . . know. . . .

FLASH: Miss Knowland! It's Miss Knowland! [CURTISS *enters Right*]

CURTISS: Madam! What happened!

[INGALLS, TONY, *and* ADRIENNE *enter from the garden.* INGALLS *is supporting* ADRIENNE. *She is trembling and out of breath*]

INGALLS: All right. Take it easy. Now what is it?

ADRIENNE: It's Walter . . . out there . . . in the garden. . . . He's dead. [*Silence, as they all look at her*] It was dark . . . I couldn't see. . . . He was lying on his face. . . . And then I ran. . . . I think he's shot. . . . [HELEN *gasps and sinks into a chair*]

INGALLS: Did you touch anything?

ADRIENNE: No . . . no. . . .

INGALLS: Curtiss.

CURTISS: Yes, sir?

INGALLS: Go down there. Stand by. Don't touch anything. And don't let anyone near.

CURTISS: Yes, sir.

ADRIENNE: [*Pointing*] There . . . to the left . . . down the path. . . . [CURTISS *exits into the garden*]

INGALLS: Tony, take Helen to her room. Flash, go to Billy. Don't tell him. Put him to bed.

FLASH: Y-yes, sir.

[*Exits Right.* TONY *helps* HELEN *up the stairs and they exit, while* INGALLS *reaches for the telephone*]

ADRIENNE: Steve! What are you doing?

INGALLS: [*Into phone*] Operator? . . .

ADRIENNE: Steve! Wait!

INGALLS: [*Into phone*] Give me District Attorney Hastings.

ADRIENNE: No! . . . Wait! . . . Steve, I—

INGALLS: [*Into phone*] Hello, Greg? Steve Ingalls speaking. From the house of Walter Breckenridge. Mr. Breckenridge has been—[ADRIENNE *seizes his arm. He pushes her aside, not violently, but firmly*]—murdered. . . . Yes. . . . Yes, I shall. . . . Yes, the new house. . . . [*Hangs up*]

ADRIENNE: Steve . . . you wouldn't let me tell you . . .

INGALLS: Well? What is it?

ADRIENNE: [*Pulls a man's handkerchief from her pocket and hands it to him*] This. [*He looks at the initials on the handkerchief*] It's yours.

INGALLS: Yes.

ADRIENNE: It was caught on a branch—there—near the . . . body.

INGALLS: [*Looks at the handkerchief, then at her*] It's good evidence, Adrienne. [*Slips the handkerchief calmly into his pocket*] It's evidence that you still love me—in spite of everything—in spite of what happened this afternoon.

ADRIENNE: [*Stiffening*] Merely circumstantial evidence.

INGALLS: Oh, yes. But one can do a lot with circumstantial evidence.

CURTAIN

ACT II

SCENE 1

*Half an hour later. Before the curtain rises we hear the
sound of Chopin's "Butterfly Etude" played on the piano. It is played violently, exultantly—the gay notes
dancing in laughter and release. The music continues
as the curtain rises.*

*STEVE INGALLS is alone on stage. He is pacing the
room impatiently; he glances at his wristwatch. Then
there is the sound of a car driving up. He looks out. He
walks to the entrance door Left and throws it open suddenly, at the right moment, before the bell is rung.
SERGE stands outside.*

SERGE: [*As he enters, angrily*] How thoughtful of you.
[*Pulls the* Courier *out of his pocket and throws it to him*]
There is nothing in the *Courier* about the Soviet Culture
and Friendship Society. Or the FBI.

INGALLS: No?

SERGE: No! I make all the long trip for nothing.

INGALLS: [*Glancing through the paper*] Guess Joe
Cheeseman gave me the wrong dope.

SERGE: And where is everybody? [*INGALLS slips the paper
into his pocket and doesn't answer*] Why is it in the
house all the windows dark? [*INGALLS stands watching
him silently*] What is the matter?

INGALLS: Serge.

SERGE: Yes?

INGALLS: Mr. Breckenridge has been murdered.

SERGE: [*Stands stock-still for a long moment, then emits one short, sick gasp—like a moan. Then snaps hoarsely and crudely:*] You are crazy! . . .

INGALLS: [*Without moving*] Mr. Breckenridge is lying dead in the garden.

SERGE: [*Sinks down into a chair, his head in his hands, and moans*] Boje moy! . . . Boje moy! . . .

INGALLS: Save it for the others, Serge. Save it for an audience.

SERGE: [*Jerks his head up, his voice harsh and deadly*] Who did it?

INGALLS: You. Or I. Or any of us.

SERGE: [*Jumping up, ferociously*] *I?!*

INGALLS: Pipe down, Serge. You see, it's the one question that none of us must ask—under the circumstances. Leave that to Greg Hastings.

SERGE: Who?

INGALLS: Greg Hastings. The district attorney. He will be here any moment. I'm sure he'll answer your question. He always does.

SERGE: I hope he's good, I hope—

INGALLS: He's very good. Not one unsolved murder in his whole career. You see, he doesn't believe that there can be such a thing as a perfect crime.

SERGE: I hope he should find the monster, the fiend, the unspeakable—

INGALLS: Let me give you a tip, Serge. Cut down on that kind of stuff around Greg Hastings. I know him quite well. He won't fall for the obvious. He'll always look further than that. He's clever. Too clever.

SERGE: [*His voice rising angrily*] But why do you say this to *me*? Why do you look at me? You do not think that *I* . . .

INGALLS: I haven't even begun to think, Serge. [TONY *enters Right*]

TONY: [*Gaily*] The cops arrived? [*Sees* SERGE] Oh, it's you, Serge, old boy, old pal.

SERGE: [*Startled*] I beg your pardon?

TONY: You look wonderful. The ride's done you good. It's wonderful to drive fast at night, against the wind, with nothing to stop you! To drive fast, so fast—and free!

SERGE: [*Aghast*] But what is this? [*Whirls on* INGALLS] Oh, I see! It was the joke. It was the horrible joke from *you*. . . . [*To* TONY] Mr. Breckenridge he is not dead?

TONY: [*Lightly*] Oh yes, Mr. Breckenridge is dead. Dead as a doornail. Dead as a tombstone. Good and dead.

SERGE: [*To* INGALLS] He has lost his mind!

INGALLS: Or just found it. [HELEN *enters, coming down the stairs*]

HELEN: Tony, why did you—

SERGE: Oh, Mrs. Breckenridge! Permit me to express the deepest sympathy at this terrible—

HELEN: Thank you, Serge. [*Her manner is now simple, young, more natural than it has ever been*] Why did you stop playing, Tony? It was so lovely. I've never heard you play like this before.

TONY: But you will hear me again. You will—for years—and years—and years—[INGALLS *exits up the stairs*]

SERGE: Mrs. Breckenridge—

HELEN: I will give you a piano, Tony. Now. Tomorrow.

[*There is the distant sound of a police siren approaching.* SERGE *looks up nervously. The others pay no attention*]

TONY: You won't give me a piano! Nobody's going to give me anything ever again! I think I can get a job at Gimbel's, and I will, and I'll save three dollars a week, and in a year I'll have a piano—a good, secondhand piano of my own! . . . But I like you, Helen.

HELEN: Yes. Forgive me.

SERGE: Mrs. Breckenridge! . . . What has happened?

HELEN: We don't know, Serge.

TONY: What's the difference?

SERGE: But who did it?

TONY: Who cares?

[*Doorbell rings.* TONY *opens the door.* GREGORY HAS-TINGS *enters. He is a man in his early forties, tall, suave, distinguished, and self-possessed. He enters calmly, he speaks quietly, as naturally and undramatically as possible—without overdoing it. He enters, stops, looks at* HELEN]

HASTINGS: Mrs. Breckenridge?

HELEN: Yes.

HASTINGS: [*Bowing*] Gregory Hastings.

HELEN: How do you do, Mr. Hastings.

HASTINGS: I am truly sorry, Mrs. Breckenridge, that I should have to be here tonight.

HELEN: We'll be glad to help you in any way we can, Mr. Hastings. If you wish to question us—

HASTINGS: A little later. First, I shall have to see the scene of—

HELEN: [*Pointing*] In the garden. . . . Tony, will you show—

HASTINGS: It won't be necessary. I'll keep my men out of your way as much as possible. [*Exits Left*]

TONY: This is going to be interesting.

SERGE: But . . . you are inhuman!

TONY: Probably. [INGALLS *enters, coming down the stairs*]

INGALLS: Was that Greg Hastings?

TONY: Yes. The police.

INGALLS: Where are they?

TONY: [*Pointing to garden*] Sniffing at footprints, I guess.

SERGE: There will not be any footprints. There will not be anything. It is going to be terrible.

INGALLS: How do you know there won't be anything, Serge?

SERGE: There never is in a case like this.

INGALLS: You never can tell. [*Pulls the* Courier *out of his pocket*] Anyone here want the evening paper that Serge was nice enough to bring us?

TONY: [*Taking the paper*] Does the Courier have any comic strips? I love comic strips. [*Turns the paper to the funny page*] They don't have "Little Orphan Annie," though. That's my favorite—"Little Orphan Annie."

HELEN: [*Looking over his shoulder*] I like "Popeye the Sailor."

TONY: Oh, no! Annie's better. But Popeye has his points—particularly when they bring in Mr. Wimpy. Mr. Wimpy is good.

HELEN: Lord Plushbottom is good, too.

TONY: Lord Plushbottom is from another strip.

SERGE: *That's* what I drive the three-quarters of an hour for!

HELEN: Oh, yes, Serge, wasn't there some story you wanted to read?

SERGE: There was! But there isn't! Not a word in the damn paper about the Soviet Culture and Friendship Society!

TONY: And not even "Little Orphan Annie" or "Popeye the Sailor."

[FLEMING *comes down the stairs. He is sober and walks calmly, steadily. There is an air about him as if he were holding his head up for the first time in his life. His clothes are still disreputable, but he is shaved and his tie is straight*]

FLEMING: Steve, you won't—by any chance—need a janitor down at the laboratory?

INGALLS: No. But we will need an engineer.

FLEMING: A has-been engineer?

INGALLS: No. A *shall-be* engineer.

FLEMING: [*Looks at him, then in a low voice:*] Steve, you're—

INGALLS:—a cold-blooded egoist. I've never been called anything else. I wouldn't know what to do if I were. Let it go at that.

FLEMING: [*Nods slowly, solemnly. Then sits down and picks up part of the newspaper*] The police are out there in the garden. Guess they'll want us all here.

INGALLS: Yes, it won't be long now.

SERGE: [*Walks to sideboard, pours himself a drink*] Do you want a drink, Mr. Fleming?

FLEMING: [*With slow emphasis*] No, thank you.

SERGE: [*Swallows a stiff drink in one gulp. Then:*] The laboratory—who will run it now?

INGALLS: I will.

SERGE: And . . . what is to happen to the invention?

INGALLS: Ah, yes, the invention. Well, Serge, only two men knew the secret of that invention—Walter and I. Walter is dead.

SERGE: He wanted to give it to mankind.

INGALLS: He did. Now I'm going to sit and loaf and collect a fortune. It's too bad about mankind.

SERGE: You have no respect for the wishes of a—

INGALLS: I have no respect for anything, Serge.

SERGE: [*Cautiously*] But if you should now carry out the wish of Mr. Breckenridge—then perhaps the police will not think that *you* had a reason to kill him.

INGALLS: Oh, but Serge! You wouldn't suggest that I try to deceive the police, would you? [HASTINGS *enters from the garden. His face looks earnest*]

HASTINGS: Mrs. Breckenridge . . . [*Sees* INGALLS] Oh, hello, Steve.

INGALLS: Hello, Greg.

HASTINGS: I'm glad you're here. It will make things easier for me.

INGALLS: Or harder—if I did it.

HASTINGS: Or hopeless, if you did it. But I know one or two things already which seem to let you out. [*To* HELEN] Mrs. Breckenridge, I'm sorry, but certain facts make it necessary for everyone here to be fingerprinted.

HELEN: Of course. I'm sure none of us will object.

HASTINGS: If you will please ask everybody to step into the library—my assistant is there with the necessary equipment. After that I should like to have everybody here.

HELEN: Very well.

HASTINGS: Steve, will you please go down there—[*Points to the garden*]—and take a look at that electrical apparatus that Breckenridge was operating? I have the butler's statement about the invention and the fireworks display that was interrupted. I want to know what interrupted it. I want you to tell me whether that machine is out of order in any way.

INGALLS: Will you take my word for it?

HASTINGS: I'll have to. You're the only one who can tell us. Besides, my men are there and they'll be watching you. But first, come to the library and get fingerprinted.

INGALLS: All right.

[*They all exit, Right.* HELEN *is the last to go. She turns out the lights, then follows the others. The stage is dark and empty for a few moments. Then a man's figure enters Right. We cannot see who it is. The man gathers quickly all the sheets of the newspaper, twists them into one roll, and kneels by the fireplace. He strikes a match and sets fire to the paper. We see his two hands, but nothing else. He lets the paper burn halfway, then blows out the fire. Then he rises and exits Right*]

[*After a moment,* HELEN *and* HASTINGS *come back, Right.* HELEN *turns on the light. We can see part of the rolled newspaper among the logs in the fireplace*]

HASTINGS: May I apologize in advance, Mrs. Breckenridge, for anything that I might have to say or do? I'm afraid this is going to be a difficult case.

HELEN: Will you forgive me if I say that I *hope* it will be a difficult case?

HASTINGS: You do not wish me to find the murderer?

HELEN: I suppose I should, but . . . No. I don't.

HASTINGS: It might mean that you know who it is. Or—it could mean something much worse.

HELEN: I don't know who it is. As to the "much worse"— well, we'll all deny that, so I don't think my denial would be worth more than any of the others. [CURTISS *enters Right*]

CURTISS: Mr. Hastings, could you ask the coroner please to attend to Mrs. Pudget?

HELEN: Good God, Curtiss! You don't mean that Mrs. Pudget has been—

CURTISS: Oh no, madam. But Mrs. Pudget has a bad case of hysterics. [FLEMING *and* SERGE *enter Right*]

HASTINGS: What's the matter with her?

CURTISS: She says that she positively refuses to work for people who get murdered.

HASTINGS: All right, ask the coroner to give her a pill. Then come back here.

CURTISS: Yes, sir. [*Exits Right*]

HASTINGS: [*To* HELEN] I understand that your son witnessed the fireworks from this room?

HELEN: Yes, I believe so.

HASTINGS: Then I'm afraid I shall have to ask you to have him brought here.

FLEMING: And get him out of bed? At this hour? [HASTINGS *looks at him with curiosity*]

HELEN: But of course, Harvey. It can't be avoided. It's quite all right. I'll ask Flash to bring him down.

FLEMING: *I* will. [*Exits Right, as* TONY *enters*]

HASTINGS: [*To* HELEN] Do you know why I think this case is going to be difficult? Because motive is always the most important thing. Motive is the key to any case. And I'm afraid I'll have a hard time finding one single motive among all the people here. I can't imagine any reason for killing a man of Mr. Breckenridge's character.

HELEN: Neither could Walter. And I hope whoever did it told him the reason before he died. [*He looks at her, astonished*] Yes, I'm really as cruel as that—though I didn't know it before. [ADRIENNE *enters Right. She is pale, tense and barely able to control herself*]

TONY: I didn't know fingerprinting was as simple as that, did you, Adrienne? Wasn't it fun?

ADRIENNE: [*Curtly*] No.

TONY: [*Taken aback*] Oh . . . I'm sorry, Adrienne. . . . But I thought . . . you'd be the one to feel better than any of us.

ADRIENNE: [*Bitterly*] Oh, you did?

HELEN: Adrienne, may I get you a drink?

ADRIENNE: [*Looks at her with hatred. Then, to* HASTINGS:] Get this over with, will you, so I can get out of here?

HASTINGS: I shall try, Miss Knowland. [INGALLS *enters from the garden*] What about the machine, Steve?

INGALLS: In perfect order.

HASTINGS: Nothing the matter with it?

INGALLS: Nothing.

HASTINGS: Doesn't look as if anybody had tried to monkey with it?

INGALLS: No. [CURTISS *enters Right*]

HASTINGS: Now, I should like to ask you all to sit down and be as comfortable as we can be under the circumstances. I won't have a stenographer taking down anybody's words or gestures. I shan't need that. Let's just relax and talk sensibly. [*To* HELEN] Is everybody here now?

HELEN: Yes, except Billy and his tutor and Mr. Fleming.

HASTINGS: Now as to the servants—there are the butler, the cook and her husband, the chauffeur. Is that all?

HELEN: Yes.

HASTINGS: And—who are the nearest neighbors?

HELEN: I . . . don't know.

INGALLS: The nearest house is two miles away.

HASTINGS: I see. All right. Now we can begin. As you see, I don't believe in conducting an investigation behind closed doors and trying to play people against one another. I prefer to keep everything in the open. I know that none of you will want to talk. But my job requires that I make you talk. So I shall start by giving you all an example. I don't believe it's necesssry—though it's usually done—to keep from you the facts in my possession. What for? The murderer knows them—and the others should want to help me. Therefore, I shall tell you what I know so far. [*Pauses. Then:*] Mr. Breckenridge was shot—in the back. The shot was fired at some distance—there are no powder burns around the wound. The body was lying quite a few steps away from the electrical machine which Mr. Breckenridge was using for the fireworks display. The watch on Mr. Breckenridge's wrist was broken and stopped at four minutes past ten. There was nothing but grass and soft earth where the body had fallen, so the watch crystal could not have been smashed like that by the fall. It looks as if someone stepped on the watch. The gun was lying on the ground, near the machine. Curtiss has identified it as Mr. Breckenridge's own gun. Only one shot had been fired. The gun shows an excellent set of fingerprints. We shall soon know whether they are the prints of anyone here. That's all—so far. Now I should like to— [FLEMING *and* FLASH *enter Right wheeling* BILLY *in.* BILLY *wears a bathrobe over his pajamas*]

HELEN: This is Billy, Mr. Hastings.

HASTINGS: How do you do, Billy. I'm sorry I had to get you out of bed.

HELEN: [*Looks questioningly at* FLEMING, *who shakes his head. She turns to* BILLY, *says gently:*] Billy, dear, you must try to be calm and grown-up about what I'm going to tell you. It's about Father. You see, dear, there was an accident and . . . and . . .

BILLY: You mean he's dead?

HELEN: Yes, dear.

BILLY: You mean he's been murdered?

HELEN: You mustn't say that. We don't know. We're trying to find out what happened.

BILLY: [*Very simply*] I'm glad. [*Silence as they all look at him. Then:*]

HASTINGS: [*Softly*] Why did you say that, Billy?

BILLY: [*Very simply*] Because he wanted to keep me a cripple.

HASTINGS: [*This is too much even for him*] Billy . . . how can you think such a thing?

BILLY: That's all he wanted me for in the first place.

HASTINGS: What do you mean?

BILLY: [*In a flat monotone*] He wanted a cripple because a cripple has to depend on him. If you spend your time helping people, you've got to have people to help. If everybody were independent, what would happen to the people who've got to help everybody?

FLEMING: [*To* HASTINGS, *angrily*] Will you stop this? Ask him whatever you have to ask and let him go.

HASTINGS: [*Looks at him, then:*] What's your name?

FLEMING: Harvey Fleming.

HASTINGS: [*Turns to* BILLY] Billy, what made you think that about Mr. Breckenridge?

BILLY: [*Looks at him, almost contemptuously, as if the answer were too enormous and too obvious. Then says wearily:*] Today, for instance.

HASTINGS: What happened today?

BILLY: They asked him to let me have an operation—the last thing they could do for me or I'd never walk at all. He wouldn't. He wouldn't, even when—[*Looks at* FLEMING. *Stops short*]

HASTINGS: [*Softly*] Even when—what, Billy?

BILLY: That's all.

FLEMING: Say it, kid. It's all right. Even when I cursed him and threatened him.

HASTINGS: You did? [*Looks at him, then:*] Mr. Fleming, why are you so concerned about Billy?

FLEMING: [*Astonished by the question, as if his answer were a well-known fact*] Why? Because I'm his father. [HASTINGS *turns to look at* HELEN] No, not what your dirty mind is thinking. I thought you knew. They all know. Billy's my own legitimate son—and my wife's. My wife is dead. Walter adopted him five years ago. [HASTINGS *looks at him, startled.* FLEMING *takes it for reproach and continues angrily:*] Don't tell me I was a Goddamn fool to agree to it. I know I was. But I didn't know it then. How was I to know? [*Points at the others*] How were any of them to know what would happen to them? I was out of work. My wife had just died. Billy'd had infantile paralysis for a year. I'd have given anything to cure him. I gave all I had to give—I gave *him* up, when Walter asked to adopt him. Walter was rich. Walter could afford the best doctors. Walter had been so kind to us. When I saw what it really was—it took me two years to begin to guess—there was nothing I could do . . . nothing. . . . Walter owned him.

HASTINGS: [*Slowly*] I see.

FLEMING: No, you don't. Do you know that we came from the same small town, Walter and I? That we had no money, neither one of us? That I was the brilliant student in school and Walter hated me for it? That people said I'd be a great engineer, and I'd made a good beginning, only I didn't have Walter's gift for using people? That he wanted to see me down, as far down as a man can go? That he helped me when I was out of work—because he knew it would keep me out of work, because he knew I was drinking—when my wife died—and I didn't care—and it seemed so easy. . . . He knew I'd never work again, when he took the last thing I had away from me—when he took Billy to make it easier for me—to make it easier! If you want to finish a man, just take all burdens—and all goals—away from him! . . . He gave me money—all these years—and I took it. I took it! [*Stops. Then says, in a low, dead voice:*] Listen. I didn't kill Walter Breckenridge. But I would have slept prouder—all the rest of my life—if it was I who'd killed him.

HASTINGS: [*Turns slowly to* HELEN] Mrs. Breckenridge . . .

HELEN: [*Her voice flat, expressionless*] It's true. All of it. You see, we couldn't have any children, Walter and I. I had always wanted a child. I remember I told him once—I was watching children playing in a park—I told him that I wanted a child, a child's running feet in the house. . . . Then he adopted Billy. . . . [*Silence*]

BILLY: [*To* FLEMING] I didn't want to say anything . . . Dad. . . . [*To* HELEN, *a little frightened*] It's all right, now?

HELEN: [*Her voice barely audible*] Yes, dear. . . . You know it wasn't I who demanded that you . . . [*She doesn't finish*]

BILLY: [*To* FLEMING] I'm sorry, Dad. . . .

FLEMING: [*Puts his hand on* BILLY'S *shoulder, and* BILLY *buries his face against* FLEMING'S *arm*] It's all right, Bill. Everything will be all right now. . . . [*Silence*]

HASTINGS: I'm sorry, Mr. Fleming. I almost wish you hadn't told me. Because, you see, you did have a good motive.

FLEMING: [*Simply, indifferently*] I thought everybody knew I had.

TONY: What of it? He wasn't the only one.

HASTINGS: No? And what is your name?

TONY: Tony Goddard.

HASTINGS: Now, Mr. Goddard, when you make a statement of that kind, you're usually asked to—

TONY:—finish it? What do you suppose I started for? You won't have to question me. I'll tell you. It's very simple. I'm not sure you'll understand, but I don't care. [*Stretches his hands out*] Look at my hands. Mr. Breckenridge told me that they were the hands of a great surgeon. He told me how much good I could do, how many suffering people I could help—and he gave me a scholarship in a medical college. A very generous scholarship.

HASTINGS: Well?

TONY: That's all. Except that I hate medicine more than anything else in the world. And what I wanted to be was a pianist. [HASTINGS *looks at him.* TONY *continues, calmly, bitterly:*] All right, say I was a weakling. Who wouldn't be? I was poor—and very lonely. Nobody had ever taken an interest in me before. Nobody seemed to care whether I lived or died. I had a long struggle ahead of me—and I wasn't even sure that I had any musical talent. How can you ever be sure at the beginning? And the road looks so long and so hopeless—and you're hurt so often. And he told me it was a selfish choice, and that I'd be so much more useful to men as a doctor, and he was so kind to me, and he made it sound so right.

HASTINGS: But why wouldn't he help you through a music school, instead?

TONY: [*Looks at him, almost pityingly, like an older man at a child, says wearily, without bitterness:*] Why? [*Shrugs in resignation*] Mr. Hastings, if you want to have men dependent on you, don't allow them to be happy. Happy men are free men.

HASTINGS: But if you were unhappy, why didn't you leave it all? What held you?

TONY: [*In the same wise, tired voice*] Mr. Hastings, you don't know what a ghastly weapon kindness can be.

When you're up against an enemy, you can fight him. But when you're up against a friend, a gentle, kindly, smiling friend—you turn against yourself. You think that you're low and ungrateful. It's the best in you that destroys you. That's what's horrible about it. . . . And it takes you a long time to understand. I think I understood it only today.

HASTINGS: Why?

TONY: I don't know. Everything. The house, the horse, the gift to mankind . . . [*Turns to the others*] One of us here is the murderer. I don't know who it is. I hope I never learn—for his sake. But I want him to know that I'm grateful . . . so terribly grateful. . . . [*Silence*]

HASTINGS: [*Turns to* INGALLS] Steve?

INGALLS: Yes?

HASTINGS: What did *you* think of Walter Breckenridge?

INGALLS: [*In a calm, perfectly natural voice*] I loathed him in every way and for every reason possible. You can make any motive you wish out of that. [HASTINGS *looks at him*]

ADRIENNE: Stop staring at him like that. People usually prefer to look at me. Besides, I'm not accustomed to playing a supporting part.

HASTINGS: You, Miss Knowland? But *you* didn't hate Mr. Breckenridge.

ADRIENNE: *No?*

HASTINGS: But—why?

ADRIENNE: Because he kept me doing a noble, useful work which I couldn't stand. Because he had a genius for finding people of talent and for the best way of destroying them. Because he held me all right—with a five-year contract. Today, I begged him to let me go. He refused. We had a violent quarrel. Ask Steve. He heard me screaming.

HELEN: Adrienne, I'm so sorry. I didn't know about this.

ADRIENNE: [*Looks at her, doesn't answer, turns to* HASTINGS] How soon will you allow us to leave? It was bad enough staying here when it was Walter's house. I won't stand it for very long—when it's hers.

HASTINGS: *Why,* Miss Knowland?

TONY: Adrienne, we don't have to—

ADRIENNE: Oh, what's the difference? He'll hear about it sooner or later, so he might as well have it now. [*To* HASTINGS] This afternoon, Walter and I and the others came in from the garden just in time to interrupt a love scene, a very beautiful love scene, between Helen and Steve. I've never been able to get any leading man of mine to kiss me like that. [*To* HELEN] Was Steve as good at it as he looked, my dear? [HELEN *stands staring at her, frozen.* ADRIENNE *whirls to* HASTINGS] You didn't know that?

HASTINGS: No. I didn't know either of these two very interesting facts.

ADRIENNE: Two?

HASTINGS: First—the love scene. Second—that it should have impressed you in this particular manner.

ADRIENNE: Well, you know it now.

INGALLS: Adrienne, you'd better stop it.

ADRIENNE: Stop what?

INGALLS: What you're doing.

ADRIENNE: You don't know what I'm doing.

INGALLS: Oh, yes, I think I do.

HASTINGS: Well, I don't know if any of you noticed it, but I've made one mistake about this case already. I thought nobody would want to talk.

INGALLS: I noticed it.

HASTINGS: You would. [*Turns to* BILLY] Now, Billy, I'll try not to hold you here too long. But you were here in this room all evening, weren't you?

BILLY: Yes.

HASTINGS: Now I want you to tell me everything you remember, who left this room and when.

BILLY: Well, I think . . . I think Steve left first. When we were talking about the operation. He walked out.

HASTINGS: Where did he go?

BILLY: In the garden.

HASTINGS: Who went next?

BILLY: It was Dad. He went upstairs.

FLASH: And he took a bottle from the sideboard with him.

HASTINGS: You're Billy's tutor, aren't you?

FLASH: Yes. Flash Kozinsky—Stanislaw Kozinsky.

HASTINGS: And you stayed here with Billy all evening?

FLASH: Yes.

HASTINGS: Now who went next?

BILLY: Mr. Breckenridge. He went into the garden. And he said that he didn't want anybody to follow him.

HASTINGS: What time was that?

FLASH: About ten o'clock.

HASTINGS: And then?

FLASH: Then Mrs. Breckenridge got up and said "Excuse me" and went upstairs. And then Tony told me to . . . to do something with the fireworks which I couldn't possibly do—and went into the library.

BILLY: And then we heard Tony playing the piano in the library.

FLASH: Then the fireworks started—and nobody was there to see it but us two and Miss Knowland. They were very beautiful fireworks, though. And Miss Knowland said that it was lovely, good target shooting, or something like that—and suddenly she kind of screamed and said she had thought of something and wanted to find Mr. Breckenridge right away.

[INGALLS *makes a step forward*]

HASTINGS: Ah. . . . What did you think of, Miss Know-land?

ADRIENNE: I thought . . . [*Looks at* INGALLS. *He is watching her*]

INGALLS: [*Slowly*] What did you think of, Adrienne?

ADRIENNE: I thought . . . I thought that Steve would take advantage of Walter's absence and . . . and that Steve would be upstairs with Helen, and I wanted to tell Walter about it.

HASTINGS: I see. And what did you do?

ADRIENNE: I went out into the garden—to find Walter.

HASTINGS: And then?

BILLY: Then the fireworks stopped.

HASTINGS: How soon after Miss Knowland left did the fireworks stop?

FLASH: Almost immediately. Almost before she could've been a step away.

HASTINGS: And then?

FLASH: Then we waited, but nothing happened. We just talked and—[*Stops. Gasps:*] Jesus Christ!

HASTINGS: What is it?

FLASH: Jesus Christ, I think we heard it when Mr. Breckenridge was murdered!

HASTINGS: *When?*

FLASH: Bill, do you remember the dud? Remember there was a kind of crack outside and I thought the fireworks were starting again, but nothing happened and I said it was a dud?

BILLY: Yes.

CURTISS: I heard it too, Mr. Hastings. But there had been so many rockets outside that I thought nothing of it at the time.

HASTINGS: Now that's interesting. You heard it *after* the fireworks had stopped?

FLASH: Yes. Quite a bit after. Five minutes or more.

HASTINGS: What happened after that?

BILLY: Nothing. Then Steve came back from the garden, and we talked, and then Flash took me to my room.

HASTINGS: You didn't see Mrs. Breckenridge or Mr. Fleming come back down these stairs while you were here?

BILLY: No.

HASTINGS: Now, Curtiss, you were in the pantry all that time?

CURTISS: Yes, sir. I was polishing the silver.

HASTINGS: Could you see the back stairway from the second floor all the time you were there?

CURTISS: Yes, sir. The pantry door was open.

HASTINGS: Did you see anyone coming down the stairs?

CURTISS: No, sir.

HASTINGS: [*To* FLEMING] Well, I guess that lets *you* out.

FLEMING: [*Shrugging*] Not necessarily. There's a window in my room.

HASTINGS: What were you doing in your room? Getting drunk?

FLEMING: *Staying* drunk.

HASTINGS: And you, Mrs. Breckenridge, were you in your room?

HELEN: Yes.

HASTINGS: Since I can't see you climbing out of a window, I presume at least that it lets you out.

HELEN: Not necessarily. There's a balcony outside my room with a perfectly functional stairway leading to the garden.

HASTINGS: Oh. . . . What were you doing in your room?

HELEN: Packing.

HASTINGS: *What?*

HELEN: My suitcase. I wanted to go back to New York.

HASTINGS: *Tonight?*

HELEN: Yes.

HASTINGS: Why?

HELEN: Because I felt that I couldn't stay in this house. [HASTINGS *looks at her. She continues quietly:*] Don't you see? I had always wanted a house of my own. I wanted a small, very modern house, simple and healthy, with huge windows and glass brick and clean walls. I wanted to hunt for the latest refrigerators and colored washstands and plastic floor tiles and . . . I wanted to work on it for months, to plan every bit of it. . . . But I was never allowed to plan anything in my life. . . . [*Controls herself. Continues in a matter-of-fact voice:*] I was ready to leave. I came downstairs. Steve and Tony were here. I was about to go when we heard Adrienne scream . . . and . . . [*Finishes with a gesture of her hand, as if to say: "And that was that"*]

HASTINGS: I see. . . . Now, Miss Knowland. What were you doing in the garden?

ADRIENNE: I was looking for Walter. But I went in the wrong direction. I went toward the lake. I got lost in the dark. Then I came back and—I found him. Dead. [*Looks at* HASTINGS, *adds:*] Of course, I could have been doing anything.

HASTINGS: Is that what you want me to think?

ADRIENNE: I don't care what you think.

HASTINGS: You know, I *would* think it—if it weren't for one fact. The fireworks stopped too soon after you left. You wouldn't have had the time to get from here to the spot where Mr. Breckenridge was found. And I think it was the murderer who stopped those fireworks— or interrupted Mr. Breckenridge and caused him to stop. Because there's nothing wrong with the machine itself. I think the murderer got there when the fireworks stopped. Perhaps earlier. But not later. [*Turns to* INGALLS] Now, Steve. What were you doing in the garden?

INGALLS: I have no alibi at all, Greg.

HASTINGS: None?

INGALLS: None. I just went for a walk through the grounds. I saw no one and no one saw me.

HASTINGS: Hm. . . . Now, Mr. Goddard. You were playing the piano in the library?

TONY: Yes.

HASTINGS: [*To* BILLY *and* FLASH] How long did you hear him playing? Till after the fireworks stopped?

BILLY: Yes, till quite a bit after.

FLASH: Yes.

HASTINGS: [*To* TONY] Well, that lets *you* out.

TONY: Not necessarily. If you look through the phonograph records, you will see that there is one of Rachmaninoff's Prelude in G Minor.

HASTINGS: [*Leans back in his chair, disgusted*] Is there anyone here who does *not* want to be the murderer?

FLASH: Oh, *I* don't.

SERGE: I think it is horrible! It is horrible that these people should act like this after the death of their benefactor!

HASTINGS: [*Turns to look at him with curiosity. Then, to* HELEN:] Who is this gentleman?

HELEN: Mr. Serge Sookin. A friend of my husband's.

HASTINGS: Mr. Sookin, we seem to have forgotten you. Where were you all that time?

SERGE: *I* was not here at all.

HASTINGS: You weren't?

BILLY: That's right. I forgot him. Mr. Sookin left long before everybody else. He went to Stamford.

HASTINGS: [*Interested, to* SERGE:] You drove to Stamford?

SERGE: Yes. To get the evening newspaper.

HASTINGS: What newspaper?

SERGE: The *Courier.*

HASTINGS: What time did you leave?

SERGE: I am not certain, I think it was—

INGALLS: A quarter to ten. I looked at my watch. Remember?

SERGE: That is right. You did.

HASTINGS: When did you get back?

SERGE: Just a few minutes before you arrived here.

HASTINGS: Which was at ten-thirty. Well, you made pretty good time. You couldn't have gotten to Stamford and back any faster than that. I presume you didn't stop anywhere on your way?

SERGE: No.

HASTINGS: Did anyone see you buying that newspaper?

SERGE: No. It was the drugstore, you know, with the newspapers on the box outside the door, and I just took the newspaper and left the five cents.

HASTINGS: What drugstore was it?

SERGE: It was . . . yes, it was called Lawton's.

HASTINGS: You didn't speak to anybody at Lawton's?

SERGE: No. [*Begins to understand, looks startled for a second, then laughs suddenly*] Oh, but it is funny!

HASTINGS: What is?

SERGE: [*Very pleased*] You see, there is no place between here and the Lawton's drugstore where I could buy a newspaper.

HASTINGS: No, there isn't.

SERGE: And Mr. Ingalls he said that the Lawton's drugstore they do not get the last edition of the *Courier* until ten o'clock, so I could not have had it with me earlier. And I left here at one quarter to ten. And I came back with the last edition of the *Courier.* And I could not have waited somewhere till four minutes past ten and killed Mr. Breckenridge, because then I could have only twenty-six minutes to get to Stamford and back, and you say that this would not be possible. And it is funny, because it was Mr. Ingalls who gave me the real alibi like that.

INGALLS: I sincerely regret it.

HASTINGS: Where is the paper you brought, Mr. Sookin?

SERGE: Why, right here . . . right . . . [*Looks around. Others look also*] But that is strange. It was right here. They were reading it.

TONY: That's true. I saw the paper. I read the comic strips.

HASTINGS: It was the *Courier*?

TONY: Yes.

HASTINGS: Who else saw it here?

INGALLS: I did.

HELEN: I did.

FLEMING: I did, too.

HASTINGS: Did any of you notice whether it was the last edition?

INGALLS: No, I didn't. [*The others shake their heads*]

HASTINGS: And Mr. Sookin did not seem to mind your reading that paper he brought? He did not seem in a hurry to take it away from you?

HELEN: Why, no.

[INGALLS, TONY, *and* FLEMING *shake their heads*]

HASTINGS: No. What I'm thinking wouldn't be like Mr. Sookin at all.

SERGE: [*Still looking for it*] But where is it? It was right here.

HASTINGS: Did anyone take that paper?

[*They all answer "No" or shake their heads*]

SERGE: But this is ridicable!

HASTINGS: Oh, I guess we'll find it. Sit down, Mr. Sookin. So you have a perfect alibi . . . unless, of course, you telephoned to some accomplice to get that paper for you.

SERGE: *What?!*

HASTINGS: Did anyone see Mr. Sookin using the telephone? [*They ad-lib denials*] And, of course, there's no other place to phone from, closer than Lawton's. No, I don't really think you phoned, Mr. Sookin. I just mentioned it. . . . How long have you been in this country, Mr. Sookin?

SERGE: I escaped from Russia during the World War Number Two.

HASTINGS: How long have you known Mr. Breckenridge?

SERGE: About three months.

HASTINGS: What do you do for a living?

SERGE: In my country I was a physicist. That is why Mr. Breckenridge he took an interest in me. Now I am unemployed.

HASTINGS: What do you live on?

SERGE: I get from the Refugees' Committee the fifteen dollars each week. It is quite sufficient for me.

HASTINGS: And Mr. Breckenridge didn't help you?

SERGE: Ah, Mr. Breckenridge he offered many times to help me. But money I would not take from him. I wanted to get work. And Mr. Breckenridge wanted to give me the job in his laboratories. But Mr. Ingalls refused.

HASTINGS: Oh? [*To* INGALLS] Is that right, Steve?

INGALLS: That's right.

HASTINGS: Why did you refuse?

INGALLS: Well, I'll tell you: I don't like people who talk too much about their love for humanity.

HASTINGS: But how could you override Mr. Breckenridge's wish?

INGALLS: That was a condition of our partnership. Walter received seventy-five percent of the profits and he had sole authority over the disposition to be made of our products. But I had sole authority over the work in the laboratory.

HASTINGS: I see. . . . Now tell me, Steve, how many hours a day did you usually spend in the laboratory?

INGALLS: I don't know. About twelve, I guess, on the average.

HASTINGS: Perhaps nearer to sixteen—on the average?

INGALLS: Yes, I guess so.

HASTINGS: And how many hours a day did Mr. Breckenridge spend in the laboratory?

INGALLS: He didn't come to the laboratory every day.

HASTINGS: Well, average it for the year. What would it make per day?

INGALLS: About an hour and a half.

HASTINGS: I see. . . . [*Leans back*] Well, it's very interesting. Any of you could have committed the murder. Most of you have halfway alibis, the kind that make it possible, but not probable. You're worse off than the rest, Steve. You have no alibi at all. At the other end—there's Mr. Sookin. He has a perfect alibi. [*Pauses, then:*] Here's what makes it interesting: someone deliberately smashed Mr. Breckenridge's watch. Someone was anxious that there should be no doubt about the time of the murder. Yet the only person who has a good alibi for that particular time is Mr. Sookin—who was, at four minutes past ten, just about driving into Stamford.

SERGE: Well?

HASTINGS: I'm just thinking aloud, Mr. Sookin.

[DIXON *enters Right, carrying some papers in his hand. He is an energetic, efficient young man who does not waste much time. He walks to* HASTINGS, *and puts one paper on the table before him*]

DIXON: The statements of the cook and the chauffeur, Chief.

HASTINGS: [*With a brief glance at the paper*] What do they say?

DIXON: They went to bed at nine o'clock. Saw nothing. Heard nothing—except Curtiss in the pantry.

HASTINGS: Okay.

DIXON: [*Handing him the other papers. His voice a little less casual:*] And here are the fingerprints off the gun— and another set.

HASTINGS: [*Looks carefully at two cards of fingerprints.*

Then puts them on the table, facedown. Then raises his head and looks slowly at all the people in the room, from face to face. Then says slowly:] Yes. The fingerprints on that gun are those of someone in this room. [*Silence. He turns to* DIXON] Dixon.

DIXON: Yes, Chief?

HASTINGS: Have the boys examine the shrubbery and the ground under Mr. Fleming's window. Have them examine the balcony and the stairs leading down from it. Look through the phonograph records and see if you find one of Rachmaninoff's Prelude in G Minor. Search the house and bring me all the newspapers you find. Look particularly for a copy of today's *Courier*.

DIXON: Okay, Chief. [*Exits Right*]

SERGE: [*Jumping up suddenly*] Mr. Hastings! I know who did it! [*They all look at him*] I know! And I will tell you! You are wasting the time when it is so clear! I know who did it! It was Mr. Ingalls!

INGALLS: By us in America, Serge, when you say a thing like that—you're expected to prove it.

HASTINGS: Now, Mr. Sookin, why do you think that Mr. Ingalls did it?

SERGE: Mr. Ingalls hated Mr. Breckenridge, because Mr. Breckenridge was fine and noble, and Mr. Ingalls is cold and cruel and without principles.

HASTINGS: Is he?

SERGE: But is it not clear? Mr. Ingalls he seduced the wife of Mr. Breckenridge. Mr. Breckenridge discovered it this afternoon.

HASTINGS: Now there, Mr. Sookin, you have an interesting point. Very interesting. There's never been any trouble between Mr. Ingalls and Mr. Breckenridge—until this afternoon. This evening, Mr. Breckenridge is found murdered. Convenient. A bit too convenient, don't you think? If Mr. Ingalls murdered Mr. Breckenridge—wouldn't it be dangerous for him to do it tonight? On the other hand, if someone else murdered Mr. Breckenridge—wouldn't he choose precisely tonight, when suspicion could be thrown so easily on Mr. Ingalls?

SERGE: But that is not all! Mr. Breckenridge he wanted to

give this great invention to all the poor humanity. But Mr. Ingalls wanted to make the money for himself. Is it not to his advantage to kill Mr. Breckenridge?

HASTINGS: Sure. Except that Steve never cared for money.

SERGE: No? When he said so himself? When he shouted so? When I heard him?

HASTINGS: Sure. I heard him, too. Many times. Except that Steve never shouts.

SERGE: But then, if you heard it, too—

HASTINGS: Come on, Mr. Sookin, you can't be as stupid as you're trying to appear. Who doesn't care for money? You name one. But here's the difference: the man who admits that he cares for money is all right. He's usually worth the money he makes. He won't kill for it. He doesn't have to. But watch out for the man who yells too loudly how much he scorns money. Watch out particularly for the one who yells that others must scorn it. He's after something much worse than money.

INGALLS: Thanks, Greg.

HASTINGS: Don't thank me too soon. [*Picks up the fingerprint cards*] You see, the fingerprints on that gun are yours. [*The others gasp*]

ADRIENNE: [*Jumping up*] That's horrible! It's horrible! It's unfair! Of course they're Steve's. Steve handled that gun today! Everybody saw him do it!

HASTINGS: Oh? . . . Tell me about that, Miss Knowland.

ADRIENNE: It was . . . it was this afternoon. We were talking about Walter being afraid of guns. Walter said he wasn't, said he had a gun and he told Steve to look in that drawer. Steve took the gun out, and looked at it, and then put it back. And we all saw it. And someone . . . someone got the horrible idea . . .

HASTINGS: Yes, Miss Knowland, I think so, too. [*Walks to cabinet, opens the drawer, looks in, then closes it*] Yes, it's gone. . . . Sit down, Miss Knowland. There's no need to be upset about this. Nobody who's ever seen a movie would commit murder holding a gun with his bare hand. Now, if Steve did it, he would certainly think of wiping off the fingerprints that he'd left on that gun earlier. But if somebody else did it, he'd certainly be damn glad to leave Steve's fingerprints where they were. Convenient, isn't it? . . . Now, who saw Steve handling that gun today? All of you here?

ADRIENNE: All—except Billy and Flash and Curtiss.

HASTINGS: [*Nods*] Interesting. . . . You see, Steve, that was one of the reasons why I said I thought certain things let you out. I saw that there were prints on that gun and I didn't think you'd be stupid enough to leave them there. I didn't think you'd drop the gun like that, either. Not with a deep lake close by. . . . The other reason was that I don't think you'd shoot a man in the back.

TONY: [*Gasps at a sudden thought*] Mr. Hastings! . . . I just thought of something!

HASTINGS: Yes?

TONY: What if Serge is a Communist spy? [SERGE *gasps and leaps to his feet*]

HASTINGS: [*Shakes his head at* TONY *reproachfully*] Why, Tony. You didn't really think that I hadn't thought of that already?

SERGE: [*To* TONY] You swine! *I*—a Communist? I who go to church? I who have suffered?

HASTINGS: Look, Mr. Sookin, be sensible about it. If you're not a Communist spy—you'd be angry. But if you *are* a Communist spy—you'd be much angrier, so where does it get you?

SERGE: But it is the insult! I, who have faith in the Holy Mother Russia—

HASTINGS: All right. Drop it. [*To* TONY] You see, Mr. Goddard, it's possible, but it doesn't jell. If Mr. Sookin were a Soviet agent, he'd be after the invention, of course. But nobody touched that machine. Besides, I understand that Mr. Sookin heartily supported Mr. Breckenridge in his decision to give this invention away to the world.

SERGE: I did! I am a humanitarian.

HASTINGS: What? Another one?

INGALLS: He did more than that. It was he who gave Walter the idea of the gift in the first place.

SERGE: That is true! But how did you know it?

INGALLS: I guessed it.

HASTINGS: Tell me, what is that invention actually good for? I mean, in practical application.

INGALLS: Oh, for a source of cheap power. For lighting the slums, for instance, or running factory motors.

HASTINGS: Is that all?

INGALLS: That's all.

HASTINGS: Well, you see? If it's a purely commercial invention, why should the Soviets be anxious to get exclusive control of it? They would try to steal it, of course. But once Mr. Breckenridge had decided to save them the trouble and give it away, they would cheer him as their best friend. They spend billions trying to prompt giveaways of that kind. They would guard his life—at least until tomorrow noon. They wouldn't send any spies around to kill him.

SERGE: But Mr. Hastings!

HASTINGS: Yes?

SERGE: I am *not* a Soviet spy!

HASTINGS: Okay. I haven't said you were. [*To the others*] Well, here's how we stand. On one side, we have Steve, who had not one, but two possible motives. He has no alibi at all and his fingerprints are on the gun. On the other side, we have Mr. Sookin, who has a perfect alibi and no possible motive.

SERGE: But then why do you not act? What more do you want? When you have the so good case against Mr. Ingalls?

HASTINGS: That's why, Serge—because it *is* so good. It's *too* good.

SERGE: Why do you not let the jury decide that?

HASTINGS: Because I am afraid that the average jury would agree with you.

[DIXON *enters from the garden. He carries on his palm a tiny object wrapped in cellophane. He hands it to* HASTINGS]

DIXON: Found in the grass near the machine.

HASTINGS: [*Unwraps the cellophane. Looks, sighs with disgust*] Oh Lord! . . . A cigarette butt. . . . I didn't think murderers went around doing that anymore. [*Waves to* DIXON, *who exits into the garden.* HASTINGS *picks up the cigarette butt, examines it*] A Camel . . . burned just to the brand. . . . How convenient. . . . [*Puts the butt down. Says wearily:*] All right, who smokes Camels around here? [INGALLS *takes out his cigarette case, opens it, and extends it to* HASTINGS. HASTINGS *looks and nods*]

INGALLS: It doesn't surprise you?

HASTINGS: No. [*To the others*] Does anyone else here smoke Camels? [*They shake their heads*]

ADRIENNE: *I* do.

INGALLS: You don't smoke, Adrienne.

ADRIENNE: I do—on the stage. . . . I'm very good at staging things.

HASTINGS: I'm not too sure of that.

INGALLS: [*In a warning tone*] Adrienne . . .

ADRIENNE: [*To* HASTINGS] Keep him out of this. Are you running this investigation or is he? You've been reviewing things a lot around here. How about my doing that for a change?

HASTINGS: Go right ahead.

ADRIENNE: Well, for instance, look at me. I had two motives. I wanted to break my contract. If you wish to know how badly I wanted it—well, I tried to kill myself a year ago. If I'd try that, wouldn't I try something else, as desperate—or worse? Today I asked Walter, for the last time, to release me. He refused. That alone would be enough, wouldn't it? But that's not all. I love Steve Ingalls. I've been in love with him for years. Oh, it's all right for me to say that—because he doesn't give a damn about me. Today—I learned that he loves Helen. [*Looks at* HASTINGS] Well? Am I going to finish? Or will *you*?

INGALLS: [*To* ADRIENNE] You're going to shut up.

HASTINGS: No, Steve, I'd rather let Miss Knowland finish.

ADRIENNE: All right. Wouldn't I be smart enough to kill Walter and frame Steve for it? Wouldn't I figure that even if he's not convicted, Helen will never be able to get him—because if he married her, it would be like signing a confession? How's that? Pretty good case?

HASTINGS: Very good.

INGALLS: [*Stepping forward*] Adrienne . . .

ADRIENNE: [*Snaps angrily*] It's your turn to shut up! [*To* HASTINGS] And besides, that business about the murderer interrupting the fireworks—that's nothing but your own guess. What is there to prove it? Drop that—and my alilbi is as bad as Steve's. Worse. Because I went out looking for Walter. Nothing wrong with *this* case, is there?

HASTINGS: Yes. There is. That's why it's good.

INGALLS: Greg, I won't allow this.

HASTINGS: Come on, Steve, that's the first foolish thing I've heard you say. What's the matter with you? How can you stop me? [*To* ADRIENNE] Miss Knowland, have you noticed that you're the only one here who's been contradicting herself?

ADRIENNE: How?

HASTINGS: That's why I like your case. Because it's not perfect. I don't like perfect cases. . . . How? Well, if Steve was framed, I see only two people who had a motive for framing him. Mr. Sookin and you. Mr. Sookin hates Steve. You love him—which is much more damning. Now look at Mr. Sookin. If he framed Steve, he's been acting like a fool here, laying it on too thick. Now what would he do if he weren't a fool?

SERGE: [*With a new kind of dangerous, mocking note in his voice*] He'd pretend to be one.

HASTINGS: [*Looks at him with new interest, says slowly:*] Quite so. [*Then lightly again:*] Congratulations, Mr. Sookin. You're beginning to understand my ways of thinking. You may be right. But there's another possible method of being clever. The person who framed Steve might do his best to act afterward as if he were *protecting* him.

INGALLS: Greg!

HASTINGS: [*His voice driving on intensely*] Keep still, all of you! Do you see, Miss Knowland? You've put on a beautiful show of protecting Steve. And yet, it was you who gave away the story of that interrupted love scene.

Why? To show us that you were jealous? Or to damn
Steve?

INGALLS: [*In a tone of such authority that* HASTINGS *has to
remain silent*] All right, Greg. That's enough. [*His tone
makes everyone look at him*] You wanted to know how I
could stop you? Very simply. [*Takes a notebook out of
his pocket and throws it down on the table. Takes out a
pencil and stands holding it in his hand, over the paper*]
Unless you leave Adrienne out of this, I'm going to
write a confession that *I* did it.

[ADRIENNE *stands stock-still, like a person hit over
the head*]

HASTINGS: But, Steve, you didn't do it!

INGALLS: That's your concern. Mine is only that *she* didn't
do it. I'm not going to put on a show of protecting her—
as she's been trying to protect me, very crudely. I'm
not going to hint and throw suspicion on myself.
That's been done for me—quite adequately. I'm simply
going to blackmail you. You understand? If I sign a
confession—with the evidence you have on me, you'll
be forced to put me on trial. You'll have no choice. You
might know that I didn't do it, but the jury won't be so
subtle. The jury will be glad to pounce upon the obvious. Have I made myself clear? Leave Adrienne out of
this, unless you want an unsolved murder on your
record—and on your conscience.

ADRIENNE: [*It is a scream of terror, of triumph, of release
all at once—and the happiest sound in the world*] Steve!
[*He turns to look at her. They stand holding the glance.
It is more revealing than any love scene. They look at
each other as if they were alone in the room and in the
world. . . . Then she whispers, choking:*] Steve . . . you,
who've never believed in self-sacrifice . . . you, who've
preached selfishness and egoism and . . . you wouldn't
do this, unless . . . unless it's—

INGALLS: [*In a low, tense voice, more passionate than the
tone of a love confession*]—unless it's for the most self-

ish reason in the world. [*She closes her eyes. He turns away from her slowly.* HELEN, *who has been watching them, lets her head drop, hopelessly*]

HASTINGS: [*Breaking the silence*] God help us when people begin protecting each other! When they start that— I'm through. [*Throws the notebook to* INGALLS] All right, Steve. Put it away. You win—for the moment. I'll have a few questions to ask you about this—but not right now. [*To* ADRIENNE] Miss Knowland, if you were actually protecting him, you have no respect for my intelligence at all. You should have known I wouldn't believe that Steve is guilty. I know a frame-up when I see one. [*To the others*] And for the information of the scoundrel who did this, I'd like to say that he's an incredible fool. Did he really expect me to believe that Steve Ingalls—with his brilliant, methodical, scientific mind—would commit a sloppy crime like this? I could readily accept Steve as capable of murder. But if he ever committed one, it would be the finest job in the world. There wouldn't be a hair's weight of a clue. He'd have an alibi—as perfect as a precision instrument. But to think of Steve leaving fingerprints and cigarette butts behind! . . . I'd like to get the bastard who planned this and punch him in the nose. It's not a case, it's a personal insult to me!

TONY: And to Steve.

HASTINGS: [*Rising*] I've had enough of this for tonight. Let's get some sleep and some sense. I shall ask everybody not to leave this house, of course. I'll have my men remain here—in this room and in the garden. I'll be back early in the morning. I won't ask you who killed Walter Breckenridge. I'll know that when I find the answer to another question: *who framed Steve Ingalls?* . . . Good night. [*Exits into the garden, calling:*] Dixon! [*As the others move to rise slowly or look at one another,* INGALLS *turns and walks to the stairs.* ADRIENNE—*who has looked at no one but him—makes a step to follow him. He stops on the stairs, turns to her, says calmly:*]

INGALLS: I told you to wait. Sound vibrations travel very

slowly, Adrienne. Not yet. [*Turns and exits up the stairs, as she stands looking after him*]

CURTAIN

SCENE 2

Early next morning. The room seems to be glowing. There is a clear blue sky outside and the house is flooded with sunlight.

HELEN *and* FLEMING *are sitting at a table, deep in conversation. It is a serious conversation, but their voices are simple, light, natural.*

FLEMING: Would we go by boat or by train?
HELEN: A plane would be best, don't you think? Easier for Billy and he'll enjoy it.
FLEMING: Do we have to make arrangements with Dr. Harlan in advance?
HELEN: I think so. I'll telephone him today.
FLEMING: Long-distance?
HELEN: Yes, of course. Why not?
FLEMING: Helen . . . is it going to be very expensive—the operation and all?
HELEN: We don't have to worry about that.
FLEMING: Yes, Helen. We do.
HELEN: [*Looks at him. Then:*] Of course. Forgive me. Bad habits are very hard to lose.
FLEMING: I thought—

[ADRIENNE *comes down the stairs. She walks as if her feet do not need to touch the ground. She wears a gay, simple summer dress. She looks like a person whose presence in a room would compete with the sunlight. But her manner is very simple; it is the manner of so profound a happiness that it cannot be anything but simple*]

ADRIENNE: Good morning.
FLEMING: [*Brightly*] Good morning, Adrienne.

HELEN: [*With a little effort*] Good morning.

ADRIENNE: Mr. Hastings arrived?

FLEMING: Not yet.

ADRIENNE: [*Looking through cigarette boxes*] Any Camels around here? I think I'll take up smoking. Camels are wonderful things. God bless every Camel butt in the world! [*Finds a cigarette and lights it*]

FLEMING: Never saw you look like that, Adrienne. Slept well?

ADRIENNE: [*Walking to French doors*] Haven't slept at all. I don't see why people insist on sleeping. You feel so much better if you don't. And how can anybody want to lose a minute—a single minute of being alive?

FLEMING: What's the matter, Adrienne?

ADRIENNE: Nothing. [*Points to the garden*] It's the Fourth of July. [*Exits into the garden*]

HELEN: [*Looks after her, then forces herself to return to the conversation*] When we go to Montreal—

FLEMING: Look, Helen, here's what I thought: I'll have to take the money from you for Billy's operation. That's one time when it's proper for a man to accept help. But don't *give* me the money. Lend it. And charge me a fair interest on it. That, you see, would really be an act of humanity.

HELEN: Yes, Harvey. That's what we'll do.

FLEMING: [*In a low voice*] Thank you.

HELEN: And, of course, we'll take legal steps to make him "Billy Fleming" again. . . . But you won't forbid me to visit him, will you?

FLEMING: [*Smiles happily, shaking his head. Then, at a sudden grim thought:*] Helen. There's one more thing. It's still possible that they'll decide that one of us . . . that . . .

HELEN: Yes. That one of us is the murderer.

FLEMING: Well . . . shall we agree that . . . if it's one of us . . . the other will take Billy to Montreal?

HELEN: Yes, Harvey. And if it's not one of us, then we'll go together.

[INGALLS *enters, coming down the stairs*]

INGALLS: Good morning.

HELEN: Good morning, Steve.

FLEMING: [*Looks at the two of them, then:*] Is Billy up yet?

INGALLS: Don't know. I haven't been downstairs.

FLEMING: Guess I'll go to see if he's up. [*Exits Right*]

INGALLS: [*Turning to* HELEN] Helen.

HELEN: [*Quietly*] I know.

INGALLS: Helen, will you marry me?

HELEN: [*Looks at him, startled, then shakes her head slowly*] No, Steve.

INGALLS: Do you think that I am afraid?

HELEN: No. But if I told you what I think of this, you'd be very angry. You're never angry, except when people say nice things about you. [*As he is about to speak*] No, Steve. You don't love me. Perhaps you thought you did. Perhaps you didn't know who it was that you really loved. I think you know it now. I do. You can't hurt me, Steve, except if you refuse to admit this. Because, then, I'll know that you have no respect for me at all.

INGALLS: [*In a low voice*] I'm sorry, Helen.

HELEN: [*Nods her head slowly. Then forces herself to say lightly:*] Besides, you should have noticed that I never said I loved you.

INGALLS: I noticed something else.

HELEN: Oh, that? Well, you must be generous, Steve. You mustn't hold a moment's weakness against me. After all, you're very attractive, and ... and Adrienne was right about your manner of making love.

INGALLS: Helen, I'm making it harder for you.

HELEN: [*Calmly, her head high, looking straight at him*] No, Steve, no. I wanted to say it. And now I want you to forget it. No, I don't love you. I've never loved you. I've known you all these years—I've seen you so often—I've looked at you—I've heard your voice. . . . But I never loved you.

INGALLS: Helen . . .

HELEN: And that, Steve, is all you have a right to remember.

[*She turns, walks to stairs. The doorbell rings. She stops on the stairs.* INGALLS *opens the door.* HASTINGS *enters*]

HASTINGS: Good morning.

HELEN: Good morning, Mr. Hastings.

INGALLS: Hello, Greg.

HASTINGS: [*To* INGALLS] It would be your face that I'd have to see first. All right, I suppose I'd better take you first. [*To* HELEN] Will you excuse me, Mrs. Breckenridge? This case has upset all my theories. I'll have to revert to the conventional and question some of the people in private.

HELEN: Yes, of course. I shall be upstairs if you want me. [*Exits up the stairs*]

HASTINGS: [*Sitting down*] Goddamn this case. Couldn't eat a bite of breakfast this morning.

INGALLS: Oh, I did. I had scrambled eggs and bacon and fresh strawberries and coffee and—

HASTINGS: All right, all right. It doesn't prove anything. You'd eat as well whether you'd done it or not. Did you do it?

INGALLS: What do you think?

HASTINGS: You know what I think. But damn it, Steve, if I don't solve this, it's you that they'll throw to the lions. The jury lions.

INGALLS: I don't think I'm a good type for a martyr.

HASTINGS: No. But a swell type for a murderer.

INGALLS: Oh yes.

[DIXON *enters Right, carrying a stack of newspapers and a phonograph record*]

DIXON: Good morning, Chief. Here it is. [*Deposits his load on a table*]

HASTINGS: What about the shrubbery outside and the balcony?

DIXON: In perfect order. No broken branches. No footprints. Nothing. [*Picking up the record*] Rachmaninoff's Prelude in G Minor all right. And the newspapers.

HASTINGS: [*Looks through the newspapers, stops at one*] *Who* reads the *Red Worker*?

DIXON: Mrs. Pudget.

HASTINGS: [*Having gone to the bottom of the pile*] No *Courier*?

DIXON: No *Courier*.

HASTINGS: Damn it, Dixon, we've got to find it—or prove that it wasn't here at all!

INGALLS: But it was here. I saw it.

HASTINGS: That's the hell of it! Too many of you saw it. I don't think that little Holy Russian rat would've had the guts to fake it with an earlier edition. And yet I know there's something phony about that alibi. Dixon, look through the garbage cans, the incinerators, everything!

DIXON: We did.

HASTINGS: Look again.

DIXON: Okay, Chief. [*Exits Right*]

HASTINGS: Steve, don't be too damn noble and tell me who'd really have a reason to frame you around here!

INGALLS: If you'll take my word for it—and I wish you would—no one.

HASTINGS: No one?

INGALLS: I wouldn't vouch for Serge. But I know of no reason why he'd kill Walter.

HASTINGS: You know, I'm sure he's done it. Look at how it was done. So crude, so obvious. I don't see anyone else staging a frame-up quite so blatantly and hoping to get away with it. It just smells "Serge" all over. A dull, presumptuous, Communist mind that counts on its insolence to overcome the intelligence of anyone else.

INGALLS: But you've got to prove it.

HASTINGS: Yes. And I can't. Well, let's see about the others. Tony Goddard? No reason for him to frame you. Fleming? Possible. Out of fear. Drunkards are not very strong people.

INGALLS: I'll vouch for Fleming.

HASTINGS: Mrs. Breckenridge? No reason. Miss Knowland? . . . Now don't pull out any notebooks. Steve, don't refuse to answer this. I've got to ask it. You're in love with Adrienne Knowland, aren't you?

INGALLS: Desperately. Miserably. Completely. For many years.

HASTINGS: Why "miserably" for many years—when she loves you?

INGALLS: Because neither of us thought it possible of the other. . . . Why did you have to ask this?

HASTINGS: Because—what, then, was that love scene with Mrs. Breckenridge?

INGALLS: [*Shrugging*] A moment's weakness. Despair, perhaps. Because I didn't think that I could ever have the woman I wanted.

HASTINGS: You chose a nice day to be weak on.

INGALLS: Yes, didn't I?

HASTINGS: [*Rising*] Well, I think I'll have a little talk with Fleming now.

INGALLS: Will you be long?

HASTINGS: I don't think so. [SERGE *enters Right.* HASTINGS *turns at the stairs*] Ah, good morning, Commissar.

SERGE: [*Stiffly*] That is not funny.

HASTINGS: No. But it could be. [*Exits up the stairs*]

SERGE: [*Sees the papers, hurries to look through them*] Ah, the newspapers. Have they the *Courier* found?

INGALLS: No.

SERGE: But that is unbelievable! I cannot understand it!

INGALLS: Don't worry. They'll find it—when the time comes. . . . You have nothing to worry about. Look at *me*.

SERGE: [*Interested*] You are worried?

INGALLS: Well, wouldn't you be? It's all right for Greg to amuse himself with fancy deductions and to believe the most improbable. A jury won't do that. A jury will love a case like mine. It's easy on their conscience.

SERGE: [*As persuasively as he can make it*] That is true. I think the jury it would convict you. I think you have no chance.

INGALLS: Oh, I might have a chance. But it will take money.

SERGE: [*Attentively*] Money?

INGALLS: Lots of money. I'll need a good lawyer.

SERGE: Yes. You will need a very good lawyer. And that is expensive.

INGALLS: Very expensive.

SERGE: Your case it is bad.

INGALLS: Very bad.

SERGE: You feel certain that you will be put on trial?

INGALLS: Looks like it.

SERGE: And . . . you do not have the money?

INGALLS: Oh, I suppose I can scrape some together, but you see, I've never made very much. Not like Walter. And what I made I put back into the laboratory. Oh, I guess I could raise some cash on that, but what's the use? Even if I'm acquitted, I'll be broke when I get out of it.

SERGE: You are not the type of man who will like it—being broke.

INGALLS: I won't like it at all.

SERGE: And besides, you believe that your own interest— it comes first?

INGALLS: That's what I believe.

SERGE: [*Throws a quick glance around, then leans over the table, close to* INGALLS, *and speaks rapidly, in a low, hard, tense voice—a new* SERGE *entirely. Even his English is better, but his accent remains*] Listen. No jokes and no clowning about what you knew or what you guessed. We haven't the time. And it's your neck to be saved. Five hundred thousand dollars—now—in your hands—for that invention.

INGALLS: [*Whistles*] Why, Serge, at the rate of fifteen dollars a week, it will take you—

SERGE: Cut it out. You know. You knew all the time. I knew that you knew. And it didn't do you any good, did it? There's no time for showing how smart you are. Now it's either you want it or you don't. And it must be quick.

INGALLS: Well, looks like you've got me, doesn't it?

SERGE: Yes. So don't start talking about your conscience or your patriotism or things like that. You and I, we understand each other.

INGALLS: I think we've understood each other from the

first. [*Chuckles*] A gift to mankind, eh, Serge? Just to light the slums and put the greedy utility companies out of business?

SERGE: We have not time for laughing. Yes or no?

INGALLS: Do you carry five hundred thousand bucks, like that, in your pocket?

SERGE: I will write you a check.

INGALLS: How will I know it's any good?

SERGE: You'll know it when you see on whose account it's drawn. Beyond that, you'll have to take the chance. Because I want that graph right now.

INGALLS: Now?

SERGE: I can't come for it when you're in jail, can I? [*Pulls a sheet of paper and a pencil out of a drawer and throws them down on the table*] Now. On this sheet of paper. Before you touch the check.

INGALLS: Aren't you afraid of giving me a check? It could be used as evidence against you.

SERGE: You had evidence against me yesterday. You didn't use it. You saved me. Why?

INGALLS: I think you know that.

SERGE: Yes. There was one thing which you said yesterday—and when you said it, I knew I could have you.

INGALLS: I know what that was. But Greg Hastings didn't notice it.

SERGE: There were many things he didn't notice. Of course, you and I we know who killed Breckenridge.

INGALLS: I'm sure one of us does.

SERGE: It was Adrienne Knowland.

INGALLS: Was it?

SERGE: Good God, it's obvious, isn't it? But we don't care who did it, you and I. It was very convenient, that's all.

INGALLS: Yes.

SERGE: Well, do I get the graph?

INGALLS: I have no choice, have I? I suppose I'll get used to it in time, but it's rather uncomfortable—becoming a scoundrel.

SERGE: That won't bother you for long.

INGALLS: No, not for long. . . . Write that check.

[SERGE *takes a checkbook and a pen out of his pocket, sits down at the table, across from* INGALLS, *writes the check, then extends it, showing it to* INGALLS, *but not letting him touch it.* INGALLS *looks at the check, reads:*]

"The Soviet Culture and Friendship Society." Fancy that! What a coincidence.

SERGE: [*Contemptuously*] If I were doing what you are doing, at least I would not laugh about it.

INGALLS: That's the trouble with you, Serge. You have no sense of humor.

SERGE: You are a very contemptible person.

INGALLS: But I thought you knew that. [*Extends his hand for the check*]

SERGE: [*Pulls the check back, puts it down on the table in front of himself, and pushes the sheet of paper toward* INGALLS] Now get to work. Quick.

INGALLS: Why quite so much hurry? Can't you let me degrade myself gracefully?

SERGE: Shut up! The graph now!

INGALLS: [*Picking up the pencil*] Oh yes, the graph. [*Taps his chin with the pencil thoughfully*] Have you ever thought, Serge, what a strange thing life is? There's so much about it that we don't understand.

SERGE: Hurry up, you fool!

INGALLS: Oh yes. [*Leans over the paper, the pencil ready, then looks up*] And when we don't understand things, we make mistakes.

SERGE: Shut up! Write!

INGALLS: What? Oh, the graph. Well you see cosmic rays are tiny particles which bombard the earth from outer space, carrying an electric charge of—[*Looks up*] For instance, we never understood that incident when someone shot at Walter a month ago. Or did we? [SERGE *looks at him.* INGALLS *holds the glance. Then:*] Shall I write?

SERGE: What about that incident?

INGALLS: Doesn't anything strike you as funny, Serge?

SERGE: What about that incident?

INGALLS: Oh, I thought you knew that I knew everything.

Well, I know, for instance, that what you planned then—has succeeded now. Brilliantly, completely, and as you wanted it. Only much better planned than the first time. And a little late. One month too late. [SERGE *jumps up*] I'm sorry. You want the graph. Cosmic rays, when drawn into a single stream by means of . . . Incidentally, you're not a good shot, Serge. You're much better at housebreaking—or at breaking locks on bags, to be exact. You should have searched that bag, though. It would have looked less obvious.

SERGE: You understood—

INGALLS: Of course, Serge. If that murder had succeeded, the gun would have been found in my bag. And you wouldn't have had time to break the lock *after* the shot. You were very foresighted. But obvious.

SERGE: You can't prove that.

INGALLS: No. I can't prove it. And the gun in my bag wouldn't have proved much, either. Not much. Just enough to put me on trial. And you would have had one man who knew that graph dead, and the other in desperate need of money. But you're a bad shot. You're a much better psychologist. The gift to mankind idea worked smoother and safer.

SERGE: You can't prove—

INGALLS: No. I can't prove anything. And you know, Serge, I don't really think that you did it, this time. But doesn't it strike you as funny that someone has done it for you?

SERGE: I don't care what you think or know. It worked.

INGALLS: Yes. It worked.

SERGE: Then write, Goddamn you!

INGALLS: If you wish.

[*There is the sound of a door opening upstairs.* SERGE *whirls around.* INGALLS *slams his right hand, palm down, over the check on the table, as* HASTINGS *comes down the stairs*]

HASTINGS: [*Notices* INGALLS' *hand at once, says lightly:*] I'm not interrupting anything, am I?

[SERGE *stands by the table, doing a very bad job of disguising his anxiety.* INGALLS *is perfectly calm*]

INGALLS: No. No.

HASTINGS: Imagine finding the two of you in a friendly tête-à-tête.

INGALLS: Oh, we were discussing going into vaudeville together. In a mind-reading act. We're very good at reading each other's mind. Though I think I'm better at it than Serge.

HASTINGS: [*Looks at* INGALLS' *right hand on the table, imitating his tone*] You have an interesting hand, Steve. Ever had your palm read?

INGALLS: No. I don't believe in palmistry.

HASTINGS: [*Takes out a cigarette*] Give me a light, Steve. [INGALLS *reaches into his pocket, takes out his lighter, snaps it on, and offers it to* HASTINGS—*all with his left hand*] Didn't know you were left-handed.

INGALLS: I'm not. I'm just versatile.

HASTINGS: Come on, Steve, how long are you going to play the fool? Lift that hand.

INGALLS: Well, *Serge* enjoyed it. [*Lifts his hand as* SERGE *leaps toward it, but* HASTINGS *pushes* SERGE *aside and seizes the check*]

HASTINGS: [*Reading the check*] "Pay to the order of Steven Ingalls . . ." Well, well, well. Had I come down a minute later, you'd have been half-a-millionaire, Steve.

INGALLS: Yes. Why did you have to hurry?

SERGE: [*Screams at the top of his voice, whirling upon* IN-GALLS] You swine! You did it on purpose!

HASTINGS: [*In mock astonishment*] *No?*

SERGE: [*To* INGALLS] You lied! You betrayed me! You never intended to sell yourself! You're unprincipled and dishonest!

INGALLS: You shouldn't have trusted me like that.

[HELEN *and* TONY *enter hurriedly at the top of the stairs*]

HELEN: [*Anxiously*] What's going on here?

HASTINGS: Nothing much. Just Serge throwing five-hundred-thousand-dollar checks around.

[HELEN *gasps.* TONY *follows her down the stairs*]

SERGE: [*Screaming defiantly to* INGALLS *and* HASTINGS] Well? What are you going to do about it? You can't prove anything!

[FLEMING *hurries in Right and stops short at the door*]

HASTINGS: [*Reproachfully*] Now, Serge. We can prove that you're defrauding the Refugees' Committee out of fifteen bucks a week, for instance. And we can prove that I'm right about people who have no motive.

TONY: [*Almost regretfully*] Gee, I hoped it wouldn't be Serge. I hate having to be grateful to Serge for the rest of my life.

[ADRIENNE *comes in from the garden, followed a little later by* DIXON]

SERGE: What motive? What can you prove? That I tried to buy an invention from a murderer who needed the money—nothing else. It's just a simple commercial invention. *Isn't* it, Mr. Ingalls?

INGALLS: Yes.

HASTINGS: Goddamn it, we've got to find that newspaper!

SERGE: Now you understand, Mr. Hastings? Prove that I wasn't in Stamford! Prove it! I don't care whether you find that paper or not! Your own dear friends will have to swear they saw it!

HASTINGS: They don't know what edition it was.

SERGE: That's right! They don't know! Then how do they know it wasn't the last one? Prove that!

FLEMING: [*Looking around the room uselessly, frantically*] We ought to tear this house down and find the lousy sheet! [TONY *joins him in searching*]

SERGE: Prove that I lied to you! Find a jury, even a dumb

American jury, that will want to look at me, when they hear of this very heroic genius—[*Points at* INGALLS]— alone in the garden, leaving his fingerprints on the gun!

[*During the last few speeches,* INGALLS *takes out his cigarette case, takes a cigarette, takes a match folder from the table, strikes a match, lights the cigarette and tosses the lighted match into the fireplace.* ADRI- ENNE, *who has been looking at him, follows it with her eyes, screams suddenly, and dives for the fireplace to put out the fire set to the charred, rolled remnant of a newspaper*]

ADRIENNE: Steve! Look! [*Rises from her knees, with the rolled newspaper in her hand.* HASTINGS *seizes it from her. He unrolls it frantically, looks for the upper front page. Stands perfectly still and silent for a moment. Then raises his head to look at the others, and says quietly, almost wearily:*]
HASTINGS: The early edition of yesterday's *Courier.*

[*Silence. Then* SERGE *lunges for the paper*]

SERGE: You're lying!
HASTINGS: [*Pushing him aside*] Oh no, you don't!

[DIXON *steps to* SERGE'S *side.* HASTINGS *extends the newspaper headline toward* SERGE, *but at a safe distance*]

See for yourself. But don't touch it.
SERGE: It's not the paper! It's not the same paper! It was the last edition! I know it was! I looked for the mark when I got it! It was the last edition that I specially wanted!
HASTINGS: [*Shaking his head*] And that, Serge, proves I'm right about people who have good alibis.
SERGE: Who put it in that fireplace? Who burned it like this? I didn't do that! [*Whirls on* INGALLS] He did it! Of course! I gave it to him! When I arrived I gave the paper

to him! He changed it for this one! He put it there in the
fireplace and—

HASTINGS:—and almost burned the evidence, just now,
that's going to save his life? Come on, Serge, how much
do you expect me to believe?

SERGE: But I didn't—

HASTINGS: You did. But very badly. Like all the rest of it.
You were in a hurry when you started burning that paper. You were interrupted. So you stuck it there, hoping
to get it later. But you couldn't—not with my man here
all night. . . . Well, I'm almost as big a fool as you are.
Do you know why I took that alibi of yours seriously?
Because I didn't think you'd have the guts to pull what
you pulled. You could shoot a man in the back all right.
But to risk showing a paper to all those people—when
your life depended on whether they'd notice the edition
or not—*that* took the kind of courage you haven't got.
Or so I thought. I owe you an apology there.

SERGE: But you can't prove I did it! You can't prove this is
the paper I brought!

HASTINGS: All right, produce the other one.

SERGE: You can't convict me on that!

HASTINGS: I can have a pretty good try at it.

SERGE: [*Real terror showing in his face for the first time*]
You're going to—

HASTINGS: I'm going to let you explain it all to a jury.

SERGE: [*Screaming*] But you can't! You can't! Listen! I'm
innocent! But if you put me on trial, they'll kill me,
don't you understand? Not your jury! My own chiefs!
All right! I *am* a Soviet agent! And they don't forgive an
agent who gets put on trial! They'll kill me—my own
chiefs at home! Don't you understand? Even if I'm acquitted, it will be a death sentence for me just the same!
[*Pulls a gun out*] Stand still, all of you!

[SERGE *whirls around and rushes out through the
French doors.* DIXON *flies after him, pulling out his gun.
They disappear in the garden, as* HASTINGS *starts to fol-
low them. There are two shots. After a moment,* HAS-
TINGS *comes back slowly*]

HASTINGS: That's that.

HELEN: Is he dead?

HASTINGS: Yes. [*Then adds:*] Perhaps it's best this way. It saves us from a long and painful trial. The case is closed. I'm glad—for all of you. [*To* HELEN] I hope, Mrs. Breckenridge, that when you've been a neighbor of ours longer, you will forgive us for giving you on your first day here—

HELEN: I shall be a neighbor of yours, Mr. Hastings— perhaps—later. Not this summer. I'm going to sell this house. Harvey and I are going to Montreal.

TONY: And I'm going to Gimbel's.

[HASTINGS *bows as* HELEN *exits up the stairs with* TONY. FLEMING *exits Right*]

HASTINGS: [*Walks to door Left, turns to* INGALLS] It's as I've always said, Steve. There *is* no perfect crime.

INGALLS: [*Who has not moved from near the fireplace*] No, Greg. There isn't.

[HASTINGS *exits Left.* INGALLS *turns to look at Adrienne*]

ADRIENNE: What are you going to do now, Steve?

INGALLS: I'm going to ask you to marry me. [*As she makes a movement forward*] But before you answer, there's something I'm going to tell you. Yesterday, when you looked at those fireworks and suddenly thought of something—it was not of me or of Helen, was it?

ADRIENNE: No.

INGALLS: I know what you thought. You see, I know who killed Walter Breckenridge. I want you to know it. Listen and don't say anything until I finish.

[*The lights black out completely. Then a single spotlight hits the center of the stage. We can see nothing beyond, only the figures of the two men in the spotlight:* WALTER BRECKENRIDGE *and* STEVE INGALLS. BRECKENRIDGE *is operating the levers of a portable electric switchboard.* INGALLS *stands beside him.* INGALLS *speaks slowly, evenly, quietly, in the expressionless tone of an irrevocable decision*]

INGALLS: If, tomorrow ·at noon, Walter, you give this invention to the world—then, the day after tomorrow, Soviet Russia, Communist China, and every other dictatorship, every other scum on the face of the earth, will have the secret of the greatest military weapon ever invented.

BRECKENRIDGE: Are you going to start on that again? I thought we had settled it this afternoon.

INGALLS: This afternoon, Walter, I begged you. I had never begged a man before. I am not doing that now.

BRECKENRIDGE: You're interfering with the fireworks. Drop it, Steve. I'm not interested.

INGALLS: No, you're not interested in the consequences. Humanitarians never are. All you see ahead is lighted slums and free electric power on the farms. But you don't want to know that the same invention and the same grand gesture of yours will also send death through the air, and blow up ammunition depots, and turn cities into rubble.

BRECKENRIDGE: I am not concerned with war. I am taking a much farther perspective. I am looking down the centuries. What if one or two generations have to suffer?

INGALLS: And so, at a desperate time, when your country needs the exclusive secret and control of a weapon such as this, you will give it away to anyone and everyone.

BRECKENRIDGE: My country will have an equal chance with the rest of the world.

INGALLS: An equal chance to be destroyed? Is that what you're after? But you will never understand. You have no concern for your country, for your friends, for your property, or for yourself. You don't have the courage to hold that which is yours, to hold it proudly, wisely, openly, and to use it for your own honest good. You don't even know that that takes courage.

BRECKENRIDGE: I do not wish to discuss it.

INGALLS: You are not concerned with mankind, Walter. If you were, you'd know that when you give things to mankind, you give them also to mankind's enemies.

BRECKENRIDGE: You have always lacked faith in your fellow men. Your narrow patriotism is old-fashioned, Steve. And if you think that my decision is so dangerous, why don't you report me to the government?

INGALLS: There are too many friends of Serge Sookin's in the government—at present. It's I who must stop you.

BRECKENRIDGE: You? There's nothing you can do about it. You're only a junior partner.

INGALLS: Yes, Walter, that's all I am. Sixteen years ago, when we formed our partnership and started the Breckenridge Laboratories, I was very young. I did not care for mankind and I did not care for fame. I was willing to give you most of the profits, and all the glory, and your name on my inventions—they were *my* inventions, Walter, mine alone, all of them, and nobody knew it outside the laboratory. I cared for nothing but my work. You knew how to handle people. I didn't. And I agreed to everything you wanted—just to have a chance at the work I loved. You told me that I was selfish, while you—you loved people and wanted to help them. Well, I've seen your kind of help. And I've seen also that it was I, I the selfish individualist, who helped mankind by producing the Vitamin X separator and the cheap violet ray and the electric saw—[*Points to machine*]—and this. While you accepted gratitude for it—and ruined all those you touched. I've seen what you've done to men. It was *I* who gave you the means to do it. It was I who made it possible for you. It is my responsibility now. I created you—I'm going to destroy you. [BRECKENRIDGE *glances up at him swiftly, understands, jerks his hand away from the machine and to his coat pocket*] What are you looking for? This? [*Takes the gun out of his pocket and shows it to* BRECKENRIDGE. *Then slips it back into his pocket*] Don't move, Walter.

BRECKENRIDGE: [*His voice a little hoarse, but still assured*] Have you lost your mind? Do you expect me to believe that you're going to kill me, here, now, with a house full of people a few steps away?

INGALLS: Yes, Walter.

BRECKENRIDGE: Are you prepared to hang for it?

INGALLS: No.

BRECKENRIDGE: How do you expect to get away with it? [INGALLS *does not answer, but takes out a cigarette and lights it*] Stop playing for effects! Answer me!

INGALLS: I am answering you. [*Indicating the cigarette*] Watch this cigarette, Walter. You have as long a time left to live as it will take this cigarette to burn. When it burns down to the brand, I'm going to throw it here in the grass. It will be found near your body. The gun will be found here—with my fingerprints on it. My handkerchief will be found here on a branch. Your watch will be smashed to set the time. I will have no alibi of any kind. It will be the sloppiest and most obvious murder ever committed. And that is why it will be the perfect crime.

BRECKENRIDGE: [*Fear coming a little closer to him*] You . . . you wouldn't . . .

INGALLS: But that's not all. I'm going to let your friend Serge Sookin hang for your murder. He's tried once to do just what I'm going to do for him. Let him take his punishment now. I'm going to frame myself. And I'm also going to frame him to look as if he'd framed *me*. I'll give him an alibi—and then I'll blow it up. Right now, he is in Stamford, buying a newspaper. But it won't do him any good, because, at this moment, up in my room, I have an early edition of today's *Courier*. Do you understand, Walter?

BRECKENRIDGE: [*His voice hoarse, barely audible*] You . . . Goddamn fiend . . . !

INGALLS: You wanted to know why I let you see me kissing Helen today. To give myself a plausible motive of sorts. Just the kind that would tempt a Serge to frame me. You see, I can't let Greg Hastings guess my real motive. I didn't know that Helen would play her part so well. I never dreamed that possible or I wouldn't have done it. It's the only thing that I regret.

BRECKENRIDGE: You . . . won't . . . get away with it. . . .

INGALLS: The greatest chance I'm taking is that I must not let Greg Hastings guess the real nature of my invention. If he guesses that—he'll know I did it. But I have to take that chance. [*Looks at his cigarette*] Your time is up. [*Puts the butt out and tosses it aside*]

BRECKENRIDGE: [*In utter panic*] No! You won't! You won't! You can't! [*Makes a movement to run*]

INGALLS: [*Whipping the gun out*] I told you not to move. [BRECKENRIDGE *stops*] Don't run, Walter. Take it straight for once. If you run—you'll only help me. I'm a good shot—and nobody would believe that I'd shoot a man in the back. [*And now* this *is the real* STEVE INGALLS— *hard, alive, taut with energy, his voice ringing—the inventor, the chance-taker, the genius—as he stands pointing the gun at* BRECKENRIDGE] Walter! I won't let you do to the world what you've done to all your friends. We can protect ourselves against men who would do us evil. But God save us from the men who would do us good! This is the only humanitarian act I've ever committed—the only one any man can ever commit. I'm setting men free. Free to suffer. Free to struggle. Free to take chances. But free, Walter, *free*! Don't forget, tomorrow is Independence Day!

[BRECKENRIDGE *whirls around and disappears in the dark.* INGALLS *does not move from the spot, only turns without hurry, lifts the gun, and fires into the darkness*]

[*The spotlight vanishes. Blackout*]

[*When the full lights come back,* INGALLS *is sitting calmly in a chair, finishing his story.* ADRIENNE *stands tensely, silently before him*]

INGALLS: I've told you this because I wanted you to know that I don't regret it. Had circumstances forced me to take a valuable life—I wouldn't hesitate to offer my own life in return. But I don't think that of Walter. Nor of Serge. . . . Now you know what I am. [*Rises, stands looking at her*] Now, Adrienne, repeat it—if you still want me to hear it.

ADRIENNE: [*Looking at him, her head high*] No, Steve. I can't repeat it now. I said that I was inexcusably, contemptibly in love with you and had been for years. I can't say that any longer. I will say that I'm in love with you—so terribly *proudly* in love with you—and will be for years . . . and years . . . and forever. . . .

[*He does not move, only bows his head slowly, accepting his vindication*]

CURTAIN

"Do you think," Ayn Rand said to me when I finished reading, "that I would ever give the central action in a story of mine to anyone but the hero?"

(This page constitutes an extension of the copyright page:)

A fascinating and illuminating guide to
Ayn Rand's Objectivist philosophy

THE AYN RAND LEXICON

Objectivism from A to Z

Edited by Harry Binswanger
With an Introduction by Leonard Peikoff

A comprehensive, alphabetical encyclopedia of
Objectivist thought, this is the definitive guide
to the works of one of the most important
writers of our century. A highly accessible
compilation of key statements on over 400
topics in philosophy and related fields, selected
from Ayn Rand's articles, essays, lectures and
books. This unique volume brings together for
the fist time all the key ideas of Objectivism, as
brilliantly dramatized in Miss Rand's novels
We the Living, The Fountainhead,
and *Atlas Shrugged.*

0-452-01051-9

Available wherever books are sold or at
www.penguin.com

S468/Rand